ROUTLEDGE LIBRARY EDITIONS: INTERNATIONAL SECURITY STUDIES

Volume 6

ESTIMATING FOREIGN MILITARY POWER

ESTIMATING FOREIGN MILITARY POWER

Edited by
PHILIP TOWLE

Routledge
Taylor & Francis Group
LONDON AND NEW YORK

First published in 1982 by Croom Helm Ltd

This edition first published in 2021
by Routledge
2 Park Square, Milton Park, Abingdon, Oxon OX14 4RN

and by Routledge
52 Vanderbilt Avenue, New York, NY 10017

Routledge is an imprint of the Taylor & Francis Group, an informa business

© 1982 Philip Towle

All rights reserved. No part of this book may be reprinted or reproduced or utilised in any form or by any electronic, mechanical, or other means, now known or hereafter invented, including photocopying and recording, or in any information storage or retrieval system, without permission in writing from the publishers.

Trademark notice: Product or corporate names may be trademarks or registered trademarks, and are used only for identification and explanation without intent to infringe.

British Library Cataloguing in Publication Data
A catalogue record for this book is available from the British Library

ISBN: 978-0-367-68499-0 (Set)
ISBN: 978-1-00-316169-1 (Set) (ebk)
ISBN: 978-0-367-71445-1 (Volume 6) (hbk)
ISBN: 978-0-367-71446-8 (Volume 6) (pbk)
ISBN: 978-1-00-315091-6 (Volume 6) (ebk)

Publisher's Note
The publisher has gone to great lengths to ensure the quality of this reprint but points out that some imperfections in the original copies may be apparent.

Disclaimer
The publisher has made every effort to trace copyright holders and would welcome correspondence from those they have been unable to trace.

Estimating Foreign Military Power

EDITED BY PHILIP TOWLE

CROOM HELM LONDON

©1982 Philip Towle
Croom Helm Ltd, 2-10 St John's Road, London SW11

British Library Cataloguing in Publication Data

Estimating foreign military power.
  1. Military history
  2. Foreign relations – History
  I. Towle, Philip
  355'.033   U42

ISBN 0-7099-0434-7

Typesetting by Elephant Productions, London SE15
Printed and bound in Great Britain
by Billing and Sons Limited
Guildford, London, Oxford, Worcester

CONTENTS

List of Figures

List of Abbreviations

Introduction   11

Part One: Russia and the Soviet Union

1. British Views of Russia: Russian Views of Britain
   C.D. Bellamy   37

2. Estimating Soviet Military Expenditure R. Huisken   77

3. Western Assessment of Soviet Strength G. Jukes   88

Part Two: The Power of the New States

4. British Estimates of Japanese Military Power,
   1900-1914 P.A. Towle   111

5. Australian Estimates of the Japanese Threat,
   1905-1941 D.M. Horner   139

6. Perceptions of Naval Power Between the Wars:
   the British Case G. Till   172

7. Nine Examples from Recent Indian Experience,
   1962-1980 R. Rikhye   194

8. Assessing the Arab-Israel Military Balance K.R. Singh   237

Part Three

9. The Forgotten Dimensions of Strategy M.E. Howard   261

Notes on Contributors   273

Index   275

FIGURES

1.1	Russia in the Thirteenth Century Showing Foreign Invasions	43
1.2	The Expansion of Russia	45
1.3	Soviet Russia, 1918	46
1.4	Russia and Britain in Asia, 1846-1907	63
4.1	The Far East in 1904-5	113
7.1	China, Northern India and East Pakistan	196
7.2	The Indo-Pakistan Frontier	201
8.1	The Middle East	238

I am grateful to Mr K. Blissett for providing the maps.

ABBREVIATIONS

CID	Committee of Imperial Defence
CIGS	Chief of the Imperial General Staff
UAE	United Arab Emirates
SSM	Surface to surface missile
ECM	Electronic counter measures
RPV	Remotely piloted vehicle
PGM	Pecision guided munition
PLO	Palestine Liberation Organisation
SP	Self propelled
APC	Armoured personnel carrier
ATGW	Anti-tank guided weapon
SAM	Surface to air missile
IAEA	International Atomic Energy Agency
ICBM	Intercontinental ballistic missile
IISS	International Institute for Strategic Studies
SAL	Strategic Arms Limitation
RUSI	Royal United Services Institute
ACDA	Arms Control and Disarmament Agency
CIA	Central Intelligence Agency
GNP	Gross National Product

Introduction to the 2021 Edition

When this book was published in 1982, we were still in the later years of the Cold War between the Soviet bloc and the West which had been raging for more than three decades. We thought it was important to assess what could be gleaned from past arms races to raise some of the appropriate questions about the existing situation; was the tendency to exaggerate or underestimate the power of a potential enemy, and why? Was correct intelligence about enemy forces available for those who would need to know it to prepare for war and, if not, why not?

Thus we divided the book into two sections, the first looking at Russia and the Soviet Union because they were the focus of Western anxieties, the second at what would now be called 'rising powers', Japan in the first half of the 20th Century and India in the second. We also included Israel and the Arab states, not so much because of their military strength, though that was considerable, but because the area had unfortunately been the focus of so much tension and conflict since 1945. The greatest omission was that we did not look at China because we failed to foresee that it might shake off the economic trappings of communism and unleash the age-old spirit of the entrepreneur in its people.

The three contributors to the first section of our book, Chris Bellamy, Ron Huisken and Geoffrey Jukes were all cautious about much of the commentary on the balance of conventional military power and expenditure between NATO and the Warsaw Pact. They stressed the difficulties caused by Moscow's secrecy which made it somewhat easier to count the numbers of their tanks, aircraft and other weaponry than their quality. After the end of the Cold War, when Western officers could examine Warsaw Pact weapons, they found that many were old and in very poor condition. If counting equipment led to exaggeration of Soviet capability, Western belief that the Soviets were devoting a large proportion of their gross national product to defence proved correct. To this day, Russian people have apparently been willing to spend a much higher proportion of their budget on their armed forces than Western publics but then they have suffered more from foreign occupations than some Western states have done.

In the second section we looked at Japan because it was the only country to join the great powers in the first half of the 20th Century and a very restless new power it had been. Lord Salisbury once jibed that 'you never should trust experts. If you believe the doctors, nothing is wholesome: if you believe the theologians, nothing is innocent: if you believe the soldiers, nothing is safe.' But Western countries were frequently surprised by Japan's power and actions at that time. British leaders negotiated an alliance with Japan in 1902 to balance growing Russian naval power in East Asia yet they were surprised two years later when Japan attacked Russia and its armies defeated the Russians in every battle on land and sea. Despite this Geoffrey Till showed that in the 1930s many British naval and air force officers underestimated the Japanese threat out of cultural prejudice. They could not believe that the Japanese would make good aircraft carrier pilots. Yet British army officers who alone of the three Services were attached to their Japanese counterparts were impressed by their competence and efficiency. The problem was that their reports were not widely circulated. Naval officers had also forgotten the laudatory views which their predecessors had held of the Japanese Navy when Japan was Britain's ally. Nor did the Australians agree with British underestimates. David Horner explained this partly by geopolitics: to Australians the Japanese forces just looked more menacing than they did in London because they were so much closer. It is generally better to exaggerate than underestimate the strength of a potential enemy to formulate appropriate defence and foreign policies and, if war does still come, it will be less demoralising to military and civilian alike. The obvious disadvantage is that it leads to arms races.

In this same section Ravi Rikhye examined India which was an obvious candidate for great power status because of the size of its population and its diplomatic role during the Korean War and establishment of the Non-Aligned Movement. He focused on India's frequent confrontations with its neighbours, China and Pakistan, which had diminished its wider role on the world stage and unfortunately continues to do so. Its defeat by China in 1962 was particularly demoralising and, so Rihye argued, was caused by the army's refusal to believe intelligence reports. K.R. Singh suggested that it was divisions between the Arab nations, and Israeli links with the US which largely determined that Israel would be the dominant power in the region. But his suggestion that the Arabs might work together and force Israel to the negotiating table still seems unlikely to come about.

Today we see even more clearly the importance of societal strength in determining military power, a factor which Michael Howard emphasised in the last chapter of our book alongside logistical strength, technical efficiency and operational competence. He had to hand a good example of this because the United States had just emerged from its struggle against the Vietnamese guerrillas battered and divided, despite its vast superiority in weaponry and manpower. Similarly, today Washington is trying to extricate its forces from Afghanistan after a decade of wearying struggle against guerrilla forces which have limited weaponry but the backing of a section of the indigenous people. As the anti-colonial struggles showed after 1945, the day is long passed when foreign troops can change a country's culture.

To determine the military power of another state, we need imagination, together with as much knowledge as we can amass about its history and social cohesion. Our intelligence services need to be working effectively and to be respected as the Indians were not in 1962. Available reports have to be circulated to the right people as the British failed to do with their military reports in the 1930s, even if this risks leakage. Understanding the balance of power correctly is important in efforts to prepare for war and to formulate measures to avoid it including arms control and deterrence, hence the continuing significance of this collection.

INTRODUCTION

Now that we are well into the fourth decade of peace between the Great Powers the problem of assessing their military capabilities is becoming steadily greater. Reputations won or lost on the battlefields of the Second World War are increasingly irrelevant to the way states would fight in a major conflict over the next decades. Although the Great Powers have been involved in limited wars since 1945 such wars can be a very misleading guide to the way they would fight in a world war, to whether they are in fact still great military powers and to whether the ranks of such powers have been joined by new states. Wars which follow a long period of peace have often provided dramatic surprises about the balance of military power. The Prussian army in 1806 could no longer play the role in Europe which it had carried out under Frederick the Great, while the French army, which held all Europe at its mercy for two decades before 1814, was easily defeated by Prussia 56 years later.

This book therefore examines previous attempts to estimate the military power of foreign countries in order to see whether any general trends or patterns emerge. Such a task could easily degenerate into ridicule of previous generations for their failings; there are only too many ways of explaining past military defeats, but there are also only too many difficulties in the way of forecasting future ones. Preparing for war and assessing the military power of potential enemies and allies are the two most important and most difficult tasks of the armed forces in peacetime. Such ridicule is therefore not the intention, nor would it be wise since, if previous mistakes were very great, this was only a reflection of the magnitude of the task attempted.[1]

In order to keep the book within manageable proportions, we have concentrated on the two main areas which have been of most concern to Western statesmen and strategists over the last decades and which are likely to continue to be of most concern for the rest of the century: Russian and Soviet military power and the power of the 'new' states — Japan before 1941 and the Third World countries subsequently. Thus, C.D. Bellamy looks at the perceptions which Britain and Russia have had of each other over the centuries, R. Huisken discusses the current debate over the extent of Soviet defence expenditure and G. Jukes examines the ways in which Western intelligence may distort the picture of Soviet strength. P.A. Towle and D.M. Horner look at British and

12 *Introduction*

Australian estimates of Japanese military power before the two world wars, while G. Till examines the misperceptions of the British naval staff in the interwar period of the naval power of Japan and other countries. R. Rikhye and K.R. Singh analyse the two areas where most of the conventional wars have taken place since 1945 — South Asia and the Middle East — and M.E. Howard reassesses some of the fundamental assumptions on which Western strategy has rested in recent years.

The Basis of Power

For reasons of space we have concentrated mainly on the assessment of military power but it is clear that such power is only an aspect of the fundamental strengths and weaknesses of a particular state. In a famous essay, which was written thirty years ago, the American political scientist, Hans Morgenthau, suggested that there were eight key elements in national power; geography, natural resources, industrial capacity, military preparedness, population, national character, national morale and diplomacy.[2] Of these, geography is more or less a constant, although the rapid development in turn of railways, automobiles, aircraft and intercontinental ballistic missiles (ICBMs) has drastically altered the effects of geography on warfare. Similarly the importance of the possession of various natural resources depends on the prevailing technology. In 1936 one statistician estimated that coal was twice as important as oil in the constitution of national power. Few would say the same today, although the situation may have changed again by the year 2000.

Changes in the size of populations are notoriously difficult to predict. Beginning in the eighteenth century, European populations began to expand very much more rapidly than they had in the past and consequently demographic calculations became important in the assessment of national power. The fact that the French population only rose from 28 million to 41.9 million between 1800 and 1940, whilst the British population rose from 11 million to 46.4 million, the German population rose from 22.5 million to 70 million and the population of the United States rose from 5.3 million to 131.7 million during the same period, could hardly fail to revolutionise the balance of world power.[3]

Yet observers have to compare the effect of such changes in population with other changes in the basis of power. Since the beginning of the nineteenth century industrial strength has come to play an ever greater role in conventional wars and those leaders who ignored it have done so

Introduction 13

at their peril. The German military commanders who contemptuously dismissed American military power in the First World War,[4] or the Japanese leaders who gambled the future of their country on the supposedly unwarlike characteristics of American society, paid dearly for their mistakes. Such misunderstandings came naturally to conservative military leaders who considered military traditions more important than industrial power. On the other hand, industrial might can also be overemphasised. American strategists who believed that they could defeat a guerrilla force by fire power alone discovered in Vietnam that, in unconventional wars at least, national morale and resolve are still crucial.

Like the other bases of national power, even national character may change, or appear to change, as the transformation of England from the country of revolutions in the seventeenth century into the epitome of stability in the nineteenth, or the metamorphosis since 1945 of Jewish shopkeepers into the most powerful nation in the Near East, has demonstrated. In past centuries Kings and their advisers in Europe knew well enough that they could not estimate the power of their allies and enemies from such straightforward factors as the size and wealth of their populations and territories, since the character of the people, the state of national morale and the quality of leadership also played a vital role. England's size and wealth did not change significantly during the period when it was successively triumphant against Spain under Queen Elizabeth, humiliated by the continental powers under James I and Charles I and brilliantly successful under Cromwell. As one commentator has pointed out, 'political units did not differ from each other by the number of men or the potential of manufacture, as by the unequal capacity to mobilise resources' and for this national leadership was an essential factor.[5]

The relative importance of certain types of industry also changes with the nature of warfare. Until the Second World War, iron, coal and steel production were considered the key elements in industrial and consequently in military power but it is not clear that they would play so great a part in future conflicts. Even in the Second World War submarines and bomber aircraft were defeated as much by developments in electronics, particularly radar, as by the ships and aircraft which their opponents could mobilise. Electronics would undoubtedly play a much greater part in a future war, although the Soviet Union and China sometimes still measure their industrial growth in terms of iron and steel production rather than in computers and radios.

Technology has advanced with sufficient rapidity since 1945 to raise question marks over the continued utility of whole weapon systems such as surface ships, armoured fighting vehicles and aircraft. Yet precipitate rejections of these traditional symbols of military power may be as dangerous as their retention through conservatism rather than military necessity; the French Jeune Ecole was simply wrong to argue that battleships were obsolete before 1914 and it decisively handicapped French naval power, whilst Duncan Sandys' assumption that manned aircraft were obsolescent at the end of the 1950s reduced British air power for two decades. Small wars in Asia and Africa provide little guidance as to the continued adequacy of weapons systems in a major war between the Great Powers and, by the time such a major war breaks out, it may be too late to remedy peacetime deficiencies.

Military preparedness is of course most important when wars begin, but excessive military expenditure may reduce a country's ability to invest in new industries upon which its future prosperity and military strength may largely depend. Moreover, with rapid advances in military technology, excessive expenditure at one period may leave a country with great quantities of obsolete equipment.[6] The time needed to develop and produce major weapons has increased, even compared to the interwar period, hence the nervousness with which the Great Powers watch the military developments of their potential enemies. Other things being equal, victory or defeat may go to those countries which have best absorbed the latest products of modern technology and built their tactical and strategic doctrines around them: howitzers and machine-guns before the First World War, tanks and aircraft in the interwar period and possibly precision guided munitions and electronic counter-measures today. Alternatively, as one commentator has pointed out, 'when everybody starts wrong, the advantage goes to the side which can most quickly adjust itself to the new and unfamiliar environment and learn from its mistakes'.[7]

The Duration of War

Clearly 'potential' power is not the only factor to be considered. A country with vast potential inadequately mobilised may yet be defeated in a war by an unexpected attack, particularly when preparations take so long. Even in the First World War it took six months before shells could be manufactured in large numbers in France or Britain, it took nearly a year before artillery could be produced in quantity and it was not until 1916 that France began to mass produce aeroplanes. Today

Introduction 15

such preparations would take far longer because the equipment involved is infinitely more complex. On other occasions a country may be unable to bring its full power to bear sufficiently quickly on an enemy, as Russia was unable to bring its forces to bear on Japan in 1904.

The conventional wisdom today is that any future great war is likely to be short and therefore that it may have to be fought with the forces in being at the start of the conflict, thereby reducing the significance of the sources of potential power analysed by Morgenthau. However great the size of a country's population, however extensive its industrial potential, unless these are mobilised, and mobilised in the most effective way, defeat may follow in weeks if not in days. Thus Japan is regarded as an economic rather than a military power, although in an extended war it could use its vast industrial resources, particularly in shipbuilding and electronics, to become a military power of the first importance. As a leading authority has put it, 'it is unlikely that there will be either the need or the time to apply the techniques we learned in the two World Wars for the switching over of the national economy from a peacetime to a wartime footing'.[8] Above all this would be true in a great nuclear war between the super powers but, even in a conventional or a tactical nuclear war in Europe, the decision is expected to be reached quickly. Small-scale wars in Asia and Africa appear to confirm this hypothesis since the 'attrition rate' in equipment is so high that the contestants are often forced to cease fighting through lack of supplies. The result in the Middle East and South Asia has been a series of very short wars, followed by *de facto* armistices while the enemies prepare for the next round.

All the same, the historian must hesitate before accepting the conventional wisdom. Prophecies about the length of future wars have too often been falsified by events to be accepted unreservedly and so it would be unwise to base all calculations about the balance of military power on forces in being. Before the First World War the prevalent opinion was that future wars would be short, despite the arguments to the contrary by the Polish banker, I.S. Bloch, and certain artillery and engineer officers.[9] The consensus was that military solutions would be achieved quickly and that arms and ammunition would too rapidly be consumed to allow for a prolonged conflict. However a military solution was not rapidly achieved and the contestants were prepared to await the production of more arms and ammunition. The idea of defeat, or even of an armistice, was not accepted by any of the belligerents until, as Bloch had forecast, their entire societies were on the brink of collapse. It is not impossible that such a situation could be repeated in a great war amongst the major powers.

Public Debates

In Western societies public debate on the power of potential enemies and allies has assumed increasing importance since 1945. This tendency has gone furthest in the United States where the national press and Congress take a close interest in military matters and the legislature pronounces even on the value of individual weapons. Precisely because the debate is held in public this can lead to distortions, particularly as participants often behave as though they have to exaggerate to make themselves heard.

Domestic debates on military power in one country interact with similar debates in other lands. Criticisms by informed individuals of their own country's armed forces may lead foreigners to underestimate these forces; thus Winston Churchill's attacks on the unpreparedness of the Royal Air Force in the 1930s led some foreign observers to underplay the RAF's competence.[10] Conversely, before the First World War, foreign observers attached an exaggerated importance to Russian claims that they were improving their armed forces.[11] Before the Second World War they were equally taken in by what they thought was 'the vigorous tendency now operative in French military thought towards modernisation and re-equipment and a readiness to stake everything on the card of quality'.[12]

Public debates on military power are necessarily distorted because statesmen and soldiers may wish to avoid offending allies or encouraging potential enemies to repair the gaps in their defences. These considerations may persuade them both to ignore deficiencies in the power of potential enemies and to exaggerate the power of allies. On the other hand, military men also have to appeal for funds to build up their country's forces. Consequently they may tend to err in public on the side of caution in estimating the military balance between their country and any other. In private military men may be sceptical about the military power of other states and they may focus on the intangibles of leadership, fighting capacity and national morale; in public they may focus on the tangible evidence provided by equipment and numbers.

The situation is further complicated because some states may deliberately inflate their national power in order to frighten their enemies. Hitler followed this policy with immense success before the Second World War when the 'British service chiefs took German figures [for air strength] at their face value, or rather regarded them as less than reality. The truth was exactly the reverse; Germany never had the arms she claimed to have.' Similarly 'by the outbreak of war British production

Introduction 17

of tanks was greater than German which was only 45 per cent of the figures estimated by British intelligence'.[13] A bombastic leader may inflate the importance of his country out of all proportion to its real strength. Thus Mussolini inflated the power of Italy in the 1930s and Nasser exaggerated the importance of Egypt two decades later. In retrospect we can see that neither country had the financial or industrial resources to back up its foreign pretensions.

The tendency of dictatorial or totalitarian states to exaggerate national strength may have increased in the age of deterrence. Mr Khrushchev greatly exaggerated Soviet power at the end of the 1950s in order to persuade the West to agree to his policies over Berlin and other questions. But the Soviet Union's attempts to magnify its missile and bomber forces backfired when the West built up its forces to the purported rather than to the actual level of Soviet forces. It is much more difficult for democratic states to 'bluff' about their military power when the strength and weakness of their armed forces have been discussed at great length in public. But this is not always a disadvantage in diplomatic negotiations. The reasons for changes in the military policies of democratic states are usually clear and they can respond appropriately to foreign actions. The reasons for decisions taken by dictators must always remain obscure and therefore their diplomatic and military signals are often misconstrued.

The capabilities and intentions of foreign nations are frequently confused. Sometimes this is deliberate. According to the 1967 British Defence White Paper, 'the government believes that NATO cannot provide a strategy appropriate to the real threat facing Western Europe unless it takes into account the political intentions as well as the military capability of the Soviet Union and other Warsaw Pact powers'.[14] Thus a government which feels that it cannot balance the power of its potential enemies may make a virtue of necessity and claim that the political threat has declined. More unconsciously, if the likelihood of an attack by a foreign power is estimated to be small, its capabilities may also be played down. If the assessed danger of an attack is great, estimates of the power of potential enemies may be correspondingly high. This may help to explain why the Australians thought the Japanese a much greater threat than the British did for two decades before 1941.[15]

Once wars have taken place, historians biographers and journalists stress the importance of the personalities of the leaders and generals, and the part they played in winning or losing the war. But in peacetime the public usually knows little about the personalities of the military leaders. Moreover, even the most acute and knowledgeable observer can be misled by peacetime performance. Thus Sir Basil Liddell Hart underestimated the future Field Marshal Montgomery before the Second World War began.[16] Yet it is possible for a brilliant military leader to compensate for weaknesses in numbers and material, as Field Marshal Rommel showed in North Africa in the Second World War. Even the fall of France was not due to German material superiority in 1940 so much as the superiority of German strategy, will-power and tactics. Thus military leadership can easily upset the calculations of those strategists who rely for their assessments of military power on tangibles alone.

National reputations built up in wartime frequently last longer after the battles from which they derived have been forgotten. As two American commentators have written, 'a third of a century and more than a generation later, reputations forged or lost in World War II continue to have considerable significance for the political influence of the various armed forces'.[17] However, the West German and Japanese armed forces have deliberately turned their backs on the past and now have only tenuous links with the armies which fought in that war. For China, France and the East European countries, the war marked an equally decisive break in their military traditions. Moreover armed forces may be effective in one type of combat and ineffective in another. France and Britain tended to underestimate Prussian power up to 1866 because the Prussian army lacked the continuous battle experience which was so much a feature of the British and French armies in the nineteenth century. The Franco-Prussian War showed that organisation, efficiency and training were more important ingredients of success in European wars than proficiency in small-scale conflicts in Asia and Africa. Thus it is very difficult to tell whether the failure of US forces in Vietnam demonstrates their inefficiency for conventional wars, or whether, on the contrary, it shows precisely that their equipment and training has been designed for conventional operations and that defeat in a guerrilla war casts no reflection on their other skills.

Soviet Power

If Vietnam has set a question mark over the power of the United States — a state which Morgenthau considered in 1949 might be strong enough to defeat all the other countries in the world put together — the strength of the other superpower has always been a matter of the greatest dispute.[18] Russia was underestimated throughout the interwar period partly at least because of the Russian Revolution. Yet the French

Revolution of 1789 had led to a massive increase in French power; was this analogy sufficiently borne in mind when the views of Western experts on Russia, such as Dr E.J. Dillon and Colonel W.H.H. Waters, were ignored when they reported that Soviet power was steadily increasing?[19] According to Sir James Cable:

> in 1937 the Soviet Ambassador in London anxiously inquired of the British Foreign Secretary whether a British ship . . . chartered by Russia to help evacuate Spaniards (after the defeat of the Republican forces in Spain) could count on Royal Naval protection. The request and the condescension with which it was granted would be inconceivable today, but not because of any ideological upheaval . . . it is the objective capability of the countries that has altered beyond the recognition of either.[20]

There are a number of interesting aspects of this modern judgement. According to the calculations of the British War Office in 1936, Britain had 166 medium tanks of which 164 were obsolete, the USA had 19, Germany had 300 to 400, France had 180 and Russia, 4,000.[21] Thus, even if all the other countries had united against her, Russia would have had a superiority in number of armoured fighting vehicles of about five to one. Yet few thought of Russia as the predominant military power in Europe. It seems likely that the objective capabilities of Britain and the Soviet Union have changed less in the intervening period than Sir James Cable suggested, and that it is the perceptions of Soviet power both by the Russian government and by outsiders which has changed as a result of the battle of Stalingrad and other experiences in the Second World War. Western estimates of Soviet power were handicapped in the 1930s by Soviet secretiveness but even more by certain assumptions about the strength and weaknesses of Soviet society. The great quantities of Soviet equipment were ignored and the weaknesses of the Soviet political system (as exemplified by the execution of so many of the political and military leaders) were stressed. Today this situation is reversed.

Were the Soviet Union to emerge victorious from a major conventional war, historians would emphasise its massive military preparations, the simplicity and robustness of its military equipment and the ferocity of its military and social discipline. Were the Russians to be defeated in a future conventional war subsequent historians would wonder why the weaknesses of Soviet society had been ignored for so long. They would stress the conservatism of Soviet military doctrine which looks forward

20 *Introduction*

to a replay of the Second World War and the technical backwardness of Russian society. The Russians import their computer and automobile technology from the West and still use valves (vacuum tubes) in their radios long after these have been abandoned by Western societies.[22] The morale of Soviet armed forces is difficult to assess and is rarely discussed in Western literature about the Soviet Union. A fighter pilot who hijacked a Soviet MiG 25 to Japan descanted on the grim life of a Soviet airman and 'was astonished to find [a US] carrier crew handling landings and takeoffs without being given orders and without anyone shouting at them'.[23] But such a man was obviously prejudiced in favour of the Western system and may have felt that it was to his advantage to stress the superiority of Western ways. Again the mutiny of the crew of the Soviet warship *Storoshevov* in 1976 and their attempt to take the 3,500 ton destroyer to a Swedish port may or may not indicate the state of Soviet naval morale.[24] Finally, the Second World War did reveal great cleavages in Soviet society. Thousands of Russian prisoners volunteered to fight for the Germans and many Russian peasants initially welcomed the invading German armies. Would such scenes be repeated in another war or has the demise of Stalin and the improvement in Soviet living standards united the country? No doubt much would depend in any future war on the initial success of Soviet armies; if the battle were successful Soviet society would hold together but, in defeat, giant fissures might once again appear.

Material and Morale

While Western strategists tended to underestimate the importance of the great quantities of Soviet equipment in the interwar period, there is a tendency today, particularly amongst civilian strategists, to assess military power by examining lists of military equipment. There are exceptions to this; all commentators take Israeli training and skills into account when assessing the balance of power between the Arabs and Israelis. But this is possible because the frequent wars in the Middle East remind people that there are other aspects of military power than the simple tangible ones. Had these wars not taken place, Israeli power would undoubtedly be grossly underestimated because collectively the Arabs have greater numbers of men and equipment, because of the casual appearance of the Israeli citizen army and because of the non-military tradition of the Jews.

For the major military powers, such as the United States, the Soviet

Introduction

Union and China, recent military experience is so specialised, ambiguous in its portents or limited that the tangible factors of equipment and numbers are given precedence in most Western calculations over the intangible factors of leadership and national morale. This appears to be a contrast to the Chinese who, like the French before the First World War, tend to emphasise the human factor in their public statements and tell Western visitors that 'the role played by the soldier is decisive. The man who knows why he fights and for what he fights will be victorious.'[25]
If this sums up the views of those at one end of the spectrum, the views of those at the other are perhaps epitomised by one of the official British histories of the First World War which concluded that 'in time of war, mens' lives, the morale of armies, victory or defeat depend upon the safety and efficiency of the fighting equipment with which the soldier is provided'.[26] Undoubtedly the provision of adequate military equipment can raise the morale of a force but it is not decisive. Armies with inferior equipment (such as the Japanese forces in the Russo-Japanese War) have fought well; armies with superior equipment have been defeated. Thus morale does not depend entirely on equipment, although it can be greatly influenced by it. Nor does victory depend on morale alone; Polish soldiers knew what they were fighting for in 1939 but this knowledge was of little avail against German and Soviet tanks. Again peacetime training may be a positive handicap to drawing the right conclusions. As a British General commented recently,

> Active operations such as those of Dhofar war remind us again that man is more important than his equipment. In peacetime we tend to be mesmerised by the latter. Its maintenance detracts from training and its handling on exercises from more important issues. During peacetime manoeuvres the most difficult part of the business is the coordination required to get armoured personnel carriers, helicopters, armour and other paraphernalia to the objective at the right time with everything working; when the infantry debouch the problem is virtually over. In war the real problem has just started.[27]

In any prolonged conflict the cohesion of a nation will be a very important factor, although it is also one of the most difficult to assess beforehand. If a country loses in the field, its internal divisions will be exacerbated. Thus historians have stressed the divisions in French society in 1940 although the effect these would have was by no means so obvious before the event. One commentator wrote in 1938,

22 *Introduction*

if, however, war should come, there is not a Frenchman, whatever his political party may be, who would oppose a government which had made every effort to ward off the catastophe. Once again the nation would rise as one man to defend French territory and French freedom.[28]

Similarly an expert on the French army had written the previous year, 'what gives it unity is the inner fighting patriotism which crisis reveals to what is often an astonished world'.[29] Thus it was not clear to even the most knowledgeable commentators before 1940 that France was more deeply divided than other European nations, all of which had been effected by the economic crisis of the 1930s. Moreover, outsiders who have banked on internal divisions handicapping an enemy have usually been disappointed. Britain was not greatly troubled during the First World War by disagreements over Ireland, despite the hopes entertained by the authorities in Berlin. A successful war may unite a nation, as some Russian politicians hoped in 1904, an unsuccessful war may tear the fabric of a society to pieces. Even American society was threatened by the prolonged conflict in Vietnam.

The development of satellite verification techniques may reinforce the trend in the West to emphasise tangible factors over intangibles like national morale. Satellites can locate aircraft and even tanks and help to assess their numbers; they cannot tell how efficient such weapons are, much less the competence of the crews who man them. From time to time Soviet equipment sold to Third World countries or spirited out of the Soviet Union by defectors may give Western observers some idea of the quality of Soviet equipment, but these will be rare opportunities. Similarly mobilisation tables and divisional lists may tell Western observers much about the size of the Soviet armed forces, just as Soviet military periodicals reveal something about their tactics, but the quality of Soviet military leadership must remain an enigma.

The problem faced by the Russians and Chinese initially in assessing Western societies is different from our own. They have so much information about Western armed forces that their problem is to sift it rather than to unearth it (though this has not prevented the Russians at least from attempting to increase their information through spies). Western societies publish detailed and accurate information about their military budgets, force levels and equipment. Yet the problem for the East is still to assess the adequacy of Western equipment and the leadership and morale of the armed forces. Is the morale of the European armies reflected in unrest amongst French conscripts or resistance to national service amongst West Germans, or are these temporary and atypical

Introduction

aberrations? Did the race riots on US ships during the Vietnam War reflect permanent divisions within the US navy and does the persistence of drug addiction in the US armed forces reveal the low state of US morale?[30] Such questions must baffle Soviet strategists as much as they baffle Western ones. This bafflement may encourage the Soviet Union to exaggerate the importance of numbers and equipment, much as Western states do.

Disarmament and Military Power

Such exaggeration is also encouraged by the disarmament negotiations which are usually designed to equalise the number of forces maintained by potential enemies in the hope that equality will reduce their propensity to go to war. The inadequacy of such methods of equalising power has long been recognised. In the 1920s the French government pointed out that it was not enough simply to count numbers of soldiers or pieces of equipment but that economic strengths and strategic weaknesses should also be taken into account. The French hoped to be able to work out a 'coefficient' to express a country's military needs and to reduce all its armed forces down to this level. Military needs, in terms of the length of the frontiers, the location of the towns and colonies to be defended would be made to equal military strength represented both by forces in being and by potential forces such as population, industrial resources, etc. However in order to keep Germany disarmed and France powerful, the French gave a very high value to industrial power and a low value to military power. This, as commentators gleefully pointed out, could produce absurdities; Denmark with very little industrial power could be allocated more soldiers to meet its 'needs' than the USA with its vast industries.[31]

Even French calculations in the 1920s were an oversimplification of the real balance of forces between the nations because they ignored such intangibles as leadership, training and morale. But how could such factors be considered in the negotiations? No country was likely to ask to be allowed more men to meet its 'needs' on the grounds that its government was unpopular and national morale therefore low, or that its forces were inefficiently trained and led. Nor would any country have granted such a request. Subsequent disarmament proposals have usually been much simpler than efforts in the 1920s and have reverted to straightforward numerical comparisons of armed forces. In May 1952, for example, the Western governments proposed that the United States, the Soviet Union and China should have a maximum armed strength of between one million and one and a half million men, and that the British and French armed forces should be limited to between 700,000 and 800,000 men. [32] The Russians responded that they had much longer frontiers to defend than any of the other Great Powers and that this should be taken into account. They also disputed Western figures for existing force levels. Similarly in the current MBFR negotiations the West is trying to equalise the number of East European and Western forces in Central Europe, while the Russians argue that there is already a substantial degree of equality and that disarmament agreements should not upset the existing military balance.

Nuclear Power

If the disarmament negotiations in general focus attention on numerical comparisons between armed forces, this tendency is, not surprisingly, most in evidence in (and fostered by) the nuclear disarmament negotiations. Here is the civilian strategist's and particularly the mathematician's dream. The nuclear firepower of the Soviet Union and the United States, the French, the British and the Chinese can simply be added up to see which nation is the most powerful in terms of numbers of missiles or the destructive power that they can carry. The vulnerability of each country can be assessed by adding up the number of its military installations or cities above a certain size. That, even here, where the intangible factors of morale and leadership can be ignored more than in any other area,[33] 'balancing' agreements have been so difficult to achieve in the strategic arms limitation (SAL) negotiations shows how much more complicated achieving a genuine conventional balance would be.

Of course, it may be said that, before the outbreak of war, the influence of nuclear weapons may be much greater if the leadership of the nuclear weapon state can convince potential opponents that it will use them in certain eventualities. National leadership obviously played an important role during the nuclear crisis over Cuba, as indeed did national morale. A nation deeply divided over nuclear weapons, as Britain was during the Campaign for Nuclear Disarmament, might be handicapped in such a crisis and, more importantly, an opponent might doubt its willingness to make use of its nuclear arsenal. Some of the traditional bases of national strength could also be important if tactical nuclear weapons were used to 'win' battles in a war in Europe or elsewhere. Some commentators have suggested that the West would surrender

Introduction

first in these circumstances because of the weak nerves of its peoples, others have speculated that the threat of nuclear war might exacerbate differences within the Soviet Union.[34] How the use of nuclear weapons would effect national morale or the morale of armies can only be imagined and, perhaps because of this, such effects are usually ignored and the discussions are channelled back to the safer area of comparable megatonnage.

Outside the East-West and Sino-Soviet military balances it is doubtful whether nuclear weapons add much to the military power and influence of the Great Powers. The Americans have been defeated by the North Vietnamese, their diplomats were seized by the Iranians, and the Russians fought with the Afghan rebels without nuclear weapons entering into the calculations of the contestants. If these conflicts were relatively peripheral, it is difficult to think of a feasible scenario where the issue would be less peripheral from the point of view of the superpower. The use of nuclear weapons by the existing nuclear weapon states in a limited war has become progressively less likely with the passing years. The actual and potential power of the superpowers may have increased but this power has often become less usable. As one commentator pointed out 17 years ago, 'a curious inversion has taken place. Never before has the gap been wider between the Great Powers and the miniscule Powers. Many of the latter are dependent for their very existence on the assistance afforded by the powerful. Yet the Great Powers are strangely inhibited in pursuing their interests amongst the miniscule states.'[35]

The fact that nuclear weapons can be quantified so readily, the growing importance of satellite reconnaissance, the protracted disarmament negotiations and the prolongation of peace all contribute to the tendency amongst strategists to concentrate on material and numbers, at the expense of less tangible factors, when they are assessing the power of other states. Only the outbreak of a major war will show how much this tendency has undermined their judgements.

The Estimators

Have estimates of foreign military power become more or less accurate over the last 80 years? Historic calculations were frequently wrong. An acute observer might pick out many of the salient features of a society without understanding how they would effect its behaviour in wartime. I.S. Bloch forecast many of the features of the First World War, including the stalemate of the trenches, over a decade before its outbreak. But he completely misjudged the ability of the Russian state to stand up to the strains of war. He believed that Russia would survive a long war better than the other European states because 'Russia [was] the only country in Europe which produce[d] sufficient food for her people' and thus 'she [was] in a position to carry on a serious and prolonged struggle — such a struggle as would not even be dreamt of by the states of Western Europe'.[36] In the event it was Russian morale and cohesion which collapsed before that of any of the other major European states.

The growing professionalism of nineteenth-century armies and navies certainly made them more concerned than their predecessors to investigate the character of foreign military forces. Even Britain with the most isolated of European armies sent teams of investigators to Europe to examine the quality of the military education provided for the armies of other states.[37] The rise of a military press, often of a very high quality, also kept informed those members of the armed forces who took an interest in the activities of foreign armed forces. Armies were rarely secretive about their activities and scores of foreign journalists and military attachés followed the main battles of the nineteenth century. Even if they were taken by surprise when hostilities began, the pace of the campaign usually allowed them to see something of the fighting. Moreover many of the nineteenth-century battles were compact enough to allow observers to gain some idea of the course of the fighting; by the beginning of the twentieth century not only was this ceasing to be so but censorship was closing around the war correspondents.[38] Such censorship was particularly effective during the two world wars and few of the wars since 1945 (with the exception of Vietnam) have been observed as openly and minutely as the campaigns of the nineteenth century.

The appointment of military attachés to study the armed forces of other countries and to report back to their own government did help in the nineteenth century to keep armed forces in touch with the power of their potential rivals. Prussia began to send attachés abroad in 1817; other countries such as Britain were slow to follow this lead. During the Crimean War of 1854-5, Britain had attachés in France and Turkey but it was not until after the war had ended that the peacetime employment of military attachés became an established institution.[39] By 1860 Britain had a naval attaché in Washington and military attachés in Paris, Berlin and Vienna. The effect of such appointments depended not only on the ability of the attachés, their open-mindedness and their relationship with the armed forces to which they were attached, but on the receptivity of the authorities at home. For example, when Von Schlieffen

Introduction 27

was Chief of the German General Staff he asked for far less advice from his attachés than his predecessor Count Waldersee.

Despite their professional training, military attachés are as subject to failures of judgement as others. They cannot be immune to the conventional attitudes towards foreign powers which are prevalent in the societies from which they spring. Often this conventional wisdom is based on half-forgotten historical experiences, from mythical events or from newspaper reports of varying quality. National stereotypes play a necessary role in making judgements about other nations. Yet an army may not necessarily reflect the salient characteristics of the society to which it belongs. The British army in the nineteenth century lived for the most part in the imperial world of Kipling and Henty while British society as a whole was closer to the world of Dickens and Thackeray. Thus, while British prosperity was based increasingly on industry and science and its military power was derived largely from the same sources, British officers were extremely reluctant to become involved in anything which savoured of industry, although such involvement was essential for the satisfactory development and production of the weapons needed in European wars.

Even if an armed force does reflect the characteristic features of a society, outsiders may be simply wrong about what those features are. The French colonial administrator, Lyautey, described the Vietnamese people living in the Mekong Delta in 1895 as 'peaceful, very domestic and law-abiding'. He contrasted them with the people from the highlands who, he said, were 'stronger, more warlike, prouder but less industrious than the Annamites . . . They carry firearms; the Annamites prefer umbrellas.'[40] Events between 1945 and 1975 were to show that the fighting capabilities of the lowland Vietnamese were not to be scorned. Thus prolonged contact between armies or peoples was not a guarantee against such misjudgements. Britain sent more than 150 officers to live with the Japanese army between 1900 and 1939. Yet they did not reach a correct estimate of Japanese military power, partly because they believed that the Japanese army was purely imitative and therefore that it would 'always be one pace behind those whom it copies'.[41]

Today the task of the military attaché has become much harder. He is regarded with grave suspicion, particularly if he works in a totalitarian country, while on postings in the Third World he may become more of a salesman for his country's military equipment than a commentator on the strength of the state where he is stationed. The day when attachés and journalists were allowed to view the military manoeuvres of potential enemies and to fraternise closely with their armed forces has passed.

28 *Introduction*

Such freedom became less prevalent with the rise of totalitarian states in the interwar period and almost disappeared during the Cold War. The Conference on Security and Co-operation in Europe has attempted to turn the clock back and to ensure that military attachés might view manoeuvres above a certain size in Europe but the East European authorities have limited the practical effects of this concession by inviting the minimum number of attachés and handicapping them as much as possible.[42]

The significance of spies may have increased as the conventional military attaché has declined in importance. Spies and electronic intelligence gathering played a major part in the Second World War and information which attachés can no longer gather may be obtained by covert operations of these sorts. According to recent press reports, for example, East German spies in West Germany 'gave the Warsaw Pact authorities comprehensive information about the strength and state of the West German armed forces, their future plans, their crisis and standby arrangements and their own knowledge of the state of the Warsaw Pact forces'.[43]

Because of advances in scientific methods of monitoring, the USA and the Soviet Union have managed to reach agreement in the SAL negotiations to limit the number of their delivery systems. Each superpower should therefore know how many delivery systems are possessed by its potential adversary. The United States and the Soviet Union now lie open to each other's satellites and many aspects of their defences which would formerly have been the most closely guarded secrets have been revealed to the whole world. The United States began sending photographic reconnaissance satellites into orbit on Atlas launchers in 1966. Later US satellites have become larger, more adaptable and more effective. On average the United States sends about five reconnaissance satellites into orbit each year compared with 35 orbited by the Soviet Union, but this is largely because American satellites can operate for a longer period.[44]

The number of people involved in making calculations about foreign military power has grown dramatically. Despite the handicaps they face today, military attachés have multiplied, intelligence services have expanded out of all recognition and unofficial organisations, such as the International Institute for Strategic Studies, have been established to ponder the balance of world power. Thus there are probably more people concerned with such problems today than in all the rest of men's history put together. The handful of officers who manned military intelligence departments before the First World War have been replaced by vast

Introduction

bureaucracies such as the US Central Intelligence Agency which is tasked to examine all aspects of the power of potential enemies from their oil production to their educational system. Civilians as well as military men have become involved in this process to an unprecedented degree. Before the First World War, with rare exceptions, civilians were afraid of encroaching on military matters; afterwards the prevailing view amongst civilians was that the attempt to create a balance of power had caused the outbreak of the war and that the study of military matters was morally repugnant. Today civilian strategists have a considerable impact on defence policy, particularly in the United States, where they helped to bring to an end the 'massive nuclear retaliation' policy of the mid-1950s and to institute the idea of 'flexible response' to aggression.

In any military struggle between the Great Powers nuclear weapons could play an indeterminate yet possibly decisive role. In previous world wars almost all weapons, and particularly the most decisive ones, have been used to the full.[45] But it is not absolutely certain that this would be so in a future war unless one of the Great Powers found that it was in danger of being overrun. Moreover the types of nuclear weapons vary so much that predictions become more difficult; the employment of tactical nuclear weapons at sea or in Europe would have a quite different effect on the outcome of the conflict to a full-scale nuclear exchange.

Conclusions

All this makes the calculations of military planners and statesmen much more difficult. Because of the technological and human effort put into estimating foreign military power today, we may have better reasons than our predecessors to explain the mistakes in our calculations, but that such mistakes will be made seems inevitable. The pace of technological and demographic change has increased, the European empires have disappeared and a hundred new nations have joined the international system.[46] Some of these new nations have the human and natural resources to become major powers, but their ability to do so will depend upon their political capacity to mobilise these resources. Given these uncertainties, as Hans Morgenthau pointed out,

> What the observer of international politics needs in order to reduce to a minimum the unavoidable errors in the calculations of power is a creative imagination, immune from the fascination which the preponderant power of the moment so easily imparts ... capable of

the supreme intellectual achievement which consists in detecting under the surface of present power relations the germinal developments of the future.[47]

Perhaps the only conclusion which a study of previous attempts to estimate the military power of foreign nations reaches, is that a good deal of scepticism is necessary about any assessment which purports to be exact. If this conclusion is widely accepted, it should discourage armed forces from putting their estimates to the test of battle.[48] However it has the disadvantage that it would encourage all countries to build up their armed forces to compensate for any inaccuracies in their threat assessments and thereby it may account in part for the outbreak of arms races. The inaccuracy of military assessments may also reduce the possibility of negotiating disarmament agreements. If it were possible to quantify more precisely the balance or imbalance between potential enemies, then it might be possible to decide precisely how the balance could be improved in order to decrease the risk of any state deciding for war and to persuade the states concerned to accept the desirability of such a balance.

But such precision is unattainable. Even the most despised power may prove stronger than expected, while even the greatest power may have its weaknesses. Perhaps it was her knowledge of this that prompted Dame Rebecca West to suggest that, before, a war military science seems an exact science like astronomy, while afterwards it seems more like astrology. Astrological or not, it is on judgements about the military power of our own and other states that the policies of governments and the safety of kingdoms depend.

Notes

1. The Earl of Avon, *The Eden Memoirs, Facing the Dictators* (Cassell, London, 1962), p. 99.
2. Hans J. Morgenthau, *Politics Among Nations, The Struggle for Power and Peace* (Alfred Knopf, New York, 1949), p. 74 *passim*.
3. R. Aron, *Peace and War, A Theory of International Relations* (Weidenfeld and Nicolson, London, 1966), p. 222.
4. F. Fischer, *Germany's Aims in the First World War* (Chatto and Windus, London, 1967), p. 307.
5. Aron, *Peace and War*, p. 254.
6. The classic example of this phenomenon was Italy in the 1930s. Its aircraft were amongst the most modern in Europe in 1934, by 1940 they were obsolete. See D.C. Watt, *Too Serious a Business* (University of California Press, Berkeley, 1975), p. 21.

Introduction

7. M.E. Howard, 'Military Science in an Age of Peace', *Journal of the Royal United Services Institute for Defence Studies* (hereafter *RUSI Journal*), March 1974.
8. M.E. Howard, *Studies in War and Peace* (The Viking Press, New York, 1971), p. 201.
9. P.A. Towle, 'The Russo-Japanese War and British Military Thought', *RUSI Journal*, December 1971.
10. M. Werner, *The Military Strength of the Powers* (Victor Gollancz, London, 1939), p. 243.
11. P.A. Towle, 'The European Balance of Power in 1914', *Army Quarterly and Defence Journal*, April 1974.
12. Werner, *Military Strength of the Powers*, p. 211. See also S.C. Davis, *The French War Machine* (George Allen and Unwin, London, 1937). Davis believed that the French air force had begun to improve considerably after 1935.
13. A.J.P. Taylor, *English History 1914-1945* (Clarendon Press, Oxford, 1965), pp. 410 and 411. See also Aron, *Peace and War*, p. 99.
14. *Statement on Defence Estimates* 1967, Cmnd 3203 (HMSO, London, 1967), para 9. For the opposite danger of ignoring intentions, see Raymond Garthoff, 'On Estimating and Imputing Intentions', *International Security*, Winter 1978.
15. See below D.M. Horner, 'Australian Estimates of the Japanese Threat 1905-1941'.
16. *The Memoirs of Captain Liddell Hart*, Volume 1 (Cassell, London, 1965), pp. 55-6. Such events as the fall of France take on a spurious aura of inevitability because of the superior resources of the victor. Thus the sinking by the Japanese of the Prince of Wales and Repulse in the Second World War is often seen as an inevitable result of the overstretching of British power at the time. But this is not so; the two ships were lost because of the inadequacy of their design and, above all, because they lacked air cover.
17. Barry M. Blechman and Stephen S. Kaplan, *Force Without War* (Brookings Institution, Washington, 1978), p. 7.
18. See below Part One.
19. W.H.H. Waters, *Russia Then and Now* (John Murray, London, 1935). Waters had greatly overestimated Russian power before 1914 and this may have increased scepticism about his comments. Dr E.J. Dillon, *Russia, Today and Yesterday* (J.M. Dent, London, 1929), particularly chap. XII.
20. James Cable, *Gunboat Diplomacy, Political Applications of Limited Naval Force* (Chatto and Windus, London, 1971), p. 148.
21. M.M. Postan, D. Hay and J.D. Scott, *Design and Development of Weapons, Studies in Government and Industrial Organisation* (HMSO, London, 1964), p. 309. In fact, British estimates actually underestimated the size of Soviet tank forces. One modern historian has argued that Russia may have had as many as 24,000 armoured vehicles by 1941. See E.J. Grove, 'Prelude to Disaster', *Armor* (May-June 1979). Conversely, Germany had only about 19 medium tanks by the end of 1936 and eight of these did not have real armour protection. The European tank balance is less numerically uneven today; NATO has about 11,000 tanks in Western Europe, while Russia has about 16,000 and the other Warsaw Pact countries have about 11,000.
22. David Lascelles, 'Expert Import', *Financial Times*, 13 April 1977. See also Arthur J. Alexander, *Decision-Making in Soviet Weapons Procurement*, Adelphi Paper, No. 148 (IISS, London, 1978/9).
23. 'Grim Life of a Russian Fighter Pilot', *The Times*, 14 January 1977.
24. '50 Die in Soviet Mutiny', *Daily Telegraph*, 6 May 1976; 'Mutiny on Soviet Warship', *Guardian*, 6 May 1976. This incident also made clear how quickly the Russians could respond to such events.

32 Introduction

25. Drew Middleton, 'Well Trained Manpower in China's Major Military Resource', *International Herald Tribune*, 11-12 December 1976. See also Hitler's comments in *Hitler's Secret Book* (Grove Press, New York, 1961), p. 25.

26. *History of the Ministry of Munitions* (HMSO, London, n.d.) vol. IX, part 2, p. 1.

27. Major General K. Perkins, 'Oman 1975: The Year of Decision', *RUSI Journal* (March 1979).

28. Genevieve Tabouis, *Blackmail or War* (Penguin, Middlesex, 1938), p. 8.

29. Davis, *French War Machine*, pp. 209-13. For a cogent argument for the importance of national unity in warfare see M.E. Howard, 'Total War in the Twentieth Century: Participation and Consensus in the Second World War' in B. Bond and I. Roy (eds.), *War and Society. A Yearbook of Military History* (Croom Helm, London, 1975).

30. 'US Army in Europe: Social Problems Grow', *International Herald Tribune*, 7-8 June, 1979. The very openness of the US army about its defects makes it difficult to compare its problems with those of other forces.

31. A.C. Temperley, *The Whispering Gallery of Europe* (Collins, London, 1939), p. 51.

32. *The Disarmament Question 1945-56* (Central Office of Information, London, 1956), p. 8.

33. But see below M.E. Howard, 'The Forgotten Dimensions of Strategy'.

34. This is the conclusion of the scenario envisaged by General Sir John Hackett in *The Third World War* (Sidgwick and Jackson, London, 1978).

35. R.C. Good in L.W. Martin (ed.), *Neutralism and Non Alignment* (Praeger, New York, 1962), p. 34.

36. I.S. Bloch, *Modern Weapons and Modern War* (Grant Richards, London, 1900), see particularly the interview between Bloch and W.T. Stead at the beginning.

37. See, for example, the *Report of the Commissioners Appointed to Consider the Best Mode of Reorganising The System of Training Officers for the Scientific Corps* (1857).

38. See P.A. Towle, 'The Debate on Wartime Censorship in Britain 1902-14' in B. Bond and I. Roy, *War and Society*.

39. L.W. Hilbert, 'The Role of Military and Naval Attachés in the British and German Forces 1871-1914', PhD. Thesis, University of Cambridge, 1954.

40. Marshal Lyautey, *Intimate Letters from Tonkin* (John Lane, London, 1932), p. 107.

41. M.D. Kennedy, *The Military Side of Japanese Life* (Constable and Co., London, 1924), p. 32 *passim*. See also F.S.G. Piggott, *Broken Thread* (Gale and Polden, Aldershot, 1950).

42. J.D. Toogood, 'Military Aspects of the Belgrade Review Meeting', *Survival* (July/August, 1978).

43. 'NATO Secrets Among at Least 1000 "Betrayed by Bonn Spy Ring"', *The Times*, 13 December 1977. See also C. Andrew 'Governments and Secret Services; a Historical Perspective', *International Journal*, no. 2 (Spring 1979).

44. *World Armaments and Disarmament, SIPRI Yearbook, 1977* (Almquist and Wiksell, Stockholm), p. 103 *passim*.

45. The exception was poisonous gases which were not employed in the Second World War because the possession of such weapons by both sides deterred their use. This could provide a precedent for the non-use of nuclear weapons in a future major war but chemical weapons (unlike nuclear weapons today) played a relatively small part in military planning in the 1930s and were never fully assimilated in operational doctrines. There was also considerable reluctance at the beginning of the Second World War to make use of strategic bombers. See G.H. Quester, *Deterrence before Hiroshima* (John Wiley, New York, 1966), p. 105 *passim*.

46. See below Part Two.
47. Morgenthau, *Politics Among Nations*, p. 116.
48. This conclusion might also be drawn from D.C. Watt, *Too Serious a Business*. But see also G. Blainey, *The Causes of War* (Sun Books, Melbourne, 1977), p. 122.

PART ONE:

RUSSIA AND THE SOVIET UNION

1 BRITISH VIEWS OF RUSSIA: RUSSIAN VIEWS OF BRITAIN

C.D. Bellamy

Early Years

Western Europeans were aware of the existence of a Russian state at least as early as the thirteenth century,[1] although Russia only became a power of interest to Westerners — whether as friend or foe — much later. This was not because of Russia's lack of resources or the size of its territories but because of its remoteness and internal divisions. Even by the twelfth century, the Russian principalities, although fragmented, extended from the shores of the Black Sea to the Arctic Ocean and from the Western Dvina and Dnestr rivers to the Volga. Tales of Russian wealth, reinforced no doubt by its proximity to the mysterious East, excited the imaginations of Western poets. Russia was considered distant and unconquerable and the expression 'to wage war on Russia' became a byword for an enterprise which would result in disaster. Russia is also mentioned in English folklore of the thirteenth century when Russian merchants are reported to have come to Southampton 'laden with rich goods'.[2]

Soviet historians have stressed the role of Russia in the Thirty Years War. Some have even attempted to show that Russia was part of the European balance of power as early as the sixteenth century.[3] Certainly, Ivan III (Grand Prince of Moscow 1462-1505) concluded an alliance with the Habsburg Emperor Maximilian at the end of the fifteenth century inspired by their mutual antipathy towards the Turk.[4] Ivan IV (the Terrible), who reigned as Tsar from 1547 to 1584, conducted negotiations with the English government of Mary Tudor and with Elizabeth I in 1567 and again in the 1580s. He also entered into negotiations with Erik XIV of Sweden. Some have seen in Ivan IV's attempts against Livonia the desire to give Russia 'an outlet to the Baltic Sea and open up communications with Europe' — aims fulfilled by Peter the Great (1682-1725).[5] Alliances with England and Sweden would further contribute to this, but it is likely that Ivan's aims were more pragmatic. In the Habsburgs, England and Russia had a mutal enemy. Soviet historians have also stressed the appropriateness of a tripartite alliance of Russia, England — the nascent democracy — and the 'Revolutionary

Netherlands' against 'reactionary' Spain.⁶ Seen in terms of Marxist historical philosophy this is fair enough, but it hardly reflects what people thought at the time. Furthermore, despite Russian interest in a military alliance, English interests were entirely commercial. Neither of Ivan's attempts to conclude an alliance were successful. Soviet writers see political interests behind the commercial interests which led Englishmen to visit Russia in the sixteenth century. Ironically, it is perhaps difficult for the more politically orientated Soviet mind to appreciate the true nature of English expansion, which was essentially one of profit and free enterprise. One must agree with Yu. Tolstoi writing in 1875 that Russia was a country with no 'political significance'⁷ for England until the opening of Peter's window on the west at the turn of the seventeenth century. Russia was for the west a rich and powerful country with a touch of the mysterious east, but it was not a threat, and was isolated from the mainstream of European power politics.

What of Russian perceptions of England? Despite the visits of Richard Chancellor and others, the Russians were comparatively unaware of England. Before the Mongol invasions, Russia's only immediate western contacts were with Constantinople and Bohemia and any western ideas had to pass through those filters.⁸

Ivan the Terrible imported foreign craftsmen, principally Germans, to build up his armaments industry. The 'German Quarter' in Moscow was set aside for the foreigners. Even today, the word *Nemets* (German) is used colloquially for any western foreigner. Despite some contacts with the English, it is fair to say that the only western Europeans with whom pre-Petrine Russia had any significant dealings were Germans.

The Russian Threat

Profitable though trade with Russia was for the English, it did not obscure the bad points of Muscovite society. Russians were seen as coarse and savage, if physically brave and tough. Nevertheless, Milton had to concede that Russia was 'the most northern Region of Europe reputed civil'.⁹

With the irruption of Russia into the Baltic at the beginning of the eighteenth century and its involvement in the Great Northern War, Russia became known to the English popular imagination. This process was abetted by no less a figure than Daniel Defoe. England at this time was enjoying a period of constitutional development with great emphasis on freedom and human rights. It was natural, therefore, that tales of the

Russian system should strike fear into the heart of freedom-loving Englishmen. The Tsar commanded 'the very Souls and Bodies' of his subjects, they breathed 'but by his permission'.[10] Even then, Defoe remarked on the practice of sending prisoners to Siberia, arguably the traditional epitome of Russian tyranny. Notwithstanding the fact that exile to Siberia was no worse, and probably more pleasant than transportation to the English colonies, Defoe managed to print a picture of Russian savagery and repression that mirrors our own.

Besides this negative picture Defoe also painted a positive one – Russian strength. The vast forest and mineral resources of the country impressed him. Even in the sixteenth century Russian raw materials had played a significant part in English ship construction, and by the eighteenth century not only were there sufficient naval materials to build a great Russian fleet but the navies of 'Great Britain, Holland, France and Sweden' were furnished with 'Hemp, Flax, Timber . . . and Tar' from Russia.[11] Even more striking for its modern ring is the realisation that Russia's human resources gave it tremendous military potential, a fact also noted by Milton.[12] According to Defoe

> Once his [the Tsar's] army is prepared . . . to come Hand to Hand with any of the Nations that lie thus on its Front . . . it will be much Superior to them on Account of the numberless Multitude of his People of whom he is able to raise as many thousands as some of his Neighbours can Hundreds, and *that with less Expense than any of them.*[13]

The remark about the cheapness of Russian military manpower is particularly perceptive. Defoe sensed the strength and potential of Russia and particularly its potential threat to western Europe. As if able to foretell the events of 1812 and 1941, Defoe predicted that regardless of Russian losses 'they would rise again in Armies, as if they came out of the Ground'.[14] Defoe also appreciated the great *defensive* strength of Russia. 'Wilderness . . . impassable Woods of vast Extent . . .' waited to swallow up the attacker, while his supply problems would be acute. Because of the poverty of the countryside, foraging would be impossible and provisions would have to be carried over great distances and 'thro' a thousand Dangers'.[15] With the same keen insight into the future Defoe explained why Charles XII of Sweden had not decided to rid himself of the Russian threat once and for all. 'Who would ruin a brave Soldiery, and a disciplin'd Army in fighting against Nature, struggling with Hunger, Cold and Insuperable difficulties.'[16] Here was one assessment of foreign power that would prove astonishingly accurate.*

Nevertheless, with the possible exception of the Armed Neutrality of 1780† British and Russian interests did not come into direct collision until the beginning of the nineteenth century. It was not until then that Russia's southward march in Asia and Britain's expansion in India brought the two powers within possible striking distance of each other on land. Both Britain and Russia had acquired great colonial territories, and now it was apparent that the interests of both were on a collision course from the Turkish Straits to the North Pacific. Napoleon was quick to perceive that a considerable and possibly decisive blow could be delivered at England through India. In 1800 Tsar Paul, prompted by Napoleon, conceived a scheme to attack India. The *ataman* of the Don *voiska* General Orlov received a letter suggesting he might move through Bokhara and Khiva to the Indus, destroy all English factories in India and bring the subcontinent under Russian rule.[17] It was a far-fetched scheme and came to nothing, but in 1807 Napoleon proposed an invasion of India to Alexander I at Tilsit. This would be conducted by a joint army and to this end Alexander entered into negotiations with the Shah of Persia. Napoleon intended to send his brother, Lucien, to arrange the details of the campaign.[18] This was no secret to the British, who through concern for their coveted India would come to fear the growing power of Russia. Then Franco-Russian relations took a turn for the worse and Britain and Russia found themselves allies once again. In April 1811 Napoleon requested information on the Russian and Swedish fleets. French writers were employed to proclaim that Russia was a threat to Europe, to justify the forthcoming invasion. A book containing the fabricated 'will of Peter the Great' was published by Le Sur.[19]

Although Britain was the one state not seriously threatened in the 'will', it was the one state that took it seriously. Once the French threat had receded somewhat, the Russian menace again became fully apparent. Sir Robert Wilson's *Sketch of the Military and Political Power of Russia* in 1817 sensed the great and growing power of Russia and its world vision, a theme that has permeated British assessments of Russia ever since. He saw Russia contending for world dominion with the other,

---

* A similar point was made as early as the fifteenth century. A Russian monk, writing in the fictitious 'Testament of King Magnus' (purported to be by Magnus II and VII of Denmark) wrote 'he who invades the land of Russia and ignores the kissing of the cross has the Lord God, and fire and water, against him'. Eric Christiansen, *The Northern Crusades — The Baltic and The Catholic Frontier 1100-1525* (London, 1980), p. 191.

† Russia, Sweden and Denmark banded together to oppose the British right of search at sea. Arguably, this was an earlier collision of interests.

still dangerous candidate, France.

> Such contending parties will not come out to skirmish and then mutually retire, nor will they fight for conquest to give away; the one will keep the field, and with it the Dictatorship of the World.[20]

Irving H. Smith has concluded that by the 1830s British attitudes had crystallised into a distinct Russophobia, a condition that was to persist, with few exceptions, to the present.[21] By 1838, as Anglo-Russian relations headed for a crisis over Afghanistan, the implications of Russian power for Europe were clearly understood.

> The most important political question on which modern times have to decide, is the policy that must now be pursued, in order to maintain the security of Western Europe against the overgrown power of Russia: a power that hangs in threatening darkness over the west, as the thunder cloud of the tropics hangs over the lands destined to feel the fury of the desolating tornado.[22]

With the exception of the brief invasion scare of 1859, when fear of France loomed larger, the British popular attitude to Russia remained much the same throughout the nineteenth century, and almost until the First World War.[23] A publication called *The Balance of Power* in 1888 described Russia as 'our great enemy'. The Russian threat had been with the British for so long that even after the conclusion of the Convention in 1907, the British could not believe the 'threat' had disappeared.[24] With the coming to power of the Bolsheviks in 1917 all the old ideological fears were reawakened, and although the brief period of alliance of 1941-5 cut deeply into the British consciousness, it was short-lived and died a sudden death. Before 1941, it must be remembered, Soviet Russia was formally an ally of Germany and although the British knew by 1940 that Hitler would soon attack Russia, British assessments prior to 1940, in the main, regarded Russia as a potential enemy and as an ally of the Germans from 1939-40. Furthermore, as Churchill's famous statement reminds us, it was an alliance with the Devil to deal with a more immediate problem — a Faustian pact. Even before the end of the war, the Cold War had begun.

Of course, some analysts were capable of looking beyond the immediate threats. In 1898 Sir George Clarke pointed out that even after two centuries of expansion Russia had not occupied a square yard of territory which was then or ever had been desired by Great Britain. This could not be said of France, Germany or the USA! He therefore considered that an understanding with Russia was perfectly possible.

> Until Russia advances into a defined sphere of British influence, we have no grievance against her; until such a sphere is defined, we have no claim to arrest her advance ... to remove the longstanding antagonism between the two nations and to substitute direct agreements between London and St. Petersburg for competitive manipulations of the dummy government at Peking would be a task worthy of a great statesman and a powerful guarantee of the peace of the world.[25]

The need to choose between Moscow and Peking is particularly topical.

There may be a Russian threat, and British military planners have certainly believed in it but, as Clarke said, it is wrong to accept the idea unquestioningly. A policy which appears threatening to us may seem to the Russians entirely defensive.

Russians have always seen things rather differently.

The Threat to Russia

It is very obvious, but often forgotten, that Russian fears of the West (though not of Britain) are far older and more deep-seated than Western fears of Russia. Similarly, Russians are more conscious of their own weaknesses than we are.

In the thirteenth century Russia had all the hallmarks of a rich and growing civilisation. There were 300 towns and Kiev with its golden-roofed churches was considered a 'rival of Constantinople'. Merchants from other European countries, Western Asia and the East lived in enclaves in Novgorod and Kiev. This wealth and prosperity was rudely shattered by civil war and invasion (see Figure 1.1). The effect of the Mongol invasions is well known, but it is often forgotten that the Russians were also attacked from the west. Swedes, Danes, Poles, Germans and Hungarians all invaded in the thirteenth century.[26] Of these, the memory of the Swedish crusaders is particularly detested by Russians. Against these the Russians deployed considerable forces for the time: Vladimir-Suzdal deployed 20,000 men against the German knights in the area adjacent to the Baltic Sea (*Pribaltika*) and Novgorod sent 15,000-20,000, while Galitsko-Volynsk deployed 30,000 against the Hungarians. Of course, the Tartars were still the worst of many evils: Kiev lost 10,000 dead at the battle of Kalka (1223). Before 1200 Russia

Figure 1.1: Russia in the Thirteenth Century Showing Foreign Invasions

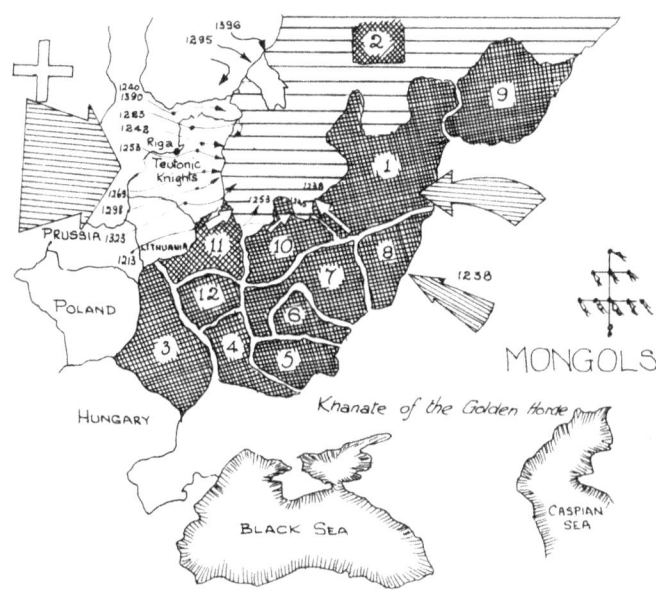

1. VLADIMAR-SUZDAL
2. NOVGOROD
3. GALITSKO-VOLYNSK (VOLHYNIA-GALICIA)
4. KIEV
5. PEREYASLAVL
6. NOVGOROD-SVERSK
7. CHERNIGOV
8. MUROM RIAZAN
9. VIATKO
10. SMOLENSK
11. POLOTSK
12. TUROV-PINSK

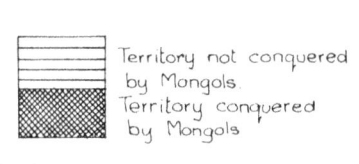

was innocent of imperial ambitions. The Mongol conquest – the most successful (but not the only) steppe incursion – changed all that. 'Russia emerged from the Tartar Yoke not only as the imperial power of Muscovy but also, after 1453, as the sole great independent orthodox power.'[27]

By the end of the fifteenth century the yoke of the Tartars had been broken and Ivan III had formed a new grouping of Russian states centred on Moscow. The natural reaction to the threats from all sides was to push the enemy further and further away. The effects of the 'Tartar Yoke' may be exaggerated by some writers but memories of degrading subjugation are deep. Even *Krest'yanin* (a peasant) comes from the word 'Christian' – those who were subjugated to the Mongols. Wars with Lithuania, Poland and the Tartar Khanates added territory to the domain of the Grand Dukes of Moscow. With some interruptions this process continued until the Russian Empire reached its fullest extent at the beginning of this century. This historical perspective is valuable because of course the early Soviet Republic found itself in the same position as Ivan IV's Russia. The nascent USSR in August 1918 was not much larger than the Principality of Moscow in 1462, expanding during 1919 to the size of Russia between 1533 and 1598 (see Figures 1.2 and 1.3).

Some of its enemies were the same too. An important point is that Western invaders had traditionally sought both to conquer and convert. This was the mission of the Knights of the Livonian order in the thirteenth century. So too after the Revolution; although the Western powers were initially motivated by the need to prop up the Eastern Front against Germany, they were also unwilling to tolerate a Communist state. The 'threat' had the vicious aspect of all ideological wars as well as the traditional aspects of invasion.[28]

By 1922, Soviet Russia had regained most of the territory occupied by the former Russian Empire. The Soviets still felt extremely vulnerable, however. They felt that the capitalists wanted to take away the considerable trade of the Russian Empire (4.2 milliard rubles in 1913) which the Soviets wanted to revive for themselves.

'The world bourgeosie has come to the conviction that it is essential to destroy Soviet Russia', wrote one commentator in 1928.[29] The principal capitalist powers were seen as 'England' (Britain) and France (not, as yet, the USA!). Britain was particularly dangerous because the Conservatives were in power at the time – 'the most evil enemies of the working class'. Britain was not a direct threat, however; she would support a 'whole range of independent countries' – countries which do not sound as if they could have posed much of a threat – Finland, Estonia, Latvia, Lithuania and Poland. In passing, it is interesting to note that these were the old enemies of medieval times. Poland, which had given the Soviets a bloody nose in 1920, was the most dangerous. The Soviets saw the balance as follows:

Figure 1.2: The Expansion of Russia[30]

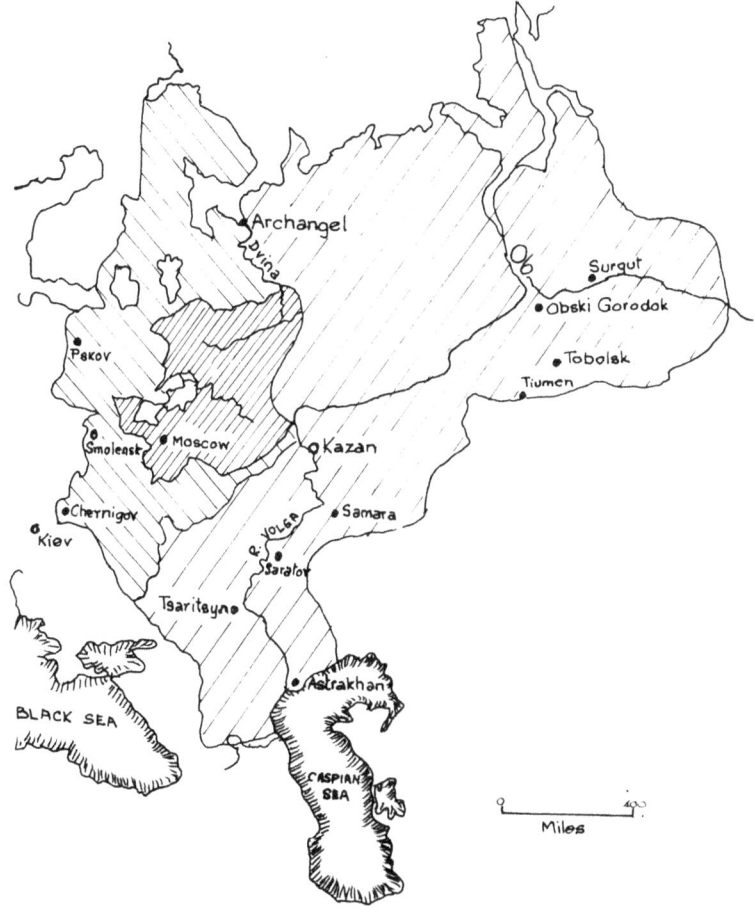

Figure 1.3: Soviet Russia, 1918[31]

(Note: This sketch map shows the approximate extent of Soviet territory in August 1918. There were other outposts (for example, Baku) which were cut off from the main Soviet territory.)

Peace time strengths	Men (000)
Poland	300
Rumania	189
Finland	32
Estonia	12
Latvia	20
Lithuania	18
Total	571
Red Army	562

Of course, the Soviets could raise more men than these allied states in the long term, but in order to beat them the Soviets would have to mobilise far more men than their standing forces. The military potential of those countries with their 55 million population posed a genuine perceived threat, the more so since French officers were busy training the Poles, and the British were training the Estonians and Finns.[32] This is one example of how the Soviets can perceive a threat of which most British people would be unaware.

The Soviets may feel the same way about NATO as they did about these countries in 1928. The situation is similar; a number of small countries whose armed forces together have a slight numerical superiority over the USSR. A Westerner's immediate reaction is 'so what?' The number of Soviet tanks, their offensive capability and their state of readiness is surely what counts. But not so to the Russian. Numbers of men matter. This is explicitly stated by the eminent Soviet historian Beskrovny who, having stressed Engels' point that population and technology are crucial determinants of military success, adds, 'for such a huge country as Russia the *quantity* and quality of the population has especial military significance'.[33] The Soviets feel that a large numerical superiority is necessary if they are to stand any chance of success. Their experience of war and particularly of the Second World War bears this out, even if we may feel that such forces are far in excess of their defensive need.

Besides perceiving threats which may not seem obvious to us, they also perceive weaknesses in capability where outsiders perceive great reserves of strength. To give an example from the Crimean War – the English publication *The Army Reformer* in 1855 considered that 'an army had sailed from the shores of Great Britain to storm a stronghold

[Sevastopol] fortified by every means which prodigal expenditure and matured ingenuity could supply'.[34] Although this might have seemed the case in retrospect, it was arguably not true of Sevastopol at the beginning of the Crimean War. The defence of Sevastopol was a triumph of concentration of resources. The difficulties of defending the country as a whole were immense. The railway network was poor, with only one principal line between Petersburg and Moscow. The road network was inadequate. The western frontier was regarded as the most vulnerable and new roads were built from Warsaw to Moscow and Petersburg, but that was all. The Russians had to guard against possible attacks in the Baltic and against Poland, and in 1853, out of 303 battalions on the western frontier only 62 were stationed in the whole south-east. They could not, therefore, anticipate the main thrust of the allies' attack and concentrating their forces to meet it the following year was no mean feat.[35]

The belief, explicitly stated here, that the western frontier is the most vulnerable is important in understanding Russian and Soviet deployments. It recurs time and time again. The major concentrations of population and the two capitals were there; so — at least until the Second World War — was most of the industry. The Russian government naturally reinforced that side first. In the Russo-Japanese War, troops were not taken from the west. The latest and best equipment continued to go first to the west, not to the east.[36] This was partly not to lose face by admitting weakness but partly because the west was what mattered. The Russians could *afford* to lose bits of Siberia in the worst event. From a NATO viewpoint it is easy to ask why the Russians keep such large forces in Europe; the reasons would appear, in part, to be deep-seated historical ones.

This raises the question of China and of the 'two-front' or 'encirclement' fear. At times in its history Russia has faced and perceived threats from east as well as west; first from the Tartar tribes and later from the Japanese. It is often asserted that the Russians are now terrified of China, but Soviet defence policy belies this view. The Chinese clearly have no intention of attacking Russia, and the Russians know it. Their 'traditional' fear of the German would also appear to be more natural to Western than to Soviet eyes. West Germany is very logically regarded as a threat because it is a member of NATO. But *East* Germany is a trusted ally. The Kremlin would appear to be highly pragmatic and not racially prejudiced or paranoiac. The evidence suggests that 'the picture of the USSR dominated by anxieties due to encirclement . . . would appear to be of our own making'.[37]

To summarise, the Russians have always considered themselves threatened and vulnerable where others would not, while others have even considered the Russians threatened where the Russians themselves would not. Russians' attitudes, however, change according to circumstances. Both the British and Russians are guilty of ethnocentrism in military perceptions.[38]

Where does Britain fit into this overall picture? Britain was not seen as much of a direct threat to Imperial Russia because of the difficulty of making an amphibious attack on the Empire. At the time of the Crimean War, the only places where the British could reach Russia were the Baltic and Black Seas. As the British Empire expanded there came other possibilities: the White Sea, and into Turkestan and the Caucasus from Iran in the Russian Civil War (in Turkestan in July and the Caucasus in August 1918). Both the British forces involved in South Russia had admittedly originally been sent to forestall Turkish invasion: after that danger disappeared they found themselves fighting the Bolsheviks. Nevertheless, they took on their new role with enthusiasm and added to Soviet fears of invasion from the south which were already of long standing.[39] Undoubtedly, the fear of an attack from British possessions in Asia was the one real land threat the Russians ever felt they faced from Britain, while the main maritime threats were perceived as lying in the Baltic and Black Seas.

Ends and Means

Ends and means in military terms are intentions and capabilities. Intentions are the non-military aspect of military power – the politics of which the means are the extension. This Clausewitzian truth has been taken to heart by Russian military writers. Few people read Clausewitz in 1869 but the eminent Russian theorist G.A. Leyer, respected in his time and by Soviet military writers since, made the same point then, at the very beginning of his greatest work on war. Lenin hammered the point home.[40] War as a tool of politics is thus very heavily stressed to the Russian. We sometimes forget it. It is the height of naïvete to say that 'we will assess capabilities because intentions can change overnight'. Intentions do not change without good reason, although they can be hidden. We assume from the mix of forces the Soviets dispose of that they have some desire to attack Western Europe. There is no hard evidence that they intend to do so. Why would they want to? They have nothing to gain from a straight thrust into West Europe that cannot be achieved by more subtle and comfortable means, and everything to lose. They would have to throw all their conventional forces into any attempt because anything less, being opposed by the 'all' of the attacked, would fail. Political will affects capability.

A striking example of political will affecting capability is the case of Russia in the First World War. As we have seen, ever since the Middle Ages, Russia had been acknowledged as having vast resources. However, the year 1915 saw her terribly short of war materiel, because the resources were not used sufficiently. At first Russia's ruling class was, in the main, not prepared to pay the social price that mobilising the economy entailed.[41] When they did, after 1915, Russia was able to produce impressive quantities of materiel. With the aid sent by the allies this should have given her a superiority on the Eastern front, had the distribution system worked.[42] It was not possible to make these supplies available at the front line quickly enough, and eventually Russia collapsed. This was, of course, partly a result of the social consequences of the mobilisation of the economy itself, and partly due to older social causes. The army proved itself competent in 1916 and, despite Lenin's assertion that it 'voted with its feet', remained an effective force well into 1917. A valuable assessment of the army's *military* capability is that of Major General John Headlam, who was posted to Russia from 25 February to 25 March 1917 (new style). Headlam visited the Southwest Front, where he saw 'no signs of slackness'. The artillery was thoroughly professional, the trenches very clean – he was particularly surprised at the absence of rats.[43] Headlam's report shows that in February 1917 the Russian army on the South-west Front, if careless in some respects, was fighting effectively.

Headlam's report contains one astonishing caveat. 'No reference has been made to the Revolution which occurred during my visit to the front. This is a matter which has formed the subject of separate reports.'[44] This does not imply criticism of Headlam. In retrospect it is impossible to think of the military ability of the army early in 1917 without thinking of the February Revolution. But Headlam's task was to report on the state of the means, not on possible changes in political ends. It is an interesting example of how the political aspect can quite happily be ignored. Of course, in assessing military power, political will is a very large-scale version of morale, which has always formed part of appreciations of the enemy.

The War Office's assessments on the other hand were very much tied up with ends. The informative *Military Resources of the Russian Empire* of 1907, whose production was inspired by the Anglo-Russian Convention of that year, devoted plenty of space to aims. These were defined as: unrestricted navigation of the Black Sea, Straits and Mediterranean; political union of all Slavs under the leadership of Russia; and political dominion over neighbouring states* *wherever their weakness permitted.* In other words, then as now, Russia sought to attain its aims wherever possible without fighting and certainly would not fight unless it felt sure of winning.[45]

During the Second World War, political will was a major factor in assessing Soviet Russia's military 'power'. The belief that Soviet Russia would not prove an effective ally in the Second World War sprang partly from a belief that Russia would not fight, and partly from a belief in Soviet weakness.

The Soviets undoubtedly wanted to keep out of the war. The War Office considered in January 1941 that Stalin would not fight an offensive war unless it became 'patent to all' that Hitler was doomed, when he would 'probably pursue opportunist tactics as he did in the case of losing Poland'.[46] Even if the Germans seized the Straits, it was thought Stalin would avoid fighting. Whereas 'a Romanov who let the Straits go without striking a blow is inconceivable', Stalin did 'not have to worry about Russian honour'. Only if he were attacked directly would he fight.[47] Whilst the Soviets might go a long way to acquiesce in German economic demands in order to avoid war, for example increasing supplies to Germany and even allowing Germans to supervise production, it was assessed that she would fight rather than allow the Germans to occupy the Ukraine or the Caucasus.[48] Russia was even more likely to fight in the spring, when she would be better prepared. It was noted that,

> the army is . . . working hard to improve its efficiency and though the fact that Germany is the chief danger is of course never officially stated, every child knows [what] these preparations are for. It is hardly conceivable that having demanded such efforts from people the Soviet government would submit without fighting . . . Further,

---

* The old cliché that 'Russia' (whoever Russia is) sought to obtain access to the open sea and possess 'warm water ports' was not quoted as a separate and definite objective of Russian foreign policy because there did not 'appear sufficient ground for so doing'. The report confirmed 'Russia already possesses upon the Murman coast excellent ice free harbours which she has never made any use of .'. . Russia no doubt desires to possess ice free harbours but only as accessories and stalking horses in her larger schemes of expansion' (War Office, General Staff, *Military Resources of the Russian Empire*, 1907, p. 254).

no Soviet government could allow a German occupation of the Ukraine and Caucasus ... and hope to survive.[49]

Stalin would not allow the armed forces to do anything that might provoke the Germans. Right up to 22 June 1941 they were forbidden to concentrate troops in frontier areas or fire on German aircraft.[50] By desperately trying to avoid a fight, Stalin tied the army's hands: will affecting capability. On the other hand, as the above quotation shows, the fact that preparations were being made further back was assessed as reinforcing resolve: in other words, capability can also affect political will.

Despite the War Office assessment, many doubted Soviet resolve. The leadership was perceived as being favourably inclined towards the Germans. There were hopes of a split between military and government circles. But the military attaché in Moscow wrote that although the Soviet government's policy towards Germany was not approved by Red Army circles who did 'not conceal their hostility toward that country', he did not believe this divergence was a major factor. He did not believe that the Red Army chiefs had sufficient power over 'the ruler of Kremlin policy' [Stalin], to turn him against Germany and any assumption based on this would be dangerous.[51] The Foreign Office thought that Stalin might be inclined to help Germany continue the struggle as this would weaken his western opponents (Britain and the USA) more than otherwise, and because he might think it would make the Germans less likely to turn on him.[52]

These assessments of ends were, in the main, accurate. In the days of Stalin's personal dictatorship, determining aims was easier than it is now — it is easier to get the measure of one man than of many. Analysing the personal views of the ruler is clearly the oldest form of assessing aims — dating from times when autocracy was the rule rather than the exception. The Russians conducted and no doubt conduct similar analyses: for example, before the Crimean War Brunnov, the Russian ambassador in London, submitted a lengthy report on the career and views of Palmerston.[53]

Assessing Means

The problem of assessing means is as old as war. Those military prodigies the Mongols, the spiritual ancestors of the Soviet army in many ways, had a sophisticated intelligence organisation, as a Russian officer noted in 1846.

In order to obtain information about the composition of states they either sent out embassies, equipped caravans, or despatched light detachments (*otryady*) on camels or horses which, burying themselves [sic] in the interior of the country, captured travellers and inhabitants and extracted from them the necessary information.[54]

Information gathering has always tended to concentrate on numbers and numbers are, as Clausewitz said, a fair guide.[55] There are few examples of military skill triumphing over much larger numbers. As early as the seventeenth century the Russian army deployed 300,000 men, according to Milton. Milton noted that the Russians fought '... without order; nor willingly give battail but by stealth or ambush; of cold and hard Diet marvellously patient'.[56] The characteristics of toughness and cunning recur in early assessments of Russian war-making, although recent works stress the straightforwardness and obviousness of Russian tactics. But Russian technical ingenuity and their proficiency in covert operations are often also stressed. Despite the bumbling image of Soviet forces in the Russo-Finnish War, they manifested 'a remarkable inventiveness', and they have been very quick to adapt new technology such as the hovercraft and helicopter to military purposes.[57]

Milton was writing not for the military, to whom Russia was not as yet a threat, but for the reading public. Governments of the time seem to have relied mostly on diplomatic intelligence — court gossip — to assess means rather than ends. An early assessment of means which has something of an official character dates from 1724. This is *The Russian Fleet under Peter the Great* by 'a contemporary Englishman'. The title implies that it was intended for publication but its comparative brevity and the technical nature of the contents suggest it was a report written by a British subject who had served under Peter. It makes the same general point as Milton, that the Russians were 'ever reputed better at ambuscade or defence of a place where they lie covered than in the bravery of open assult'.[58] The Russians could make 'a handsome defence, ever a Russian's masterpiece'. This assessment has been proved right both tactically, for example at Stalingrad, and grand strategically, in 1812 and 1941.

The report also contains an early intelligence summary, but couched in more refreshing English than most!

A list of the Russian fleet capable of going to sea the beginning of the summer 1724 before any more are launched, in case seamen can be found to man them ... Those marked with a cross are old and crazy and those marked N_3 can't carry sail, when it blows anything hard and consequently unfit for distant enterprises.

The list contains six ships of 90 guns (of which two were 'N_3') one of 80 guns, three of 70 (of which two were 'X') and eight 64s of which two — *Moscow* and *Ingermanland*,* — "'tis supposed these go no more to sea'. The overall strategic balance was also considered; 'If the Tsar attains to his aim of having forty ships of line of battle in his harbours on the Baltic he will be more than a match for the Dane or Swede.'[59]

As noted above, British and Russian interest in each other as rivals crystallised in the nineteenth century. By the 1830s the Prussians and Russians were producing objective intelligence summaries containing strengths and disposition, published openly. In 1835, the Russian *Voenny Zhurnal*, which they published under the auspices of the *Voenno-Uchěny Komitet* (Military Scientific Committee), contained a summary of the forces of European powers which included British forces.[60] It is notable that the British appear *last* among the countries covered.† It gave the total population (24 million), infantry and cavalry strengths, the strength of forces in 'East India' and naval strengths. The 1839 edition contained a 'military geography of Great Britain and Ireland'.[61]

That the Russians should have developed modern style intelligence earlier than the British is not surprising. They have always treated military affairs in a particularly scientific and objective way. They also seem to have a natural propensity for intelligence-gathering. The British did not publish a modern, objective summary of intelligence until 1853, but even so this is earlier than one might expect. The assessment — 'Organisation and Distribution of the Russian Army' — appears in *Colburn's United Services Magazine*. It was inspired by the impending crisis in Anglo-Russian relations. 'At the moment we are writing, the eyes of Europe are turned towards the lower Danube.' The pre-Crimean British army, often regarded as a fools' paradise (see the Russian assessment below, p. 58), obviously contained men of high intellectual calibre, although one can assume that most officers in the infantry and cavalry did not read the works produced by these exceptional figures. The author of the 1853 article, unfortunately anonymous, writes with the same crisp authority as a modern assessor.

---

* Ingermanland is the name of the province on the south side of the Gulf of Finland.
† Austria, Prussia, Bavaria, Saxony, Hesse, France, Holland, Belgium, Turkey and Britain.

Up to the present time no work or publication in our own language that we are aware of, – or indeed in any other save the Prussian *Wehr Zeitung* and Haxthavren's remarkable *'Stūdien über Russland'*, contains details calculated to throw light upon the military resources of the Czar or to exhibit the mode in which these forces are organised, embodied and distributed. Fragments are to be found here and there in divers publications, but no regular or connected details, dates, or returns have been given. Our tables are intended to supply this deficiency.[62]

This, therefore, was the first modern intelligence assessment of Russia in English. The tables were compiled 'with care, if not from direct official, at least from unquestionably authentic sources', especially *Wehr Zeitung*. The writer remarked that the latter should be subscribed to by all British military academies.

The raw numbers were suitably qualified. From the strength of a Russian corps or division on the march 'at least 10% must be deducted from the general amount at first starting' (they were always slightly under strength) and after 3 weeks to a month 'nearly double that amount'.[63] The total number of regular personnel borne on the returns of pay presented to the Finance Department at the end of 1852 was 1,221,164. The article pointed out, of course, that there existed a 'wide difference between the numbers of men borne on the Finance returns... and those actually effective or even in hospital'. Another problem was the large number of Cossack irregulars. The British used the *Wehr Zeitung*, whose information on such subjects was 'more correct than that of any other similar publication', which assessed the number at over 110,000 with 1500 officers holding permanent rank.[64]

It is probably more than coincidence that the British War Office series of papers WO/33, which contains official intelligence reports, among other things, began at almost exactly the same time. The first intelligence paper in this series is a *Topographical Memoir for Military Purposes*, dating from 1855. A table showing the dispositions and state of the Russian forces was compiled in the same year. Brevet Major J. McCaskill wrote a paper on the difficulty of obtaining supplies for the Russian army in the Crimea, an objective assessment of the enemy's weakness as well as of his strength.[65]

Although a few reports were therefore circulated in official circles, the military press of the time was the main forum for assessments of potential enemies and friends. The Russian journals *Voenny Sbornik* and *Morskoy Sbornik* contain a great deal of information about the

British forces, but it is not clear to what extent this was motivated by a desire for intelligence about a possible enemy and to what extent by interest in the military affairs of others as an example to be followed. This second alternative perhaps applied particularly to naval matters, where the British were unquestionably the world's leaders. The Russians were especially interested in the build-up of the ironclad fleet. In the 1860s the British were also arguably the premier industrial power with the capability for manufacturing some of the most advanced armaments.

The British were ready to adopt other people's ideas. In the 1870s, for example, they showed a great deal of interest in the system of military education in Austria, and attention was 'specially called to ... the education of Officers and Cadets by a well organised system of Lectures, Conferences, Essays ... etc.'[66]

There was at the time a veritable international intelligence community, which published profusely. Much of the material published in journals, both British and Russian, was translated from other countries' journals, especially from French and German for land matters, and from English for maritime ones. A perusal of the *Voenny Sbornik* of the 1870s reveals 'underwater Mines in England' translated from the French *Journal des Sciences Militaires*[67] in addition to details of Cardwell's reforms and British autumn manoeuvres in 1872.[68]

The amount of open discussion of detailed military matters is striking, although the Russians divided their journals into *Otdel Ofitsial'ny* (official section) and *Neofitsial'ny*. The former contained official notices, promotion lists and so on, the latter the informed discussion and interesting articles. This appears to have been for administrative reasons rather than for secrecy. The general indifference to secrecy is borne out by the fact that in the Russo-Japanese War the *Russkiy Invalid* published all orders given by the Russian War Office. Colonel Izmestiev of the Russian General Staff complained bitterly. 'Every formation of a new unit, with the dates of the commencement and completion of the formation was given to the world.' So the 'official section' could still be widely read.[69] The non-military press was also a fruitful source of information. In 1868 the Russians reported on the 'opinion of the English press concerning ironclad ships'. They were concerned as to whether the ships could survive rough seas, although more out of interest for their own developments than because of the limitations or otherwise that this might or might not impose on the scope of British maritime power.[70]

Intelligence-gathering was facilitated by the extremely free hand given to the press at the time; it was the great age of the war correspondent.

The Russians do not appear to have manifested that penchant for secrecy that westerners attribute to them now. In the Russo-Japanese War, as has been shown, they certainly gave too much away. Colonel Izmestiev's tale of woe continued:

> Notwithstanding the example of the 1870 campaign, the Russian Press published to the world everything that had to do with the Russian Army . . . anyone who cared to do so might have compiled a fairly accurate 'graphic' time table of the movements and concentration of troops by consulting the newspapers and the information given concerning the transport of units on their way to the Far East . . .[71]

After detailed treatment in military journals, the next step in the development of assessments was the publication of self-contained reports under the auspices of the General Staffs. The Germans and Austrians were again ahead, and again the British translated directly from them. The *Armed Strength of Russia*, which was the earliest of many editions published in the late nineteenth and early twentieth century, was translated from the Austrian original of 1871 by the Topographical and Statistical Department of the British War Office in 1873. The War Office expressed the hope that this volume would 'in some measure supply the want which has so frequently been felt, of a series of authentic and comprehensive works in our own language on the Organisation, Equipment & etc. of Foreign Armies'.[72]

It is noteworthy that the Russian army was the subject of the first summary. Works on the Austrian and German armies followed, in that order. This was almost certainly because the Russians, with their Asian ambitions, were the most likely land opponent in the near future. The summary was certainly not made at a convenient time, but in the middle of Milyutin's reforms, when assessment was more difficult than in a stable period.[73]

Thus, by the 1870s, foreign military power was being assessed in much the same way as now. To an extent, precision became the enemy of accuracy — any assessment which purports to be totally logical and objective fails to realise the true nature of war, which is nasty, messy and subject to the whims of the gods rather than to any rational rules.

Quality, Quantity and Experience

The first of the 'unquantifiables' is probably the quality of personnel. The Russians and the British tended to be disparaging about each other. The gallant ordinary British soldier, hero of the Crimea, was not so regarded by the Russians.

> As far as the quality of the British Army goes, it is necessary to remark that the moral level of the enlisted soldier was low and only severe discipline made up for the natural instincts of men who had come into the army because it was impossible to find other employment ... His manliness was more physical than moral ... in bivouacs he fell into a state of apathy. Being spoilt as regards material comforts [in the British army of the 1850s?] he was completely (*vovse*) unable to bear privations, and, unlike the French soldier, did not succeed in adapting himself to circumstances.[74]

Wellington might have agreed about the need to make up for some inadequacies by severe discipline, but he might have been surprised that these soldiers did not even frighten the enemy. On the other hand the Russians believed that the French soldier 'thirsted for victory and never doubted success'. He was 'independent and dextrous in combat ...'[75] The Sardinians were 'brought up in a veritable military spirit'[76] and compared favourably with the British. This is an interesting example of how 'national characteristics' can be perceived very differently by different nations.

As for the British officers, those in the infantry and cavalry were considered ignorant of 'military-academic studies', an assessment reflecting the conscious intellectualism of the Russian military, then as now. However, they acknowledged that the officers of artillery and engineers received an 'excellent specialist education' at Woolwich and Chatham respectively.[77]

As for the British opinion of the Russian, it has always respected his courage but not his intelligence, nor his capacity for taking the offensive. Fred Jane, writing on the Russian Navy in 1904, remarked with perspicacity that 'Ivan realises he exists to *be shot at;* Jack, that he exists *to shoot at others,* and this psychological difference is ... all the difference in the world.'[78] Are Russians *too* brave? Is that why they have consistently failed to perform as well in battle as their material equipment, physical toughness and undoubted military skill would indicate? There has always been a tendency to make mistakes on the day. Their performance has been inconsistent.

In the Russo-Japanese War, Colonel Waters, one of the British Military Observers, commented 'I generally found what I expected to be bad was good and vice versa.'[79] A contradiction of a different but related sort was noted by Headlam in 1917: 'that blend of contradictory qualities, which is said to be a Russian characteristic, the capacity for violent energy side by side with indolence and happy-go-lucky laissez aller . . .'[80]

How else indeed can one explain why during the Second World War one moment Russian forces would surrender in droves and the next others would fight tenaciously for some obscure, perhaps unimportant positions? How does one reconcile the ingenuity and cunning with which they blended into the terrain in defence with the obviousness of their steam-roller attacks?

Two of the most important factors influencing how people will perform in battle are training and experience. Here again, Russian performance has been contradictory. Like the British, the Russians had, before 1914, fought a 'modern' war against an enemy equipped with the latest technology. The Russians endeavoured to learn from the Russo-Japanese War, and the early days of the First World War saw them putting some of the lessons into practice. Like the British in the west, on some occasions they held firm in trenches, picking off Germans who had not fought a war since 1870 and who at first advanced in relatively dense masses.[81] But despite their advantages, and some good leadership at junior levels, poor leadership at higher levels caused a 'distinctly good' army to suffer appalling defeats. The same happened in 1939-42. After being badly handled in Finland, and with the

> whole Soviet system having been concentrated for ten years in preparing for a defensive war, they were unable in '41 and '42 to prevent a nation with 100 million fewer inhabitants than Russia from overrunning in an incredibly short time an area greater than had ever been conquered in history since . . . Alexander the Great.[82]

Yet the Red Army had proved itself highly competent in the east when it fought against the Japanese at Khalkhin Gol.

The British Foreign Office in April 1944 considered that Russian success was possible because the Soviet government 'had at their disposal vast reserves of man power and material and had been willing to sacrifice them without consideration for the future'.[83] There was an element of truth in this, but the Russians did learn from the war.

Nevertheless, it is unwise to assume that lessons are always remembered. Revision is necessary. In Finland, for example, the Russians found to their cost that a motorised division strung out along a road, surrounded on both sides by hostile terrain occupied by guerrilla forces, is liable to be cut up into 'sausages' (as the Finns called them).[84] Forty years later, in Afghanistan, they had to learn the lesson again.

The Soviets place emphasis on the value of lessons learned. For example, in 1972, a book called *Military Strength and International Relations,* in considering the US involvement in Vietnam, made the following point about so called 'local wars':

> There also remains the significance of these wars as self-contained proving grounds (*poligony*), where new types of military technology are tried out and where the structure and organisation of armed forces is proofed and perfected, principles and methods of waging war are worked out and, finally, mass training of a reserve of people possessing military experience for NATO countries is made possible. . . for example, during the years of the Vietnam war the USA put through it [such a reserve] about 3 million Americans. This reserve with military experience will continue to exist for at least a decade . . .[85]

Polemic apart, the idea that Vietnam has left the US with a reserve of trained men is interesting. Of course, that decade is now over. Again, to the Russian, when assessing foreign military power, such numbers matter. The Soviet army, which has not fought a hot war since 1945, was no doubt concerned about its lack of experience. Is it too far fetched to suggest that this thought may have added to the Russians' willingness to embark on a 'local war' in Afghanistan – a proving ground for men and equipment?

Asian Assessments

All these assessments do not tell us how the enemy or ally will actually perform, or what the outcome of a battle will be. In order to do that it is necessary first to envisage a 'scenario' – a play that is possible both from the point of view of the characters and the plot. The Russian *Voenny Sbornik* in 1868 considered a number of permutations of allies,*

---

* Prussia and Russia v. Austria;
  France and Austria v. Prussia and Russia;
  France and Prussia v. Russia and Austria;
  France and Russia v. Prussia and Austria.

and the circumstances in which they could fight each other on land in Europe, but not what the likely outcome would be. It is hardly illuminating as a study of foreign policy, and appears to have been a framework within which war games might be played.[86] Britain was not seen as a rival or even possible major participant in a European land war. She was, however, a significant land power in Asia. The Russian expedition to Khiva in 1839-40 was a direct response to the British expedition to Afghanistan in 1837.[87] The Russians were extremely cautious regarding Afghanistan and Tibet. It has been argued that the reason for this, in contrast to the tenacious and methodical policy practised in other parts of Asia (Persia and North China), was that expansion in this direction would bring the risk of war with Britain. Russia won Afghanistan over twice in the nineteenth century, in 1837 and 1878. In both cases the Russians did not take advantage of the situation, but cautiously backed down.[88] The Russian leaders' caution, and their fear of Britain, were summarised by the dynamic Ivanin:

... if we felt constrained by England's hostility to our expedition to Khiva, then could we not have said with justice 'In Asia you rule the richest of lands; 150 million are bound to you; in India you have an army of 100,000 men; your huge factories are flourishing, you can supply arms and war materiel to our enemies in Central Asia, and therefore we do not wish you to extend your dominion and influence beyond the Indus. We consider every step of yours beyond the right bank of the Indus hostile to our trade and political stance. As a naval power, you can extend your trade and political enterprises across the whole Asian littoral (*pribrezh'e*); only leave the interior countries of Asia for our trade; otherwise we must regard every step you make beyond the Indus or the Himalayan chain with suspicion.'[89]

General Skobelev, writing in 1879, felt that

Our position in Central Asia can only be considered comparatively secure so long as our influence meets no rival .... The Mussulman population of those districts, mastered by us but still quivering feverishly, will remain submissive to us *only in proportion as it believes that might is still on our side.*

If we have hitherto been able to encounter and suppress the outburst of Mussulman fanaticism amongst the population of the conquered provinces with our extremely limited fighting means [note the Russians' perception of their own weakness] we are indebted ...

to the dependence on us [of] the Khans of Khiva, leaders of the Turkoman tribes . . . and the consequent impossibility of making these districts the centres of political and religious opposition.

. . . What must not we Russians fear in Central Asia seeing that England has succeeded in entangling with a thousand snares him whom the orthodox of Central Asia consider . . . their leader in War and the representative of the Prophet? [Katta Tiouria, son of the Emir of Bokhara]

In other words, militant Islam on the Russian borders was dangerous; it might spread to within the borders, and foreign powers might use it against the Russians. The only answer was to subjugate the area from which the poison might spread. Here, a hundred years before the invasion of Afghanistan in 1980, is one probable reason why it took place.[90]

Some British assessors could see the Russian's point. Kitchener watched the expansion of Russian railways at the end of the century with alarm, considering that 'all their lines have been made for purely strategical purposes, and but with one ultimate view, the menacing of Afghanistan, Persia and India'. But the ever unflappable Sir George Clarke, who was as we have seen, a proponent of Anglo-Russian *détente*, argued that only one spur could be regarded as having been built for strategic purposes and that was 'the natural Russian answer to our forced advance to Chaman in 1892'. Furthermore, 'Anyone glancing at a map of Afghanistan could only devise the impression that, from the railway point of view, Great Britain, not Russia was the aggressive power.'[91]

Clarke's view was not shared by most Englishmen. Sir C. MacGregor, Quartermaster General in India, was of the opinion in 1884 that

The aims of Russia as regards England are altogether so aggressive and unprovoked that I hold we are justified in using every means in our power, in the event of war, towards breaking up the Russian Empire into fractions that cannot for a long time become dangerous to us.[92]

MacGregor's *The Defence of India: A Strategical Study* coolly analysed the question 'can Russia invade India?' Although MacGregor stressed that he was dealing with means, not ends, his belief in the Russian threat comes through in his writing. But even assuming that Russia would fight Britain and Turkey together, and leaving ample forces

Figure 1.4: Russia and Britain in Asia 1846-1907

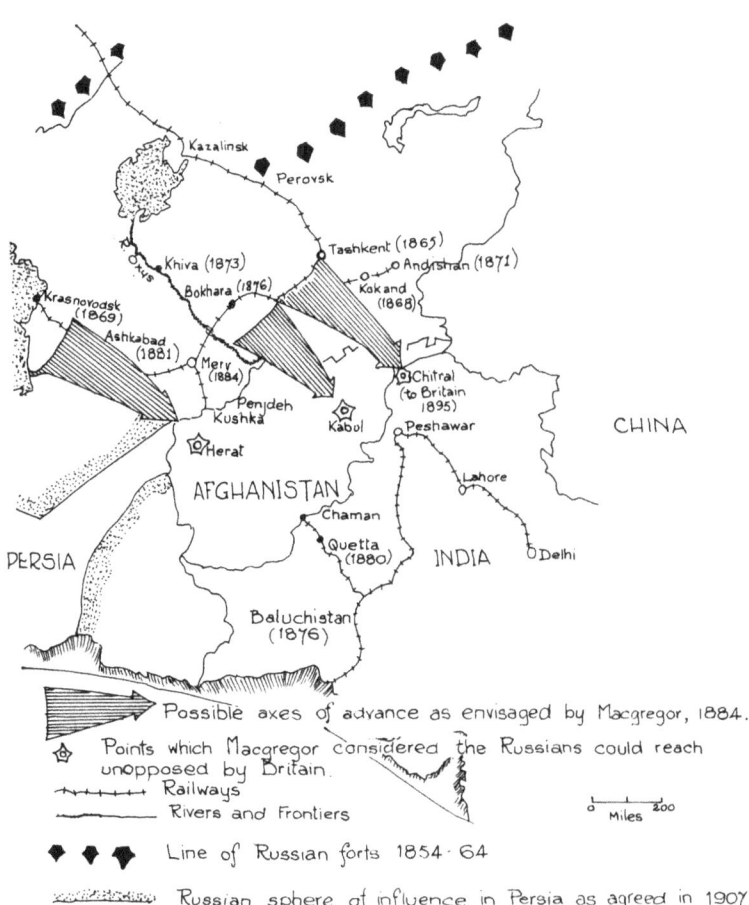

in the west to deal with the latter, Russia could deploy 185,000 infantry and 40,000 cavalry against India, even without drawing on the troops of the Balkan states.[93] As for the question of finance; then, as now, it was a question of economic priorities. The finances of Russia were known to be in a bad way, 'but as she makes no sign of reducing her forces in peace time ... we may assume that for such a popular operation as the invasion or threatening of India, money in abundance would be forthcoming'. MacGregor examined the logistics of Russian advance carefully and concluded that the Russians could reach three objectives –

Herat, Kabul and Chitral[94] – before the English could take any steps to prevent her. Once in Kabul, the Russians could raise another 20,000 'splendid and well-armed fighting men', and from Afghanistan she would be in a position to attack India.[95]

The British of this time had a healthy respect for the Russian army. The campaigns in Central Asia had given the Russians experience of warfare in a hostile environment and bred some competent and realistic commanders. There were no illusions about the superiority of the British soldier. MacGregor reminded those who underestimated Russia's power,

> ... it is not the Power of Afghanistan we shall have to meet, but that of Russia, not the efforts of a few thousand undisciplined men, but those of a *scientific, well disciplined army,* backed by an incalculable number of irregular troops drawn from the whole of Asia.[96]

Pride comes before a fall – whereas the British Empire at the height of its power was surprisingly modest. In 1903 British officials considered that 'In order successfully to oppose the 70,000 men which Russia could concentrate in the front line [in the vicinity of Kabul and Kandahar] we ought not to employ less than 80,000 men.'[97] Major J.M. Home of the Gurkhas who was sent by Britain to observe the Russo-Japanese War noted Russian claims that 'their Central Asian troops were ... vastly superior to our native troops and fully the equal of the British solder'.[98] The idea that the Russians can be beaten by smaller forces of superior quality is a fairly modern one: the Victorians and Edwardians were not so conceited. The same thought was evident in the idea of the naval two-power standard. Numerical parity *at the very least* was necessary.

Was there any substance to the belief that Russia intended to invade India? The Russian General Staff certainly compiled voluminous information on Asia, including the approaches to India. The *Sbornik po Azii* (Asian collection) was classified *Sekretno** and contained articles on topographical and military subjects. In the late 1880s articles appeared on 'The Military Communications along the Indo-Afghanistan frontier'[99] and a translation of an English article on 'The Defence of

---

* At this time the Russians only had one classification – *secret*. This was prejudicial to security as it brought it into disrepute. A list of rewards or prizes and a scheme of mobilisation would both receive the same classification – *secret*, which led to a 'serious depreciation of that most important word' (*Imestiev*, p. 1384). The British on the other hand had already worked out a most sophisticated system, ranging from *Confidential* (MacGregor's *Defence of India*) to *Most Secret*, and distinguishing between what was classified and what was merely 'private'.

India' by Bell.[100] The volumes for 1893 and 1894 contain a number of reports on routes through Afghanistan, western Persia and Russian Central Asia. It is tempting to think that the Russians were planning an invasion, but there is nothing in the *Sbornik* with the detail that a General Staff would require for war plans. Most of the articles are general briefs, often of a geographical nature. The prospects that a clash might occur were constantly under review: it is a General Staff's job to plan for all eventualities. But nothing in the *Sbornik* suggests that plans for an attack on India reached a definite or crisis stage.[101]

There were two actual schemes for an invasion, both visionary in the extreme. General Skobelev, the hero of the Akhal Tekke campaign and, one would have thought, a fairly hard-bitten soldier, formulated a scheme in 1878 which among other things would 'organize hordes of Asiatic horsemen, who to a cry of blood and plunder, might be launched against India as the vanguard, thus reviving the days of Timur'. But Sir George Clarke argued that 'reading between the lines it is clear that the author had some conception of the difficulties involved, and that in common with the projectors of all schemes for the invasion of India ... he counted heavily on assistance to be received in the invaded country'.[102] Reliance on assistance from the native population has also been a characteristic of Soviet doctrine, for example in Finland and Afghanistan, although their hopes have generally been disappointed.

A similar scheme for an advance into Afghanistan and on to India was formulated by Kuropatkin in June 1886. The British got hold of a copy from a 'most secret source' and it was despatched to Rosebery, the Foreign Secretary, from the chargé d'affaires in Tehran. Kuropatkin considered that the possibility of war existed 'beyond any doubt'. This plan was worked out in more detail than Skobelev's, and considered that it was best to begin 'in November, as the weather is healthier for the men and all Russian ports will be frozen'.[103]

The two concrete Russian schemes which have survived are both in the nature of contingency plans, and are the products of two of the most flamboyant Russian generals. The British assessments are also contingency plans, but are more sober and realistic. Commenting on Kuropatkin's scheme and likely British counters to it in 1891, Sir Frederick Roberts considered the possibility of a British attack on Russia. He concluded that the only 'effective offensive stroke of any magnitude' that was feasible was an attack on Port Arthur and the Manchurian railway, where Russia's strength could not be brought to bear (a conclusion borne out by the events of the Russo-Japanese War). An attack from India would face supply and communication problems and leave the British in a vulnerable position beyond the mountains once peace was concluded. An attack through the Caucasus was discounted because of the 'great military strength which Russia would have available to repel or attack'. They could easily concentrate half a million men there. It would only be possible if Britain with powerful allies were to attack Russia with no allies — an unlikely situation. It would require the active co-operation of Turkey — 'not a reliable factor'. The same was true of the fourth possibility, an attack in the Black Sea.[104]

Britain and Russia could not hope to injure each other in Europe. In Asia they were thoroughly frightened of each other, and neither dared risk aggression but, in the main, the Russians were more cautious than the British.

Mutual fear and plans for hostilities lasted until the Second World War. After the Anglo-Russian Convention of 1907, British fear of Russia lapsed. In the main this was not so much from a belief that she was weak, but that she was friendly, although a substantial part of British public opinion continued to fear Russia right up to 1914.[105] Furthermore, although most overestimated Russian power and tended to dismiss the effects of evidence of the Russo-Japanese War, the influential Sir George Clarke considered Russia to have been severely crippled in Asia.

> The Crimean War had the effect of deterring Russia from any great enterprises for more than twenty years. If she is now stronger, richer and more populous than in 1854, the losses of every kind arising from the present campaign are infinitely greater than those of the Crimean War, and the results will be much more wide reaching. On the whole it is not too much to assert that a Russian invasion of India of the type contemplated in the *Kriegsspiel* [a war game played at Simla in 1903] is out of the question *for twenty years.*[106]

The bogey of Anglo-Russian hostility in Asia was not finally laid low in 1914. After the revolution it revived. In 1918 Lloyd George considered that it was better for the Turks to be allowed to reach Baku than for it to remain in Bolshevik hands because 'it was not probable that they [the Turks] would ever be dangerous to our interests in the East while Russia, if in the future she became regenerated, might be so'.[107] The Soviets continued to show interest in Afghanistan. During the 1920s and 1930s the British allowed the army in India to stagnate but the Soviets retained fairly strong forces in Turkestan.

In 1929 the British produced an assessment of the military forces in

Soviet Turkestan, which contained the revealing comment that 'the Russian Army [sic] expects to fight entirely on a terrain whereon the heavy Machine Gun, which is mounted on a small pair of wheels, will not be so much handicapped by reason of its lack of tactical mobility, as in the case of an army operating in mountainous, broken or forest country'.* In other words, Russia did not intend to invade Afghanistan, but, if anything, fight a defensive war on the plains of Central Asia. The Committee of Imperial Defence considered the question of Indian defence in 1927 and decided that the maintenance of a friendly buffer state in Afghanistan should be the main object.[108] In most respects the British assessed the Soviets as being militarily weak in Asia, which they were, and, as the British harboured no aggressive designs, the tension of the nineteenth century abated. The Soviets perceived danger in Asia, but from the Chinese and Japanese, and it was in that direction that their military preparations were directed, with considerable success.[109]

The Post-war Strategic Balance

The strategic balance between Britain and the USSR has shifted so dramatically as a result of the Second World War that Britain can no longer contemplate action against the Soviet Union except as part of an alliance. The British were quick to appreciate how much Russia's world status would increase as a result of the war. In 1942 the British were, quite reasonably, preparing for action 'in the event of a Russian collapse'.[110] In 1944 the Foreign Office, considering 'Probable Post War Tendencies in Soviet Foreign Policy' believed that immediately after the war Russia's major interest would be 'to devote her main energies to the colossal task of post-war rehabilitation'. They considered that the destruction in parts of the Soviet Union which had been occupied by the Germans, and losses in young manpower, had been so great that the Soviet Union would take a very long time to recover. The 'logical deduction from this would be that she would seek friendly relations with the British and the US' provided these powers did not appear to be hostile. Despite her immense sacrifices she would emerge '(i) as the strongest land power in the world and one of the three strongest air

---

* The British were particularly impressed by the large number of machine-guns used by the Soviet infantry which was apparently to make up for the deficiencies of light weapons, which Soviet industry was at the time incapable of remedying. WO/33/1214, *Military Report on Soviet Turkestan* (1929), p. 97.

powers* and (ii) as the very successful exponent, of a new economic and social system . . .' She would have 'very great prestige and very great pride in herself'. Soviet foreign policy would be based 'on the search for absolute security until she can render herself impregnable'. She would 'dread the recovery of Germany in a way in which we have never done even in our blackest moments'. The assessment was astonishingly accurate: about the only thing the Foreign Office officials did not predict was the rise of the Soviet navy.[111]

Turning to Russian assessments of Britain, it might be supposed that Britain does not count any more. But this is not so. As is well shown, the Russians have a considerable respect for the British Royal Navy. The army does not rate so highly. Analysing the lessons of the Second World War, a Russian authority considered that the 'English armed forces' (by which he meant the army) received 'comparatively limited experience, not standing any comparison with that of the other countries [US, USSR and Germany]'. The British operated in 'second class (*vtorostepennye*) theatres of war,' and in offensive action 'the passivity of forces on adjacent sectors [to the narrow attacking sector] limited their success'. In defence, the British did not receive 'adequate experience in conducting operations against a strong enemy'.[112] Besides this, the numerical paucity of the British army makes it insignificant. The main adversary for Russians in Europe is the Bundeswehr both qualitatively and quantitatively, closely followed by US forces, and Soviet training manuals tend to concentrate on these two armies as probable opponents. The British are rated a poor third, just ahead of Belgian, Dutch and other forces.[113]

As a nation, however, Britain is still significant. In 1973 the Soviets considered military powers in the following way. The *First Class powers* were, of course (and still are), 'The two most powerful world powers – The Soviet Union and the USA.' These countries dispose of huge military potential; a high level of military technology *and* large numbers. They have nuclear weapons. Next come *Second Class powers*. These were defined as 'Developed countries with a high level of production, science and technology but limited economic and human resources.' All

---

* The two strongest air powers were the USA and Britain. The Russians were conscious of their weakness here. 'In 1946 . . . the Soviet Union had neither atomic weapons . . . nor long distance strategic bombers: the Soviet army had only weapons which are now considered as "tactical" or "conventional".' The Soviets perceived themselves at a disadvantage, with their army in Europe their only trump card. Hence their determination to hold on to 'hostage Europe' at all costs. The Russian historian Roy Medvedev interviewed in *The Guardian* 19 June 1980 p. 17.

countries in the second group possessed fully modern conventional armed forces and the British and French also had nuclear weapons:

> The military forces of those countries . . . do not have the same quality and capability as those of the first group. Nevertheless, they can be used to exert influence according both to the distribution of strength within their own region and to the politics of other countries linked with them in other regions.

These countries were divided into two groups. The first group were those with significant populations (UK, France, FRG, Italy* – in that order).[114] Furthermore, they thought that 'as against France, Great Britain disposes of a wider and more developed scientific-technical base, which, *in connection with the scientific-technical information which she receives from the USA, gives her a definite predominance* [my italics]'.[115] So Britain was top of the second class powers at the beginning of the 1970s. All the countries in the first group were 'significantly different' from the small developed countries – Belgium, the Netherlands, Denmark and Norway. Thirdly came *developing countries*, with a low level of industrial production, science and technology. In 1971 China was excluded from 'second class powers' – presumably because of her low level of industrial development (despite the fact she has nuclear weapons). It is a strange omission. The far from puny states of the Middle East were also regarded as developing countries. This reflects the traditional Russian preoccupation with Europe and, lately, with NATO, and also her regard for science and technology. China appeared technologically backward in 1972 and probably still does (she has to import much advanced military technology from the West). Nevertheless, the Soviet view in 1972 is astonishingly reminiscent of the nineteenth century, and westward-looking in the extreme. The Soviets clearly do not perceive 'third world' countries as militarily as important as we do. A recent example of this might be the Soviet invasion of Afghanistan where the Soviets underrated the opposition and clearly did not care much what the 'third world' thought.

Among countries with advanced technology, nuclear weapons confer status. They are important because they pack a big punch. Since military power confers political power, in Soviet eyes, nuclear weapons *per se*

---

* Italy is highly regarded because of her fine armaments industry. It is perhaps relevant that the Italians provided the Russians with considerable assistance in warship building in the 1930s (Meister, pp. 44-5).

confer political clout. When the Soviets criticise the British for striving to be a great power by possessing nuclear weapons, they are simply interpreting our moves in the light of their *own* perceptions: ethnocentrism again. But all the vitriol from the Russian press cannot hide the fact that in Russian eyes we are not a 'third class power'; we are a top 2:1.

Conclusions

This survey of Anglo-Russian views of each other has had to be cursory. From it, the following points emerge. The British overestimated the Russians as an enemy in the nineteenth century, as a potential friend before 1914, and underestimated her as a friend before 1942. Statistically, it would appear to be time for us to overestimate her as an enemy again. However good the Russians may look in peacetime, their performance in war has tended to be disappointing. The Russian army before the First World War *should* have been able to beat the Germans. In the Second World War a very good Soviet army took a long time to beat that of a much smaller power and suffered vastly greater losses. There are always good reasons; in the Russo-Japanese War the Russians were supplied by a single, incomplete line of railway, for example. But this cannot obscure the overall impression that their best laid schemes often go awry. Russian performance is inconsistent. Although one is reluctant to ascribe 'national characteristics' to a state comprising over 60 nationalities, some account must be taken of the tendency to combine 'violent energy . . . with indolence and a happy go lucky laissez-aller'. Russia is vast and powerful, no doubt, but we tend to look at maps drawn on Mercator's projection.

The Russians have always respected the British navy, but never thought much of the British army, apart from the somewhat condescending acknowledgement of its abilities in 1917.[116] Britain still counts in Russian eyes, because of her technological skill, her navy and above all because she has her nuclear deterrent. When considering how best to deploy resources, with deterrence in view, these Russian perceptions might be taken into account.

British and Russian assessments of each other as powers have been careful, and usually accurate in detail, although in both world wars the British drew the wrong conclusions. Throughout they have tended to fear each other, not realising that they are both only acting out of fear. Perhaps so-called 'confidence-building measures' can help to break this vicious circle of mutual suspicion and apprehension. Russia has invariably felt herself threatened, and the most astute British observers have always noticed that. It is important to remember that intention is an integral part of capability and vice versa.

Finally, a great deal of assessment is based on the outpourings of the open press. Since the Revolution, this has perhaps been more difficult for the British than for the Russians. Indeed, the sheer volume of material the West produces may well be more than the Russians can cope with. It is often assumed that intelligence-gathering is easier for the Russians because details of Western equipment and organisation are widely covered in the open press. But one can have too much of a good thing. When the vast size of the Russian intelligence-gathering effort is mentioned, it is often forgotten how much of it must be devoted to analysing open publications. Somewhere a Russian intelligence officer is reading this chapter. What will he make of this latest offering from a Western military commentator?

Notes

The transliteration system used is that of the US Board on Geographical Names, except that the adjectival ending -yy has been simplified to -y.

1. V.T. Pashuto, 'Bor'ba nashey Strany za nezavisimosti v. XIII-XV v.' in L.G. Beskrovny (ed.), *Stranitsy iz boevogo proshlogo* ('Pages from the Military Past') (Academiya nauk SSSR, institut istorii, 1968), p. 8. The Russian state was consolidated in the eleventh century under Yaroslav the Wise (1019-54), but its development was checked first by civil wars and then by the Tartar invasion. Pashuto claims that Russian wares are mentioned in the 'Song of Roland' (end of the eleventh century), and Russia itself in the *Nibelungenlied* (c. 1200) but I have been unable to find a direct reference to Russia in either. Men of 'the Slavonian Coast' are mentioned in the former (Penguin, Harmondsworth, 1957, p. 174), but the easternmost land mentioned in the latter is Hungary (the City of Gran) – see *The Geography of the Poem* (Penguin, Harmondsworth, 1965), p. 396. Awareness of the existence of the Russian state did not dawn on the West until later.

2. Pashuto, *Geography of the Poem*, pp. 427-8.

3. Ya. S. Lur'ë, 'Russko-angliyskie otnoshenii i mezhdunarodnaya politika vtoroy polovinoy XVI v.' in A.A. Zimin, V.T. Pashuto (eds.), *Mezhdunarodnye svyazi Rossii do XVII v.* (Moscow, 1961), pp. 427-8.

4. WO/33/419, 'Military Resources of the Russian Empire', War Office General Staff, 1907, pp. 1-2.

5. Karl Marx, quoted in *Sovetskaya Voennaya Entsiklopediya*, vol. 3 (Moscow, 1977), p. 483.

6. Lur'ë, 'Russko-angliyskie', pp. 442-3.

7. Yu. Tolstoy, *Pervye 40 let snoshenii mezhdu Rossiey i Anglieyu* (St Petersburg, 1875), quoted in Lur'ë, p. 419. Tolstoy's conclusions might have been reinforced by anti-English feeling in Russia at the time.

Richard Chancellor first dropped anchor in the White Sea in 1553. The English sailor then made his way to the court of Ivan the Terrible where he was welcomed by the Tsar who was anxious to establish contact with Western Europe. On his return to England, Chancellor's news resulted in the formation of the Muscovy Company, which gave Englishmen a virtual monopoly of Russia's trade with the West. This happy relationship lasted for two centuries.

8. A.P. Vlasto, *The Entry of the Slavs into Christendom* (Cambridge University Press, 1970), pp. 316-17.

9. John Milton, *A Brief History of Moscovia and of other less known countries lying Eastward of Russia as far as Cathay 1682*, with introduction by D.S. Mirsky, limited edition (London, 1929), p. 32. For Russian toughness see p. 43.

10. Defoe's newspaper, *Review* (23 August 1711), p. 262 quoted in Irving H. Smith, 'An English View of Russia in the Early Eighteenth Century', *Canadian Slavic Studies*, vol. I, no. 2 (Summer 1967), pp. 276-83.

11. Smith, 'English View of Russia', p. 280 and Lur'ĕ, 'Russko-angliyskie', p. 430.

12. Milton, *Moscovia*, p. 43.

13. Defoe, *An Impartial History of the Life and Actions of Peter Alexowitz, the Present Czar of Muscovy* (1723), p. 254, quoted in Smith, 'English View of Russia', p. 280.

14. *Review* (8 March 1707), p. 46 quoted in Smith, 'English View of Russia', p. 278.

15. *Review* (6 March 1707), p. 43 quoted in Smith, ibid., p. 278.

16. Ibid.

17. A Snesarev, *Avganistan*, Lectures given at the Red Army General Staff Academy (Autumn 1919 and Spring 1920), p. 216. See also Trench, *The Russo-Indian Question* (London, 1869), p. 3.

18. Trench, *Russo-Indian Question*, p. 4 and Sir George Clarke, *Russia's Sea Power* (John Murray, London, 1898), p. 73.

19. Sir George Clarke, *Russia's Sea Power*, p. 73.

20. Sir Robert Wilson, *A Sketch of the Military and Political Power of Russia in the year 1817*, p. viii.

21. For an excellent summary of these issues and bibliography see Smith, 'English View of Russia', p. 277.

22. Maj. Gen Sir John Mitchell, *Thoughts on Tactics and Military Organisation together with an Enquiry into the Power and Position of Russia* (London, 1838).

23. Clarke, *Russia's Sea Power*, p. 187.

24. P. Towle, 'The Influence of the Russo-Japanese War on British Naval and Military Thought 1905-14', unpublished PhD thesis, London University, 1973, pp. 286-90, 297-8.

25. Clarke, *Russia's Sea Power*, pp. 186-7.

26. Beskrovny, *Stranitsy*, pp. 9-11.

27. Vlasto, *Entry of the Slavs*, pp. 316-17; Beskrovny, *Stranitsy*, p. 11. On the invasions from the west, see I.P. Shaskol 'skii, *Bor'ba Rusi Protiv Krestonosnoy Agressii Na Beregakh Baltiki v XII-XIII vv* (Leningrad (Nauka), 1978) (Russia's Struggle against Crusading Aggression on the Baltic Shores in the 12th-13th centuries); K.M. Stetton (ed.), *The Crusades*, vol. III (University of Wisconsin, 1975), pp. 545-85 and Erik Christiansen, *The Northern Crusades, The Baltic and the Catholic Frontier*, (Macmillan, London, 1980).

28. See Stetton, *Crusades*, pp. 545-85.

29. Kh. Punga, *Ugroza voyny i zapadnye sosedi.* (The threat of war and western neighbours) (Moscow-Leningrad, 1928), p. 7.

30. Martin Gilbert, *Imperial Russian History Atlas* (Routledge and Kegan Paul, London, 1972), pp. 25-6.

31. *Sovetskaya Voennaya Entsiklopediya*, vol. 3 (1977) between pp. 32 and 33.
32. Punga, *Ugroza voyny*, pp. 6, 15-29.
33. I.G. Beskrovny, *Russkaya Armiya i Flot v xix v- voenno ekonomicheskiy potentsial Rossii* (Nauka, Moscow, 1963), p. 9. A most formidable, logical and authoritative military history of nineteenth-century Russia.
34. *The Army Reformer*, no. 1 (10 March 1855), p. 4.
35. A.M. Zayonchkovskiy, *Vostochnaya Voina* (The Eastern War) *1853-6* (St Petersburg, 1908-13), vol. 1, pp. 691, 723-5.
36. Although the war was fought in 1904-5, the model 1902 field gun does not seem to have been used. The Russians began the war armed mostly with M 1895s and replaced them with M 1900s as the war went on. The deployment of the latest tank models – T-64 and T-72 – to the west first (and even to *East German* units) is an example of similar thinking.
37. On the question of encirclement see Uri Ra'anan, 'The USSR and the "Encirclement" Fear: Soviet Logic or Western Legend', in *Strategic Review* (Winter 1980), pp. 44-50.
38. For a full analysis of the problem of ethnocentrism, vital to assessing foreign military power, see Ken Booth, *Strategy and Ethnocentrism* (Holmes & Meier, New York, 1979). On the fear of Poland see FO/371/4335 XCIA 639; 'Some Historical Tendencies in Russian Foreign Policy', 2 May 1944, p. 4. 'Russia has always been obsessed by the Fear that Poland might revive as a Great power and, indeed, after . . . 1918 she almost did so.' If the Russians had grounds to fear Poland then, they almost certainly do not fear her now to the same extent.
39. See John Silverlight, *The Victor's Dilemma* (Barrie and Jenkins, London, 1970), pp. 96-9, 207-9, 219. The leader of the August expedition to the Caucasus (Baku) was Major General Dunsterville.
40. G.A. Leyer, *Opyt kritiko istoricheskago izsledovaniya zakonov isskusstva vedeniya voiny* (1869), p. 2 'War is one of the means and what is more the extreme means in the hands of politics for the achievement of national aims.' Leyer is not studied as part of Western war studies courses which is a pity as he forms a link between the 'classical' theorists like Clausewitz and Jomini and Soviet works on war. V.I. Lenin, *Complete Works* (Poln. Sobr. Soch.) vol. 32, p. 79, and in the speech of 14 May (27) 1917; 'War and Revolution'; *Complete Works*, vol. 24, pp. 398-421. In the latter Lenin quotes Clausewitz verbatim and immediately afterwards repeats the point himself. The Soviet attribution of the phrase to Lenin is therefore not exactly wrong, but highly misleading.
41. See Lewis Siegelbaum, 'The War Industries Committees and the Politics of Industrial Mobilisation in Russia 1914-17', unpublished D Phil, Oxford, 1975, p. 42.
42. Norman Stone, *The Eastern Front 1914-17* (Hodder and Stoughton, London, 1975), p. 211. Stone argues that the Russians achieved a superiority not only in numbers of men but also in materiel. This could have been true with regard to artillery. See A.A. Manikovskiy, *Boyevoye snabzhenie Russkoy Armii v Pervoy Mirovoy Voyne* (Moscow, 1930), vol. II, p. 261. On the distribution system see Siegelbaum, 'War Industries Committees', p. 34.
43. Headlam Papers box 1 no. 5 'Report on Visit to the Russian Front' 12/25 February to 12/25 March 1917 sections 13, 14.
44. Ibid., p. 2.
45. WO/33/419 War Office, General Staff 'Military Resources of the Russian Empire', 1907, p. 254. Author's italics.
46. WO/208/1758 'Will Russia Fight' enc. 10A by Col. Mackenzie, January 1941.
47. Ibid. 'The Strategy of the Red Army in a War against Germany', November 1940.

48. Ibid. enc. 19A 12 January 1941.
49. Ibid. enc. 5A 8 January 1941.
50. John Erickson, *The Road to Stalingrad* (Harper & Row, London, 1975), p. 102.
51. WO/208/758 7A and 8A from the military attaché in Moscow, 2 and 6 January 1941.
52. WO/208/1758 enc. 18A outward telegram, FO 7 January 1941.
53. Zayonchkovskiy, vol. 1, pp. 156-61 *prilozhenie* 29.
54. M.I. Ivanin, *O voennom iskusstve i zavoevaniyakh Mongolov* St Petersburg, 1846), p. 20. Lt Col, later Lt Gen. Ivanin's work (both this and an expanded version of 1875) forms a documentary link between the study of the Mongols and the thoughts of Russian and hence Soviet military writers. (The activities of these Mongol detachments resemble those of modern 'diversionary brigades'.)
55. C. von Clausewitz *Vom Kriege* (On War) translated by Michael Howard and Peter Paret (Princeton, 1976), book 3, ch. 8: 'Superiority of Numbers', pp. 194-7.
56. John Milton, *Moscovia*, p. 43.
57. Russo-Finnish War: 'The Soviet Army's Quality', *The Times*, 18 March 1940. Quoted in Hewlett Johnson (Dean of Canterbury), *Soviet Strength*, (Frederick Muller, London, 1942). For examples of Russian inventiveness, see A. Pozdnev, *Tvortsy otechestvennogo oruzhiya* (Founders of the nation's armaments) (Moscow, 1955), although some of its assertions should be treated with caution.
58. C.A.G. Bridge (ed.), *The Russian Fleet under Peter the Great by a Contemporary Englishman* (1724) Navy Records Society, vol. xv, 1899, p. 166.
59. Ibid., pp. 112 and 126.
60. 'Nyneshnee chishtel 'noe sostoyanie voysk evropeyskikh derzhav' in *Voenny zhurnal*, no. 1 (St Petersburg, 1835), p. 121. British on p. 154.
61. *Voenny zhurnal*, no. 3 (1839), p. 107.
62. *Colburn's United Services Magazine*, no. 297 (August 1853), pp. 475-98.
63. Ibid., p. 480.
64. Ibid., pp. 494 and 498.
65. WO/33/1 no. 6 'Topographical Memoir for Military Purposes of the Sea of Azov, the Crimea and the Neighbourhood of the Konban 1855'; Ibid., no. 40, 'Tables showing the Disposition and State of Russian Forces'; McCaskill's paper, ibid., no. 59.
66. WO/33/24 p. 355 'Memorandum on the System of Military Education in Austria', 19 January 1872.
67. *Voenny Sbornik*, no. 10 (October 1874), pt II, p. 1.
68. See 'Inostrannie voennoe obozrenie' — 'British military reforms' and 'Autumn manoeuvres' in *Voenny Sbornik*; no. 4 (April 1875), pt II, p. 95 and no. 3 (March 1874), pp. 308-61 respectively.
69. Lt Col P.I. Izmestiev, 'The Importance of Secrecy in War' translated from the Russian in *RUSI Journal*, vol. LI (1907), p. 1382.
70. 'Mnenie angliskoy pressy o bronenosnykh sudakh', *Morskoy Sbornik*, no. 11 (November 1868, Otdel Neofitsial'ny), p. 15.
71. Izmestiev in *RUSI Journal*, p. 1381.
72. 'The Armed Strength of Russia' (War Office, London, 1873), pp. i-iii.
73. Ibid., p. 1.
74. Zayonchkovskiy, vol. 1, p. 675-6. This history, written in 1908 and possibly coloured by anti-British feeling, was nevertheless based on Russian reports of the 1850s.
75. Ibid., p. 671.
76. Ibid., p. 685.
77. Ibid., p. 674.

78. Fred T. Jane *The Imperial Russian Navy* (W. Thackeray, London, 1904), p. 519.
79. Quoted in Towle, 'Influence of the Russo-Japanese War', p. 297.
80. Headlam, conclusion of report.
81. N.N. Golovin *The Russian Campaign of 1914* (London, 1933), p. 27.
82. FO/371/43335 'Probable Post War Tendencies in Soviet Foreign Policy as Affecting British Interests', 29 April 1944, p. 5.
83. Ibid.
84. For a start, see Kristina Nyman, *Finland's War Years 1939-1945* (Helsinki, 1973), with a short historical introduction, p. XV. This includes an excellent bibliography of the Winter and Continuation Wars.
85. V. Kulish *et al., Voennaya Sila i Mezhdunarodnye Otnosheniya* (Akademiya Nauk SSSR Institut Mirogo Ekonomiki i Mezhdurarodnykh Otnosheniy, Moscow, 1972), pp. 128-9. This point is also made in Admiral S.G. Gorshkov's classic, *The Sea Power of the State (SPS)* (Pergamon, London, 1979), p. 238.
86. 'Strategicheskie ocherki nastoyashchego polozheniya evropeyskikh gosudarstv' in *Voenny Sbornik*, vol. 9, no. 63, (1868), p. 41.
87. M.I. Ivanin, *Opisanie Zimnyago Pokhoda* (The Expedition to Khiva 1839-40) (St Petersburg, 1874), pp. 2-3: *Quarterly Review* (1865), p. 539.
88. A. Rostovskiy, 'The Shadow of India in Russian History', *History* (October 1929), pp. 226-7.
89. Ivanin, *Zimnyago Pokhoda*, p. 4.
90. Skobelev quoted in Sir C.M. MacGregor, *The Defence of India: A Strategical Study* (Simla, 1884), pp. 140-1. Author's italics.
91. Sir George Clarke, 'Anglo Russian Relations', 16 July 1905, p. 5 in *Memoranda and Notes* by Sir George Clarke while Secretary of the Committee of Imperial Defence 1904-7, Document 37.
92. MacGregor, p. 142.
93. Ibid., p. 9.
94. Ibid., p. 48.
95. Ibid., p. 41.
96. Ibid., p. 51. Author's italics.
97. CAB 38 vol. 2 document 26 p. 2.
98. WO/33/337 quoted in Towle, 'Influence of the Russo-Japanese War', p. 297.
99. *Sbornik geograficheskikh topograficheskikh i statisticheskikh materialov Po Azii*. Voennaya Tipografiya (v zdanie General-'nogo Shtaba) (St Petersburg), vol. XLI and XLIV respectively.
100. Ibid., vol. XLIX.
101. W.B. Walsh, 'The Imperial Russian General Staff and India', *The Russian Review*, 16 (1957), pp. 53-8.
102. Clarke, *Memoranda and Notes*, 'Note on Threatened Invasions of India and their Effect on British Policy'; 3 April 1905 document no. 41 p. 5.
103. 'General Kouropatkine's Scheme for a Russian Advance upon India, with Notes thereon by Lord Roberts...', August 1891. Printed for the Committee of Imperial Defence, March 1903, pp. 1-5. CAB 38 XCIA 632.
104. Ibid., pp. 32-3.
105. Harrison, p. 11. See also P. Towle, 'The European Balance of Power in 1914', *Army Quarterly and Defence Journal* (1974), pp. 333-42 and 'Influence of the Russo-Japanese War', pp. 286-98.
106. Clarke, *Memoranda and Notes* 'The Afghanistan Problem', 20 March 1905, document 27, p. 5.
107. War Cabinet minutes CAB/23/6 quoted in Silverlight, *Victor's Dilemma*, p. 97.

108. See Snesarev; Towle, 'Influence of Russo-Japanese War', p. 321; for CID, see Adm/116/3480 'War with Russia': Naval Appreciation, August 1932, Section 1 and see WO/33/1214 'Military Report on Soviet Turkestan', 1929, p. 97.

109. N.F. Kuz'min, *Na strazhe mirnogo truda* (1921-1940) gg. ('On guard for peaceful work') (Moscow, Voenizdat, 1959). A history of the Red Army between the wars. Witness the exploits of the Special Red Banner Army of the Far East. The British are not referred to as a threat.

110. WO/208/1777 'Effects of a Soviet Collapse and Appreciation of Possible Action Required'.

111. FO/371/4335, Probable Post War Tendencies in Soviet Foreign Policy as Affecting British Interests', 29 April 1944, pp. 1-5.

112. A.D. Bagreyev, *Voennoe iskusstvo kapitalisticheskikh gosudarstv 1939-45 gg* (The Military Art of Capitalist Countries) (Moscow, 1960), p. 239.

113. See for example Ya. K. Malakhovskii, *Strel'ba na porazhenie opornykh punktov* (Moscow, 1978), and N.K. Glazunov, *Bundesver i NATO* (Moscow, Voenizdat, 1979).

114. Kulish, pp. 36-7. Britain's position as a leading technological power is also noted in Gorshkov, *SPS*, for example, p. 198.

115. Kulish, pp. 116-17.

116. See V.T. Novitskiy's interesting comments in *Moskoy Sbornik*, no. 3, March 1917, pp. 153-7.

2 ESTIMATING SOVIET MILITARY EXPENDITURE*

Ron Huisken

Official Soviet information on the financial and economic aspects of their military activities consists of a single line in the annual state budget indicating the allocation to defence. There has never been an official description of the activities that are funded by this allocation nor any information on the ministries or departments other than defence that are responsible for military activities. There is no official information on the institutional links between the Ministry of Defence, research institutions and defence industries, nor on the prices charged and paid for military goods and services. Add to this a lack of reliable and up-to-date information on how the Soviet economy functions and it is hardly surprising that estimates of the magnitude of the Soviet military effort have ranged from 4 to 40 per cent of gross national product.

Notwithstanding this high, and so far impenetrable, wall of secrecy there has been a strong demand for data on Soviet military expenditure, particularly, of course, in the United States. The level and trend of an adversary's military outlays has long been an important input in decision-making on military budgets. Indeed the influence of comparisons of military expenditure has probably grown in so far as lay decision-makers have become increasingly confused by the complexity of force level comparisons. In the United States the CIA has primary responsibility for constructing estimates of Soviet military expenditure: the first estimates were made in the late 1950s. In addition, a number of academic studies have appeared over the past 15 years. This chapter will describe the various ways in which the problem has been tackled in the past, and the manner in which the most recent estimates are constructed.

The estimates constructed by analysts outside the intelligence community were necessarily based on published Soviet financial and economic statistics. The basic assumption made in this approach is that the official statistics reflect the actual or intended allocation of all available resources or, in other words, that Soviet authorities do not keep two sets of books. It follows that all allocations to military activities are in the state budget even if the allocation for defence gives a very incomplete picture. In acting on this assumption attention is inevitably drawn to various residuals in the state budget, that is, funds that are not explicitly accounted for. However, the task of determining, with any reasonable degree of confidence, how much of these residuals represent military outlays has so far been impossible even though some analysts went to extraordinary lengths in exploring even the most indirect avenues of inquiry in an endeavour to shed some light on the residuals.

An additional and equally intractable problem concerns expenditure for military research and development. It has long been assumed, and accumulated snippets of evidence have confirmed, that most if not all military research and development is contained in the budget allocation to 'science'. It is now almost a conventional wisdom that 50 to 75 per cent of the science allocation represents military research and development but the studies on which this conclusion is based, particularly those done by Nancy Nimitz of the Rand Corporation, emphasise the high degree of uncertainty.

The residuals approach made it possible, in principle, to more than double the announced defence budget in most years. For example in 1969, the official defence budget was 17.7 billion roubles, the two main budget residuals were about 18 billion roubles and the science allocation about 10 billion roubles.

Two analysts, Anderson and Lee,[1] in a variation on the residuals approach, constructed an income and expenditure account for the state sector as a whole. The justification for this approach was that data on resource allocation in the state sector as a whole was more complete than for the budget alone. This method yields a residual which is generally larger than the budget residuals after non-military expenditures which are known or assumed to be financed from the residuals are deducted. Lee subsequently applied this approach to later years — his study with Anderson only went as far as 1965 — and estimated military outlays at about 50 billion roubles in 1970.[2] This figure is nearly three times the official budget and about double the CIA estimate prior to the upward revision that we will discuss below.

As mentioned, the CIA began producing estimates of Soviet military expenditure in the late 1950s. The primary demand was for data that could be compared with the US budget, that is, the dollar equivalent of Soviet military outlays. Given its direct access to intelligence information, the CIA adopted an entirely different approach, that of direct costing. In other words it attempted to answer the question of what it would cost the United States to run a military establishment sized and structured like the Soviet one.

Before we examine the answers to this question it is worthwhile to look at the question itself. The Soviet armed forces are the product of a unique set of circumstances: history, geo-political setting, resource endowment, social and economic structure, and political system. The US armed forces are also the product of a unique set of circumstances. Thus the question of what it would cost the US to build and run the Soviet military establishment is to a substantial extent the erection of a straw man. The US would not maintain nearly 5 million men in uniform, it would not build T-62 tanks or MiG -23 Flogger aircraft, it would not adopt Soviet practices for maintenance and repair and so on. On the assumption that the US is broadly content with the deterrent and defence capability of its armed forces, a demonstration that the dollar-equivalent of Soviet military expenditure, computed on the direct-costing method, is significantly higher than US expenditure indicates primarily that the Soviet military establishment is a less efficient one, given the conditions prevailing in the USA. The largest source of 'inefficiency' is military personnel. The average monetary cost of military personnel in the US is now well in excess of $12,000 while the average cost of a Soviet soldier is estimated at about 1,500 roubles. Direct costing produces a relatively huge outlay for military personnel, and one that increases at the same rate as pay scales in the US assuming constant military manpower in the Soviet Union. If the US were to revert to the draft then one could imagine dollar-equivalent estimates of Soviet military expenditure remaining constant or even falling, even if Soviet personnel strengths were increasing.*

In sum, comparisons of US and Soviet military expenditures in dollars should not be taken too literally. This is particularly true of the difference in the absolute levels of expenditure in a particular year because of the major distortion produced by manpower differentials. On the other hand, comparisons of the relative trend in expenditure in constant-price terms can be made with more confidence. Even here, however, the data provide only a general indication of relative military effort. While there is *some* relationship between expenditure and military capability this relationship is neither close nor invariable.

The fact that military expenditure and military power are more than coincidentally related is reflected in the fact that no country will accept expenditure limitations unless it is assured that potential adversaries do

---

* An obvious corollary of the low manpower costs in the Soviet Union is that a larger percentage of the military budget is available for procurement, construction and research and development. Lee estimates that direct personnel costs absorb less than 15 per cent of Soviet military expenditure leaving about 60 to 70 per cent for the investment categories listed above.[2] This assumes 15 to 20 per cent for operations and maintenance.

the same. On the other hand there has been a traditional reluctance to enter into military expenditure limitations because of the fear that expenditure comparisons obscure real military power relationships. The problem of specifying and ordering the contribution to real military power made by the various components of military expenditure is a very large one. For example, how does one compare, at a point in time and over time, weapons and force units with different varieties of levels of technology? Similarly, how does one assess expenditures on research and development, construction and training which contribute to future military power? These difficulties are reflected in the fact that proposals for the limitation of military expenditures inevitably generate demands for the exchange of highly disaggregated expenditive data plus comprehensive information on how the military sector interacts with the economy in general.

More generally military expenditure relations compare inputs and any two countries may differ markedly in the efficiency with which they translate inputs into effective military power, however the latter might be measured. This issue is considered further below.

The CIA estimates of the dollar-equivalent of Soviet military expenditure in any given year have tended to increase over time. The reasons given include improved data on the size and general characteristics of the Soviet armed forces, better data on the characteristics of Soviet weapons generally, showing that they are more sophisticated, and improvements in costing methodologies which permit a wider range of Soviet military activities to be costed. This also means that the expenditure series presented in, say, 1975 is not directly comparable to the one presented in 1973. This is unfortunate because the series presented in any one year is usually only for a ten-year period and it would be interesting to compare the level and trend of expenditure in the 1950s and early 1960s when some of the major changes in force levels and force structure occurred on both sides.

A by-product of the direct-costing method and what is apparently perceived as one of its main utilities is that components of total military expenditure can be directly compared. Moreover, the distortions of the manpower factor are avoided. Thus much is made, for example, of the fact that Soviet expenditure on offensive strategic forces (excluding research and development) has exceeded that for the USA since 1966 with the gap growing to 60 per cent in 1974. Similarly Soviet 'investment' expenditure (procurement plus construction) surpassed that for the US in 1969 and was 82 per cent higher in 1975. The one area in which the CIA acknowledges more than the usual uncertainty is military

Table 2.1: The Dollar-equivalent of Soviet Military Expenditure, 1965-1975[3]

Year	US $billion (constant 1974 prices)
1965	85
1966	89
1967	92
1968	96
1969	98
1970	101
1971	102
1972	104
1973	108
1974	110
1975	114

Note: These figures exclude pensions and military assistance.

research and development. This is because the Soviet military research and development programme substantially eludes the direct-costing method so that resort has to be made to Soviet budget statistics supplemented by costing of known or estimated resource inputs into research and development and such outputs as are observable. A Defense Intelligence Agency official estimated the margin of error in the research and development estimates at 20 to 30 per cent either way. This means that the estimated Soviet expenditure lead in this area, roughly 35 per cent in 1974 and 50 per cent in 1975, could have been non-existent or reduced by more than one-half respectively.[4]

A question that must be raised at this point concerns the estimates of the Soviet inventory of various types of weapons, particularly combat aircraft and naval vessels. One can presume that the CIA has the best data on such equipment but it is not made available in a form that readily permits independent analysis. Moreover the information available to the CIA and other intelligence-gathering agencies in the United States may be less than firm. An indication of this is provided by such basic sources as *Jane's Fighting Ships* and the International Institute for Strategic Studies' *Military Balance*. There is every reason to believe that these publications rely heavily on US information for their estimates of Soviet force levels and these estimates show quite significant fluctuations from year to year. If data on the force levels of a major Western power fluctuated to a similar extent it would understandably give rise to extensive debate and analysis. For the Soviet Union, tens of thousands of men or 30 major warships can be added or subtracted without comment.

Conventional wisdom is that the Soviet Union maintains weapons in its operational forces for far longer than most Western countries. Thus *Jane's Fighting Ships 1976-77* lists 126 Soviet submarines ('W', 'Z IV' and 'Q' classes) the newest of which is 20 years old. The comment is made that most of these are probably in reserve but one does not know what this means in the Soviet Union. The manner in which these vessels are costed could obviously have a significant impact on estimated total expenditure. Similar considerations apply to tanks and combat aircraft. In both cases a large fraction of the total inventory is made up of very elderly units that could well be in reserve or on reduced status with minimal operations and maintenance personnel assigned to them. In sum, while it can be assumed that US intelligence agencies have the best available data on the Soviet military establishment, the indications are that the data is deficient in important respects. Estimates of available forces and the expenditures they involve appear to be based to a significant degree on judgements rather than fact and it is very difficult for independent analysts to determine the accuracy of the judgements made or to assess their validity.

If estimates of the dollar-equivalent of Soviet military expenditure bear only a limited relationship to Soviet military capabilities they are useless for the purpose of assessing the burden of the military establishment on the Soviet economy. For this purpose rouble expenditure figures are required. Until very recently much less attention was paid to rouble figures in US official circles. The demand was for dollar figures and the direct-costing method largely obviated the need to establish a rouble base from which to derive the dollar figures. As far as can be determined the CIA broadly subscribed to the thesis that the only significant category of expenditure missing from the official defence budget was military research and development and this could be found in the allocation to 'science'. The US Arms Control and Disarmament Agency (ACDA), which gets most of its data from the intelligence community, until recently used the official defence budget plus one-half of the 'science' allocation.[5] Further, again until recently, the CIA's estimate of the burden of military expenditure in the Soviet Union was 6 to 8 per cent of GNP.

The ACDA method and the CIA's 6 to 8 per cent of GNP yield roughly the same rouble figure. In 1972 the ACDA estimate was 25.1

billion roubles while the CIA percentages yield a range of 23 billion to 31 billion roubles. For internal purposes the CIA established its rouble figure by working backwards from the calculated dollar-equivalent figure using dollar-rouble conversion ratios. The main exception is military personnel where actual rouble outlays are known with reasonable precision.

A striking feature is the magnitude of the upward translation from roubles to dollars or the downward translation in the opposite case. ACDA's 25.1 billion roubles in 1972 translates into $30.2 billion at the official exchange rate as against its published estimate of $81 billion. Similarly, in 1972, the CIA supported a rouble figure in the range 23 billion to 31 billion while its dollar equivalent (in constant 1974 dollars) was slightly in excess of $100 billion.[6]

An important part of the explanation for this has already been mentioned, namely the large disparity in the purchasing power of the rouble versus the dollar in the case of military personnel. But military personnel was only the extreme case. It was widely believed that the purchasing power of the rouble in all or most areas of military activity was substantially greater than suggested by the official exchange rate. This view was based on studies by economists on the relative purchasing power of the rouble and the dollar in relevant civilian industries such as the machine tool industry, strengthened by the argument that the military sector was a priority recipient of resources and thus more efficient than the civil economy.

Predictably, the gap – of the order of 100 per cent – between the CIA rouble figures and the estimates prepared by Lee caused controversy. According to General Graham, former head of the Defense Intelligence Agency (DIA), this controversy was resolved by a major adjustment of the CIA's dollar-rouble conversion ratios. The primary basis for the adjustment was new evidence that the Soviet Union incurred far greater costs than had previously been thought in acquiring new technologies and incorporating these technologies into military hardware. There is some indication that the evidence for this adjustment came from a specific source or a few sources. In congressional testimony in May-June 1976 former CIA Director, George Bush, claimed that the new rouble estimates were based on '. . . an intensive collection and analytical effort over the past several years . . .'[7] On the other hand, General Graham, in an article written after his resignation from the DIA, claims that by April 1975 solid proof was available of the inaccuracy of the existing conversion ratios but that the new rouble estimates were not released until July 1975 to avoid endangering the sources of information.[8]

Acquiring technological capabilities that are significantly beyond the 'state of the art' is a costly undertaking in any country. Take, for example, the Minuteman III, an extremely accurate American intercontinental ballistic missile with three independently targetable warheads. That missile went into series production in 1970 at a unit manufacturing cost of five million to six million dollars. If this had been attempted in 1965, according to one analyst, 'the entire GNP of the US *might* have purchased one overweight Minuteman III'.[9]

The same problem has complicated attempts to translate US military expenditure into roubles.[10] The Soviet Union simply does not produce many of the weapons and equipment already in the US arsenal. Nor do they produce close substitutes. For these items the rouble price is theoretically infinite. With these qualifications CIA comparisons of US and Soviet military expenditures in roubles still show a higher figure for the Soviet Union in recent years although the crossover point occurs several years later than a comparison in dollar terms. The main reason, of course, is that the large outlay for personnel in the US, more than half the total budget, is reduced by a factor of six or more.

The upshot of the adjustments in the conversion ratios was two-fold. First, the rouble estimates for the 1970s increased in absolute terms by 60 to 100 per cent and secondly there was an acceleration in the rate of growth of the estimates reflecting the Soviet Union's push into high technology areas.

Table 2.2: Estimated Soviet Military and National Security Expenditure, 1970-1975 (billions of roubles, constant 1970 prices)

	Military	National security	Official budget
1970	40 – 45	45 – 50	17.9
1971	41 – 46	46 – 51	17.9
1972	42.5 – 47.5	47.5 – 52.5	17.9
1973	45 – 50	50 – 55	17.9
1974	47 – 52	52 – 57	17.6
1975	50 – 55	55 – 60	17.4

Note: In the source[11] the data is presented in diagrammatic form so that changes from year to year may not be precise.

The ramification of this adjustment are little short of enormous. The new estimates imply that the Soviet Union diverts 11 to 12 per cent of

Estimating Soviet Military Expenditure

GNP to explicit military activities. On a broader definition of national security — including, in particular, the space programme — the CIA estimates the division at 12 to 13 per cent. Furthermore the diversion of output from specific industries is now estimated to be very large indeed. In the key machine-building and metal-working industry, the industry that supplies investment goods for the Soviet economy, the CIA estimates the defence share at 30 per cent.

Despite this drastic revision, there are still those who believe that the CIA has not gone far enough. Lee considers that national security absorbs 13 to 15 per cent of Soviet GNP and that more than one-half of machinery and equipment output goes to the military.[12] General Graham, in the article referred to earlier, maintains that 15 per cent of GNP is a minimum because several categories of military expenditure — pensions, a large part of the basic training programme and transportation — have not been added in.

Of all the various ways in which military expenditure data can be manipulated, the share in GNP is one of the more significant. Even here, however, the significance of the CIA's new estimates is not unambiguous. On the one hand it can be argued that the share in GNP reflects the priority that a government assigns to defence or, more realistically, military power. This would be particularly true in a command economy such as the Soviet Union. From this standpoint the new data might be cause for concern over the Soviet Union's intentions. Alternatively, the revelation that a *given* military effort is twice as expensive as was previously thought could be regarded as a basis for arguing that the Soviet Union will experience great difficulty in sustaining this effort and that there is much less room for accelerating it. In any case it is clear that the new rouble figures, if the CIA continues to stand by them, will make the costs of defence a far more important consideration in US assessments of future Soviet policy options.

In addition it seems that the new figures are not easily reconciled with current estimates of the size and structure of Soviet GNP and will presumably affect estimates of the real growth potential of the Soviet economy.[13] The same consistency problem arises if the new CIA figures are extrapolated backwards in time. In 1974 William Colby, then Director of the CIA, stated that the average annual rate of growth of the rouble estimate for the period 1960-73 was 3 per cent with a levelling-off in the last several years of that period. As mentioned the new estimates show an accelerated rate of growth for the 1970s, 4 to 5 per cent, but for the period 1960-70 a rate of 3 to 3.5 per cent can still be assumed. If we extrapolate the CIA's estimate for 1970, 40 billion to

50 billion roubles, back to 1960 at 3.5 per cent the result is 28 billion to 35 billion roubles or roughly 12 to 15 per cent of GNP. This can be compared with Abraham Becker's estimate of 18.5 billion roubles for military outlays in 1960, an estimate arrived at on the basis of consistency with data on the Soviet GNP.[14] The new rouble estimates also imply significant upward revisions of the share of military outlays in GNP for the 1950s. However, one analyst, Timothy Sosnovy, did produce an early figure that is broadly consistent with the new CIA data. Using a broad definition of military expenditure — including pensions for war veterans and intelligence activities — and taking large slices of all monies in the Soviet state sector not explicitly identified as non-military outlays, Sosnovy produced a figure for 1964 of 31.9 billion roubles.[15]

Conclusion

One can be mildly astonished that one of the world's two superpowers considers it necessary to keep even the financial and economic aspects of its defence effort totally secret. But this secrecy is also reason for concern. Comparative military expenditures play a not insignificant role in decision-making on military budgets and the large degree of freedom that Western analysts have in estimating the scale and trend of Soviet military outlays has clearly, on occasion, been exploited to elicit larger allocations to the national forces. The discrepancy between what the Soviet Union says and what the West believes has now reached ludicrous proportions and one wonders how long this state of affairs can prevail. One thing, however, is clear. No significant improvement in the credibility of the estimates of Soviet military expenditure can be expected until the Soviet Union makes available, officially, data on rouble expenditures, how these are distributed through the state sector and how research institutions and defence industries fit into the total picture.

Even authoritative data on force levels and information on the various levels of operational readiness of these forces would be extremely useful in that it would permit, albeit very roughly, independent verification of Soviet military expenditure estimated via the direct costing method.

Notes

*Reprinted from the *Australian Journal of Defence Studies.*

1. A critique of the financial expenditures approach can be found in 'Estimating Soviet Military Expenditure', *World Armaments and Disarmament, SIPRI Yearbook 1974,* Appendix 8B, pp. 172-204.
2. W.T. Lee, 'Military Expenditure in the USSR', *Air Force Magazine* (March 1976).
3. 'Allocation of Resources in the Soviet Union and China – 1976', Hearings before the Subcommittee on Priorities and Economy in Government of the Joint Economic Committee, May-June 1976.
4. 'Allocation of Resources in the Soviet Union and China – 1975', Hearings before the Subcommittee on Priorities and Economy in Government of the Joint Economic Committee, June-July 1975.
5. *World Military Expenditure and Arms Trade 1963-73* (US Arms Control and Disarmament Agency, 1975).
6. See note 3 supra.
7. Ibid.
8. Lt General D.O. Graham, 'The Soviet Military Budget Controversy', *Air Force Magazine* (May 1976).
9. W.T. Lee, 'Trends in Soviet Military Spending', *Air Force Magazine* (March 1977), p. 85.
10. See also A. Nove, 'Soviet Defence Spending', *Survival* (October 1971). Nove, a specialist in the Soviet economy, argued that if the real purchasing power of the rouble were as high as people claimed, Soviet products would be extremely competitive on world markets. Since this was not the case, Nove concluded that the low rouble/dollar ratios being used overstated the purchasing power of the rouble for products with the same quality and performance.
11. See note 3 supra.
12. See note 2 supra.
13. R.B. Greensalde, 'The Real Gross National Product in the USSR, 1950-75' in *Soviet Economy in a New Perspective,* a compendium of papers submitted to the Joint Economic Committee, Congress of the United States, 14 October 1976.
14. A. Becker, *Soviet National Income, 1958-1964,* Rand Corporation, RM-464-PR (August 1964).
15. T. Sosnovy, 'The Soviet Military Budget', *Foreign Affairs* (April 1964).

3 WESTERN ASSESSMENT OF SOVIET STRENGTH
Geoffrey Jukes

The only conceivable external military threat to the alliance system formed by the modern industrial states of the non-Communist world is that which the Soviet Union could pose, just as the non-Communist industrial states, and in particular the United States of America, constitute the only credible external military threat to the Soviet Union and its allies. Each system conducts continuous assessment of the other by a variety of means, ranging from diplomatic reporting through espionage to surveillance from space, and the magnitude of the effort attests to the importance of the undertaking. This discussion is devoted to the assessment of Soviet military strength by organisations collectively known as 'Intelligence', and does not attempt to consider the political forms of information which diplomatic posts exist to collect. It is therefore incomplete, because often the information conveyed by an embassy is of crucial importance. However, to the extent that an embassy gathers information on military strength, it does so through specialised personnel (the most visible of whom are the armed services' attachés), whose 'product' is fed into the 'Intelligence' machine along with many other inputs, while military strength becomes important to the day-to-day conduct of diplomacy only at rare intervals, usually during crises. For most of the time a country's military strength is part of the background to, rather than the substance of, diplomacy, which consequently has no need to concern itself with either the collection or the evaluation of detail. No basic error, therefore, is likely to result from concentrating on assessment by 'Intelligence' rather than on assessment as a whole.

Capabilities and Intentions

It is perhaps worth beginning by defining what the object of assessment is. Obviously it is not to have Soviet military strength counted down to the last round of ammunition and the last soldier; this is neither practicable nor necessary. In any event, the counting of military assets is not an end in itself; the assets are counted so that the military options open to the Soviet leadership in a variety of contingencies can be deduced.

This is not quite the same as saying that capabilities are counted so that intentions can be assessed; obviously, the *absence* of present intentions can be deduced from the absence of present capabilities, but the existence of an intention cannot be deduced from the existence of a capability. If it could, we should be forced to conclude that both the Soviet Union and the United States intend to blow up most of the world's cities, since both have the capability to do so, and island states such as Australia would have concluded that the United States represented the major threat to them, since it has the largest high seas navy and the largest marine corps. The process of deducing intentions from capabilities is not therefore as simple as that of deducing lack of intention from lack of capability. There is the further complication that intention may, and usually does, precede capability by several years, because of the time needed to design and procure the capability; so that essentially current capability represents intentions formed some years previously, which may or may not have changed in the interim, while the lack of a present capability may indicate either the lack of a present intention or only the lack of a past intention.

To make matters even worse, it can happen that capability gives rise to intention, in that weapons systems produced to meet one contingency are found to be applicable to others. But this happens infrequently and it is usually obvious when it does, because the 'new' application soon attracts attention to itself.

In the specific case of the Soviet Union, there are a number of instances where intention which could be inferred from capability has not in fact been implemented, raising the question as to whether the intention exists, does not exist, or exists only for a particular set of circumstances which have not, or not yet, arisen. To attempt to assess Soviet intentions is in any event risky, because, on the one hand, Soviet secretiveness tends to conceal intention until capability begins to become available, and then to formulate doctrine which implies completeness of capability long before the necessary numbers of the weapons system in question have been procured. The first Soviet ICBMs were a case in point: silence was maintained until a test could take place to full range in July 1957: when doubts were expressed, the dramatic launching of Sputnik I in October 1957 showed that the theoretical problems had been solved. Khrushchev then launched himself with a series of policy initiatives predicated on an implied but non-existent military superiority based on an abundance of missiles. He thereby repeated a sequence of events followed a few years earlier in respect of the first Soviet long-range bombers, and with the same result – a Western reaction in which surprise that the Soviets had achieved the result at all was followed by an exaggeration of their capacity to replicate it in quantity production, leading in turn to a US deployment far above the levels then achievable by the Soviets.

It is advisable therefore to approach the question as one of what choices the Soviets wish to provide for themselves by their military procurement rather than what specific course of action they intend to follow in particular circumstances. As regards basic defensive requirements, definition is easy. They wish to provide for the Soviet Union and, to the extent possible, for its closest allies as well, a military system that is strong enough to deter attack by the strongest possible coalition of adversaries and to win any war that it cannot deter.

That, of course, is a definition applicable to any major power, and identifies only its minimal aspiration — survival as an organised society. Beyond that, assessment becomes more prone to the intervention of subjective factors. No major power maintains armed forces solely for survival; vital interests other than survival are part of the currency of international conflict, and their definition can be extremely elastic — including in the recent past the prevention of Communist control over South Vietnam, and the preservation of Communist control over Afghanistan. One factor in this elasticity of definition is that military power comprises not merely armed forces but also real estate and the power, real or imagined, which possession of it confers in the shape of ability to control or block the movement of potential adversaries. It is also a fact that vital interests are frequently defined by what is deemed possible, and if the assessment of the possible proves wrong, are redefined as non-vital. In the case of the Soviet Union, control over Eastern Europe is considered vital, and Soviet troops are stationed in Poland, East Germany, Hungary and Czechoslovakia to assure it. Because of the geographical extent of the Soviet Union, it has borders with a large number of states, and its forces are therefore close to pieces of real estate such as the Gulf, which are deemed vital to the non-Communist world. All moves by the Soviet Union in or near these areas are therefore judged as actually or potentially threatening because of its possession of surplus military capacity above the bare minimum required for survival.

Underlying all this are tendencies to view the amount of power in the international system as fixed, of those who hold the preponderance of it at any given time to regard their continued tenure of it as beneficial not only to themselves but to the system as a whole, and of the satisfied to place order above justice. Even if the Soviet system were not based on a system of values, many of which are repugnant to the existing 'satisfied' powers, these tendencies would result in a common-sense view that any increment of power to 'them' must diminish the power of 'us', a belief that a system dominated by 'them' must of necessity be worse to live in than one dominated by 'us', and a predilection to see in leftist revolutionary movements the dead hand of the KGB, without excessive inquiry into the indigenous causes of revolution. The existence of such tendencies lends to assessment processes a subjectivity which in almost any other context would be recognised and anathematised as inimical to the analytical process.

Intelligence Organisations

A basic methodological problem is that the collection and evaluation of data, and the drawing of policy conclusions from them, are for the most part in the hands of organisations with a vested interest in the conclusions, a principle normally regarded as highly undesirable if the object were simply to 'get at the truth'. The objective of an intelligence organisation, especially in the military field, is however not this, however vehemently Directors of Intelligence claim that it is. The objectives of military intelligence consist in establishing whether or not threats exist to state political and economic interests, vital or otherwise (though with a tendency to overdefinition of interests as vital), and if they are found to exist (which, more often than not, they are) to assess their magnitude. In theory the job of countering them is the responsibility of other organisations or other parts of the same organisation, but in practice this is not the case. A 'rounded' career requires an armed forces officer to spend most of his time in operational posts, and this has several effects on the nature of military intelligence assessments, two of which are of especial importance. One is that most military assessment of adversary capabilities is performed by officers who are not professionally dedicated to the art of intelligence analysis, and the other is that analysis is not separated from decision-making, in that officers concerned with analysis of adversaries have held operational posts in the past, more importantly expect to do so in the future, and are therefore inhibited both by past training and career expectations from challenging the basic institutional values of the organisation to which they belong. The circumstances under which intelligence is conducted differ significantly from those of the law, in that to give the 'accused' the benefit of the doubt which exists (and, given the incomplete nature of the evidence, there is often a great deal of doubt) is not only seldom practised, but may well be considered by the majority of intelligence practitioners to place national interests in jeopardy. This can be prudent, but it builds in a tendency to overestimate the capacities of an adversary, especially one which, like the Soviet Union, continues to regard as state secrets matters which in most other countries are public knowledge.

Soviet Military Expenditure

In assessing the military strength of other countries, it is common to begin with the defence budget. But the one-line Soviet defence budget figure of total expenditure offers no guidance to the likely level of expenditure. All outside observers agree that it is too low for the observable size of the forces and the quantity and complexity of their equipment. But proceeding from that point to an assessment of the actual cost of Soviet defence abounds in pitfalls. To begin with, there is no precise certainty of the actual size of the forces – as pointed out elsewhere in this study, some elements of the Western assessments available in the public domain are inconsistent with other countries' armed forces and with the rest of the Soviet economy, while it is extremely difficult to cost a low-readiness division, equipped with old weapons about whose amortisation rate nothing is known, and with no reliable information on the numbers of troops and officers actually embodied in peacetime.

More than that, there is room for dispute about the categories of defence expenditure actually included in the budget. Certainly the pay, operation, maintenance and accommodation of the embodied forces are included in it, but beyond that there are some very grey areas. The border guards and internal security forces of the KGB, for example, are not included. These are not fully interchangeable with orthodox military forces, as they are not equipped with heavy weapons and are not intended for battle against enemy main forces. But clearly their availability relieves the main forces of a number of manpower-consuming tasks such as the guarding of lines of communication or rearward supply depots, and the manning of sectors of the border where the probability of enemy attack is low but not altogether negligible, or where border harassment rather than invasion in force is likely. Also excluded is some, probably most, of the cost of military research and development.

There is considerable doubt about a number of other defence-associated items. Soviet practices of accounting items within functional categories rather than by charging to 'customer' may mean that the armed forces medical services are funded within the budgetary category 'Health', that some or all military training establishments are carried on the 'Education' budget, or that administrative costs of the Ministry of Defence are included in the 'Central Government Administration' category of the budget. But there is no definite information on these points, nor on a number of others, and attempts to construct models of 'real' Soviet defence costs have come up with such widely varying results that the credibility of none of them has been established. The action of the CIA in 1975, in doubling its assessment of Soviet defence costs without in any way altering its estimates of the scope of Soviet defence programmes themselves, can be seen only as a despairing recourse, all else having failed, to common-sense reasoning that if the Soviet Union, on a GNP approximately half that of the United States, maintains a roughly comparable defence establishment, then it is highly probable that it costs proportionately twice the percentage of GNP that it costs the United States. The budgetary approach therefore is not proved fruitful: prior to the doubling of the estimated cost, it credits the Soviet Union with an ability to produce goods and services in the defence field at an incredibly low cost when compared with either the production of similar goods and services by other countries, or of comparable goods and services elsewhere in the Soviet economy. Efforts to assess the cost by calculating what the Soviet defence establishment would cost if procured by the United States have not proved fruitful either, because they involve the unjustified imposition of an American cost-pattern on to the very different Soviet socio-economic structure, and because of uncertainties at the margins of the establishment as to what is defence funded and what is not.

Force Levels

In default of reliable methods of estimating based on costs, Western estimating has predominantly been based on counting of physical assets, a process much facilitated by improvements in aerial photography, carried out from 1956 to 1960 by U-2 aircraft, and since 1961 by reconnaissance satellites, and by sophisticated radar and telemetry techniques.

There are, however, certain drawbacks associated with reliance on technological means of data-gathering. A camera can take excellent photographs of, say, a tank park, from orbit, but can say little or nothing about the readiness for action of the tanks. Repeated coverage over a long period will establish whether the tanks are in regular use or not, but if they are not can still say little or nothing about their internal condition and fitness for use. The same applies to warships and aircraft. It would seem clear that the Soviets retain equipment longer than most leading Western armed forces, but to include all such retained but obsolete or obsolescent equipment at full value in published Western estimates of the Soviet order of battle, covered by a flat assumption that 'the Soviets never throw anything away' is methodologically inadequate. It may be true that 'an old weapon is better than no weapon', but it is an equal and more observable truth that military leaders inside or outside the Soviet bloc exhibit considerable uneasiness when they feel they have too much old equipment. In any event, if the statement is true enough to be significant, there is surely a fault of methodology in the inclusion of all observed Soviet weaponry, however old, in the published order of battle, without also including items such as the serried ranks of withdrawn American aircraft lined up in the Mojave desert of Arizona, and used from time to time to replenish shortfalls among America's allies.

The overall validity of the Western estimating process in respect to Soviet military strength has not been tested by a major war since 1945, and it is to be hoped that it never will be. However, some aspects of its technical estimating have been tested and a brief review of some of the more outstanding cases of error, not intended to be exhaustive, does give some pointers as to likely causes of error, the patterns they exhibit, and the lessons to be learned from them.

Stalin's purge of the military leadership in the late 1930s created an international tendency to 'write off' the Red Army. This was reinforced by its very poor performance in the war against Finland in the winter of 1939-40, while a possible counter-indication, the very successful campaign against the Japanese in Outer Mongolia in the summer of 1939, was virtually ignored, probably because it took place in a remote area, involved only six Japanese divisions, and was overshadowed in world attention by the fact that its dénouement coincided with the outbreak of the Second World War. The tendency to underestimate Soviet military strength prompted Germany to invade and the majority of British decision-makers to expect a quick Soviet collapse.[1]

German intelligence on the Soviet armed forces in 1941 was accurate about forces deployed on the Soviet Western borders, grossly underestimated mobilisable reserves and the quality of some major items of equipment (notably the T34 tank), and was seriously inaccurate in respect to topographical features such as roads.² On a number of occasions then and later it failed to notice, misinterpreted or underestimated Soviet preparation to exploit operational possibilities, e.g. for the counter-offensive in front of Moscow in December 1941 and the encirclement operation west of Stalingrad in November 1942. However, the worst German misfortunes resulted not from the numerous partial or total failures of intelligence assessments, but from Hitler's refusal to heed professional advice when it conflicted with his own preconceptions; intelligence had detected Soviet concentrations for the Stalingrad envelopment, though it had not fully grasped their size and function, nor the imminence of the attack, as it detected the massive Soviet preparations against the German summer offensive at Kursk six months later.³ That appropriate action was not taken was a failure of decision-making rather than of assessment, and as such is outside the scope of this discussion.

In the immediate post-1945 years, overestimation of the actual size of the Soviet armed forces, and of the capacity of a country, so recently devastated by war, to fight another war, went with a tendency to underestimate Soviet scientific capability. Thus the strength of the Red Army was estimated at 175 divisions, while in a classic case of underestimation of capability, the time it would take for the Soviets to explode their first nuclear device, was variously assessed at between ten and thirty years, and it was widely believed that scientific initiative was stifled in a totalitarian society, notwithstanding the achievements of German scientists in respect to jet aircraft and rocketry under Nazism. When it proved to take only four years, a hunt for spies was instituted. Such spies were found to exist,⁴ but it is now clear that their contribution was far from decisive in the case of the fission device (1949) and probably of no importance at all in the development of fusion weapons from 1953 onwards. A trend towards overestimation then became apparent. In 1953 the Soviets displayed two aircraft – the turboprop 'Bear' and turbojet 'Bison' – which appeared to have intercontinental range, and hence to end the situation which had existed since 1945, in which American aircraft could bomb the Soviet Union but Soviet aircraft could not reach the United States. Only with the passage of several years did it become clear that both aircraft fell short in significant respects – 'Bear' in speed, 'Bison' in range/payload – of providing a true intercontinental capability and that consequently they were procured only in much smaller numbers than Western assessments anticipated at the time they were first seen.

A similar instance of overestimation occurred in respect of the first

Soviet ICBMs unveiled in 1957. US intelligence estimates of the numbers likely to be in service by the mid-1960s ranged from a hundred to several thousand.[5] The true figure turned out to be 'hardly any' because the weapon (SS-6) was too large, unwieldy and reliant on volatile fuels to be militarily useful; it was used instead in the space programme, quantity deployment being deferred until the more compact and reliable second and third generation missiles were available.

While attention was focused on Soviet strategic nuclear developments, the conventional force figure of 175 divisions went unchallenged, despite the announcement by Khrushchev in January 1960 of figures which indicated that forces manpower had fluctuated between a low of 2.87 million in 1948 and 5.76 million in 1955, then reducing to 3.62 million by 1959. These figures were totally inconsistent with the assumed maintenance of a constant number of combat-ready divisions and quite inadequate in 1959 to maintain 175 such divisions after deduction of naval and air force personnel reasonably commensurate with the equipment of those forces, of non-army ground troops such as the Strategic Rocket Forces, and ground elements of the Air Defence Forces, and non-divisional elements of the army such as the Rear (Logistical) Services. Despite this, no serious effort appears to have been made to assess the tenability of the claimed Soviet figure *vis-à-vis* the alleged 175 divisions, or the implications of the intention, announced at the same time, to reduce forces manpower by a further 1.2 million, until the advent of a new administration — that of President Kennedy — at the beginning of 1961. Civilian analysts entered the Pentagon in positions of authority, and the military intelligence organisations found themselves required to justify their figures by reference to more rigorous rules of evidence than hitherto. The result was disconcerting to the military: 35 of the divisions could not be demonstrated to exist at all, while another 30 provided considerable room for argument, since they appeared to be at most low-readiness formations maintained only at a low cadre strength. Of the 110 divisions about which there was no doubt, not more than 80 could be demonstrated as at or near full strength: the remaining 30 were apparently maintained at something around two-thirds of full strength.[6]

In short, a figure accepted without challenge for many years proved on investigation to be grossly exaggerated and the methodology which produced such a result could legitimately be questioned. Since the departure of the inquisitors in the late 1960s, the assessed strength in divisions has crept up from 140 to 169. This, however, reflects two circumstances arising in the Soviet Union: first, the entry of the Sino-

Soviet dispute into an acute phase, which necessitated an increase in forces along the Sino-Soviet border without reduction in the forces facing NATO; and secondly the advent of a phase of relative demographic abundance in Soviet military affairs, as the post-war 'bulge' of children born in 1946-59 reached military age from 1965 onwards. However, military estimating has not been subjected for over 15 years to the devastating examination it received in the early 1960s, and may stand in need of another soon. The demographic bulge in the Soviet population passes out of the Soviet armed forces in the early 1980s (most of it has gone already), and thereafter the forces' massive annual intake will have to come from a much reduced 'contingent'. There still appears to be no consensus among the Soviet military as to whether increased own firepower makes it possible to reduce manpower, or increased enemy firepower makes it necessary to increase manpower; resolution of the issue is more likely to be made on economic than on strategic grounds.[7] If the economic growth rate continues low, so will the rate of creation of new jobs, and the pressure on manpower will not be acute enough to cause significant inroads into the military contingent. But if a determined and successful effort is made to raise the growth rate, the military intake may well be affected. The extent to which it is affected will be the result of leadership decisions about priorities in resource allocation, and no assessments which confine themselves to pure strategy can hope to be anywhere near the mark.

A further case of overestimation arose in the early 1960s, over a new surface-to-air missile deployment first observed in the Baltic States and therefore known as the 'Tallinn Line'. This was for some time assessed as having some capacity against missiles, or at least of being 'upgraded' to have such a capacity, but it was eventually concluded that it could be used only against aircraft. An anti-ballistic missile (NATO codename 'Galosh'), displayed in 1964 and thereafter deployed in limited numbers around Moscow, was eventually assessed as incapable of providing defence against the US attack, though possibly of some use against attack by a small number of unsophisticated missiles such as a first-generation Chinese ICBM.[8] Recognition of the cost-ineffectiveness of ABMs in the state of the art prevailing at the time was expressed in the very low numbers permitted to be deployed under the SALT I Treaty. Research and development has continued, with periodic rumbles from the intelligence community about Soviet advances. But given the numbers of means by which nuclear warheads can be delivered to target, the essentially soft-target nature of population centres, the relatively small numbers of them which need to be destroyed in order to demolish an organised society (around 25 in the United States, something between 25 and 50 in the Soviet Union, and 3 or 4 in each of their allies), the numbers of warheads and launchers already available, and the penetration aids which can be employed to confuse the defence, the classic military syndrome under which each means of attack eventually engenders an effective defence seems unlikely to materialise. The situation is entirely different from non-nuclear wars, in which the defence needed to achieve only an attrition rate per sortie of about 5 per cent on average in order to succeed. Assertions about Soviet progress, made from within elements of the intelligence community which are not merely analysts of East-West problems, but are themselves part of the problems, must always be viewed in the context of a strategic balance in which a defence which shoots down 95 per cent of incoming warheads is still likely to find the cities it defends as effectively devastated as if it had shot down none at all.

Similarly, leaks from within the assessment process concerning the Soviet civil defence programme have to be viewed within a total war context. Since only a few elements of industrial capacity can be put underground, and almost all food must be grown on the surface, preservation of lives in a scenario of total devastation of industry, agriculture, transport and administration is not necessarily of benefit to a war effort. A distinction has to be drawn between observing the efforts of a government to reduce casualities by relatively simple and cheap civil defence programmes, and the drawing of conclusions that the same government would be more willing to place the entire society at risk because it has provided more fall-out shelters than its antagonist. This distinction is not always drawn in selective leaks about the alleged scope of Soviet civil defence programmes.[9]

The problem of selective leaks may well prove insoluble. The 'missile gap' controversy, which was prominent in the 1960 presidential campaign in the United States, originated in selective leaks which produced a totally incorrect picture of a massive Soviet lead in ICBM deployment. President Eisenhower could not refute the erroneous depiction of the strategic balance without disclosing the full scope of the intelligence effort, including the comprehensive programme of aerial coverage by U2 aircraft. The misuse of selective leaks by sections of the intelligence community in order to influence public opinion is not, strictly speaking, germane to the question of assessment in itself. But it must be remembered that most intelligence evaluation is highly compartmented, and that outside their own specialities, the assessors are part of that same public opinion. Cumulative selective leakage helps to affect the overall climate within which assessment takes place, and to remove it even further from the atmosphere of judicial enquiry. In the late 1950s, for example, assessors of Soviet military manpower who believed the (incorrect) leakages from naval intelligence sources, which credited the 'W' class submarine with sufficient range to operate effectively for long periods in the Western Atlantic, would be that much less likely to credit inconclusive (though subsequently found correct) evidence that naval construction was being severely cut back, and overall manpower of all armed forces significantly reduced. It is true that at the upper levels of assessment, there is less compartmentalisation, but it is also true that those who operate at those levels are dependent on the data provided by specialists who, outside their own fields, are as vulnerable to influence by selective leakage as the veriest layman. Problems of under- or overestimation, or of interpretation of incomplete evidence to serve parochial interests is not, therefore, totally irrelevant to the assessment process itself.

A case of interpretation of evidence in a fashion distorted by parochial imperatives concerns the status of the Soviet strategic rocket forces. Until the end of 1959 these were a branch of the ground forces, but then a change in terminology began to be noticed in references to them, suggesting that their status had been upgraded to that of an autonomous service. The matter should have been placed beyond doubt in May 1960, when Khrushchev announced the change in a speech.[10] His language was unequivocal; it referred to the new service as a 'type of armed force', and to its head as a 'Commander-in-Chief', terms applicable only to autonomous armed services and their heads. The alteration in the status of the force merely implied that it had reached a certain degree of readiness, and did not in itself add or subtract a single missile, so from the point of view of assessment of the threat to Western strategic targets it was a matter of profound unimportance. However, the question had an organisational importance to Western air forces, especially the USAF and RAF, which it totally lacked to the threat assessors, or indeed, to the Soviet High Command, because the Western strategic attack mission, whether with missiles or bombers, had been placed in the hands of the air forces, and constituted the most significant single argument for their autonomy – every other function performed by an air force (e.g. tactical air support, maritime strike-reconnaissance, transport) is performed on behalf of another service, so that the strategic attack mission has come in the West to be identified with the survival of independent air forces. Consequently, identification of the new forces as autonomous evoked a sense of threat to the autonomy of air forces, in a period when the strategic attack mission was passing from bombers to missiles, while the increasing need for air support by other forces was leading to a growth in air components within armies and navies. The incident was unimportant in itself, but illustrated the methodological irrelevancies which are liable to be introduced into a process of threat assessment, a further differentiation between intelligence and judicial enquiry.

Of greater moment was the controversy created by the first of the successful Soviet ICBM flights in 1957. The differing assumptions underlying the approach of the various armed services, CIA and State Department, made it quite impossible to derive an agreed estimate for Soviet production of the new ICBM over the period 1958-63. The 'range' of estimates presented by the different contributing authorities was from 200 (army and navy) to 800 (the air force).[11] Even the most modest estimate was to prove grossly exaggerated, because, apparently unknown to the estimators, the ICBM in question (SS-6), while a reliable and powerful space booster, was of very limited utility as a military weapon because of its bulk, use of volatile fuels and relatively low accuracy. The Soviets therefore procured very few SS-6s for military purposes, and instead used the missile widely in their non-military space programme. Deployment of missiles in quantity did not take place until the second and third generation types were available.

Fairly serious problems arise in attempting to reconcile the figures of manpower said to be available to each of the Soviet armed forces with the quantities of equipment these forces are said to deploy. Taking the Navy as the easiest case, because the number of ships involved is small relative to those of aircraft and tanks, two significant differences can be found between the Soviet navy and the other leading world navies. The first relates to the numbers of old ships said to be in service. In the latest edition of *The Military Balance*,[12] the Soviet navy is said to operate 289 major surface combatants and 257 attack or cruise missile submarines. Of the major surface combatants 80 belong to the 'Skory' and 'Kotlin' class of destroyers and the 'Riga' class of frigates, all of which were built and commissioned during the 1950s. They constitute 32.3 per cent of Soviet destroyer/frigate type ships and 27.7 per cent of the total Soviet strength in major surface combatants, yet most of them are well beyond the age at which leading Western navies would have scrapped them. Furthermore, apart from some modified 'Kotlins', the so-called 'Sam Kotlins', eight in all, none of these ships appears to have undergone any substantive modernisation since it was built. If a comparison is made with the leading Western navies, i.e. those of the

NATO countries, plus Japan, it is found that only 29.7 per cent of destroyer/frigate type ships of comparable age have been retained in service, and they are mostly concentrated in the Greek and Turkish navies.

A similar picture is found in respect to the submarine force. Here attention has to be focused especially on the diesel-powered submarine, since so few nuclear submarines are old enough to have been scrapped that reliable data on the average expected life of a nuclear submarine cannot yet be collected. The Soviet diesel-powered submarine force totals 178 units, 83 of which are of the 'Whisky', 'Romeo' and 'Zulu' classes. These ships form 46.6 per cent of the total diesel submarine force, and 31.3 per cent of all Soviet submarines. All of them were built before 1961. In the leading Western navies, only 52 submarines built before that date are still in service and they constitute a mere 22.1 per cent of the submarine strength of those navies. The wisdom of carrying such large numbers of ancient units on the active order of battle may be doubted: if they are genuinely in service, it is perhaps Soviet wisdom that needs to be questioned; if they are not, but are lying in creeks awaiting scrapping, there seems little point, from the strictly 'judicial enquiry' point of view, in counting them as still active. It is certainly rare for one of these old warships to appear outside Soviet waters, and has been so for some years. As the Soviets do not publish data either on scrapping or on new construction, there is an obvious danger that Western estimators 'play safe', by adding every identified new ship to the order of battle, but refusing to strike off old units until evidence is forthcoming that they have actually been scrapped. Such evidence can come only from satellite photography in the majority of cases. It should be noted here that ships commonly remain in physical existence for long periods after they have nominally been scrapped; the destroyer Z-1,[13] the first post-war ship of the German Federal Navy, was sent to the Mediterranean to end its days as a target ship, over four years after it had been withdrawn from service. One wonders whether it is still appearing on an order of battle in Moscow because it has not actually been sunk yet.

What would appear to be at issue is two differing concepts of maintenance of the navy. If the leading maritime countries dispose of warships when they reach a certain age, they must have good reasons for doing so. If the Soviet Navy retains such warships in service long beyond the time at which other navies scrap them, it also must have its reasons. Soviet warships on average spend less time at sea than their counterparts in some of the leading Western navies, and it is possible therefore that they do not 'wear out' so fast. However, while this may explain their apparent longevity, it does not explain why so few of them have been modernised, and it must be concluded that most of them were meant to operate only in areas where shore-based aircraft could protect them, i.e. in the Baltic and Black Sea, which were in fact the major fleet areas at the time these ships were built, and were not the spearhead of an effort to build a 'High Seas' fleet. That came much later, with post-1961 and (especially) post-1970 classes of ship.

Similar anomalies can be observed in very low ratios of manpower to weapons in all services compared to the NATO countries (95 men per aircraft compared to 150 in USAF and 126 in RAF) or in men in army per combat division (10,549 in the Soviet army versus 43,000 in the US army, for example), without any serious attempt to explain the discrepancies in terms of different structural or inventory maintenance concepts.[14] If, as is claimed, the Soviet tank inventory rose from 43,000 in 1977-8[15] to 50,000 in 1978-9,[16] it is curious that no increase in the number of tanks per division was claimed, and that only one extra division, which would account for only about 300 of the additional tanks, was said to have been established. Here too it seems more likely that old tanks were withdrawn for export to the third world or for scrapping, rather than that 7,000 tanks were added to the stock, 6,700 of them with no apparent destination. The high numbers of weapons, which Soviet forces are said to have, relative to the manpower claimed for them finds no parallel either in the armed forces of other major powers or elsewhere in the Soviet economy, where manpower is generally rather high relative to machinery and to output compared to the leading non-Communist industrial countries. It is quite possible that explanations exist for these apparent anomalies, but selective leakage has not yet brought them into the public domain, and while they exist they cannot be said to enhance confidence in the quality of assessment processes.

Underestimation of Soviet capacity has arisen more rarely than overestimation, has been more frequent in the operational field than the technical, and concerned more with assessment of intention rather than capability. In the cases of Hungary (1956), Czechoslovakia (1968), and Afghanistan (1979), short-term tactical warning was provided, in the sense that preparatory troop movements were detected by various technical intelligence means, which allowed the inference to be drawn that the invasion option was at least being provided and might be exercised. In the case of Cuba (1962) substantial progress had been made towards deployment of MRBMs and IRBMs before intelligence was obtained in a form sufficiently certain to justify action. Here the essential problems concerned the pre-existent conceptual framework; the US 'picture' of the Soviets placed low probability on a dramatic forward move, while the Soviets clearly underestimated the likelihood of dramatic US counteraction. Since contingency planning is usually done well in advance, preparatory deployment is normally visible, but orders to act are usually implemented as soon as issued; it is seldom to be expected that any form of assessment will be prophetic. The most that is likely to happen is that growing or diminishing likelihoods that an option will be exercised can be deduced from the series of movements which precede a military intervention. Most so-called 'intelligence failures' are in fact failures by the assessors to realise that assessment is a matter of identifying which of a series of options is likely to be chosen; thus Soviet deployments in 1956, 1968 and 1979 pointed to increasing probability that the military intervention option would be exercised, could do no more than that, and are not required to do more, as the decision to exercise the option can be cancelled by political decision at any moment.

Since 1945 Soviet secretiveness has diminished in some respects, notably in readiness to display current items of military equipment and, in the case of strategic nuclear weapons, to disclose or to confirm Western estimates of their capabilities, especially in negotiations with the United States. At the same time, resources with which to accumulate data for outside assessment have vastly improved through technical developments such as reconnaissance satellites; and as the Soviet Union has become a major arms exporter, much more can be gleaned, even if with some time-lags, about the characteristics of Soviet weapons systems than was the case before the Second World War. Nevertheless, many important details of the Soviet defence effort, including its total cost, the numbers of men, women and weapons, weapons performance and shortcomings, research and development programmes, are still classified as secrets and may not be referred to in the media;[17] thus data which in other countries are a matter of public knowledge must be deduced by assessment processes of varying degrees of reliability, with all the scope for misinterpretation and/or wilful mispresentation which this involves.

Since the middle 1960s, a number of developments have taken place in the strategic missile field, especially in the field of multiple-warheading, the placing of warheads programmed for different targets on the same missile, and of the possibility that warheads can be guided on to their targets by their own onboard electronics. The action-reaction phenomenon has sometimes been evoked in attempts to account for the process of competitive innovation, but it is more plausible that the real race is with technology itself. In such a race advances by one side serve to stimulate the other to emulation not merely for military reasons but in order to demonstrate that 'our' science is as good as 'theirs', or encourages the scientists of one side to persevere with their efforts by showing that the goal they are seeking is attainable. In a contest of this kind 'who started what?' becomes irrelevant and extrapolation from research and development to future deployment a potentially very misleading process, since many systems which look promising at an early stage are not deployed at all, or take much longer to convert from a scientist's toy to a serviceable military tool than was estimated by their enthusiastic proponents or by apprehensive observers. As a general proposition the United States has been 'ahead' in most innovation, but in recent years there has been a groundswell of suggestions that the Soviet Union is significantly ahead in fields such as high energy physics and is spending considerably more on research and development than is the United States. About all that can be said about this is that while all cost comparisons between the USA and USSR are difficult, research and development comparisons are the most difficult of all. There is little to be seen in the way of a costable end-product, cost allocation between the military and non-military implications of a piece of research in pure science are almost impossible to make and, while all Soviet research, military or non-military, is state-funded, much of that conducted in the non-Communist world is not, or not directly, so funded.

Alliances

The general problem of assessment of a many-factored balance can be greatly affected by the parameters chosen for emphasis. In the case of Western assessment of the Soviet Union's capacity for war, two specific tendencies can be observed: the first, to make purely bilateral comparisons between Soviet and US strengths, and to draw conclusions which may prove unwarranted in the light of the fact that war, if it occurs, is likely to be a war between two alliance systems rather than a single combat between superpowers, and, the second, to select only the parameter of military strength in being, the least unfavourable to the Soviets of all the comparisons which could be made.

It is certainly clear from their writings that the Soviet military envisage major war as a war between alliance systems,[18] and equally clear from comparison of the alliance systems that the contribution which the Soviet Union's allies make to alliance strength in no way matches that of the alliance system of the United States. Year after year the disadvantage imposed upon NATO by its lack of standardisation, compared with the Warsaw Pact, is lamented in NATO circles. Seldom is there any reference to the underlying reasons for this undoubted operational problem, namely, that the US alliance system contains all the world's major industrial powers except the Soviet Union (West Germany, France, UK, Italy and Benelux in Europe, and Japan outside it); that these countries have major arms industries of their own, and are significant producers and innovators in their own right, with a consequent impulse to resist standardisation on the products of others; and that the Soviet alliance system contains no comparable powers, so that standardisation on Soviet equipment is inevitable where all major weapons systems are concerned, but is not a source of strength in itself, rather is a partial offsetting of a weakness in the productive capacity of the Soviet alliance system as a whole. If it is logical that the existence within NATO of forces which resist standardisation constitutes a source of weakness, then the tendency towards limited independent production now apparent in Poland, Czechoslovakia and Romania must also be a source of weakness. It is more likely that the same considerations apply to both, namely that they constitute an accretion of strength, some part of which is offset by an increase in supply problems because of reduced standardisation. This is a situation frequently encountered in industry, in which the decision whether or not to change from one supplier to another is made only after consideration of all factors involved, of which compatibility with existing equipment is only one, important but not determinant. Modern armed forces are industrial organisations, and it must be assumed that NATO's relative (and it *is* only relative) reluctance to standardise is not the result of mere perversity.

The question of choice of parameters for assessment deserves further consideration. The emphasis in the Soviet armed forces on 'first day' strength, mobility and firepower would seem to confer on them significant advantages in a blitzkrieg-type war, provided their adversaries were sufficiently obliging to conform to Soviet plans, abstain from the use or threat of use of nuclear weapons against Soviet-bloc forces and territory, and cry quits as soon as Europe had been overrun.

This does not seem an overwhelmingly likely course of action for them to adopt. To begin with, 'blitzkrieg' succeeded in 1939 against a secondary power (Poland), and in 1940 against two major powers (UK and France) because of its novelty. It came near to definitive success against the Soviet Union in 1941 because the Red Army had not had time to absorb its lessons, and because of some atrociously bad leadership decisions by Stalin. Thereafter it failed, because antidotes to it had been found; the German advance to the Volga and Caucasus in 1942 netted no large Soviet formations as had been the case in 1941, and ended in a major disaster for Germany, while Rommel's advance in Africa ended in less than a year in over-extension, retreat and surrender. It is highly unlikely that NATO forces in Europe would conform to the pattern of the French army in 1940, or that Soviet military planning expects them to. That being so, it is fruitless to posit the kind of short-war scenario to which the Soviet force structure appears most suited, and advisable to note the long-war scenario implicit in the Soviet mobilisation system and reserve structure.

For a short war, differences in economic and demographic potential may well be irrelevant, for a longer war they are likely to be crucial. This is no more than a truism, frequently mentioned, but the contribution of economic and demographic potentials to deterrence tends to be either taken for granted or overlooked altogether. Omission from Western assessments of any comparison of these potentials amounts to omission of all Western military potential except that in being on Day One of a conflict, and therefore favours the Warsaw Pact by thrusting to the forefront of comparison a scenario for a most unlikely type of war — one in which the strategic nuclear power of both sides it not used, and in which Warsaw Pact conventional force is applied with complete success for a short period, after which all fighting ceases, the unsubjugated powers of the US alliance system acquiescing in whatever gains the Warsaw Pact has made in the fighting.

Essentially the Soviet Union compares well with the USA and its allies only in the military field, and does so only by making disproportionately heavy allocations of resources and skills to defence. It is inherently improbable that there exist alongside each other two Soviet industrial structures, one — the civilian — notorious for slowness to innovate, poor quality control, shortcomings in supply of spare parts, and heavy dependence on foreign technology for modernisation; the other — the military — free of all these faults. It is far more likely that quality is attained in the defence field by rejecting a high proportion of output, and modernity by incremental improvement plus occasional generational renewal, processes which place a heavy burden on the society, and reduce its ability to compete for international influence (and, hopefully, for goodwill) by trade, aid and export of skill. There have been societies in which military strength was cultivated to the virtual exclusion of all else, but their successes predate the era of industrialisation; and while the Soviet heavy industrial base is adequate to its superpower status, its relative backwardness in light industry, and especially in electronics, cannot be considered a source of military strength in an era when its potential adversaries are likely to turn increasingly to military systems which enhance the capacity of manpower by equipping it with a variety of electronic aids. In ability to innovate, there is a world of difference between societies in which defence applications grow out of a massive civil-oriented electronics industry, and one in which they lack any such base. It must be counted a fault in Western assessment of Soviet military strength that parameters such as this, or even of the ease with which children in the advanced industrial countries can acquire basic skills of military applicability, such as the ability to drive, and often to maintain, vehicles, which most Soviet citizens still cannot, are left out of account, in favour of comparisons of strength which relate mostly to the first day or first week of a hypothetical war.

The past history of Western assessments of the Soviets' military strengths therefore exhibits tendencies to overestimate their capacity but underestimate their readiness to use it, to attribute Western functions to their Soviet analogues, to interpret the data within preconceived frameworks, use only the comparisons in which the Soviets appear strongest and to depart from the spirit of judicial enquiry by a reluctance to give the 'accused' the benefit of the doubt. Soviet secretiveness is in large part responsible, in that their reluctance to release hard facts provides a monopoly of data to those organisations in the non-Communist world which have the resources for the very expensive collection process, especially those of the United States. However high the standards such organisations set themselves, it has to be recognised that they are not so much analysts of the problems of East-West relations as part of those problems; their institutional values tend to impel them, or some of them, towards worst-case assumptions or towards conclusions which are designed to enhance the status and assure the appropriations of the armed service with which they are associated; while the data which they choose to release into the public domain are disseminated on a selective basis with the intention of securing a particular outcome to public discussion rather than of merely providing a basis for it. That the dubious practices in which some of these organisations indulge have not yet led to a major catastrophe owes something to chance, but more to the fact that their forecasts are frequently in conflict with each other, their basis in self-interest readily apparent, and their reasoning not entirely impeccable. But as a basis for an informed public opinion, such practices have serious shortcomings, and all who use them in public ventilation of issues of East-West relations need to do so with considerable caution and scepticism.

Notes

1. Larry Collins and Dominique Lapierre, *Freedom at Midnight* (Vikas, New Delhi, 1976), p. 148 note.
2. Basil Liddell Hart, *The Other Side of the Hill* (Cassell, London, 1948), pp. 184 and 187.
3. Alan Bullock, *Hitler: A Study in Tyranny* (Odhams Books Ltd, London, 1964), pp. 669 and 686.
4. John Wexley, *The Judgement of Julius and Ethel Rosenberg* (Bookville, London, 1956).
5. Desmond Ball, *Politics and Force Levels, The Strategic Missile Program of the Kennedy Administration* (University of California Press, Berkeley, 1980), p. 7.
6. Alain C. Enthoven and K. Wayne Smith, *How Much is Enough? Shaping The Defense Program, 1961-1969* (Harper and Row, New York, 1971), pp. 132-42.
7. Geoff Jukes, 'Soviet Strategy 1965-1990' in Robert O'Neill and D.M. Horner (eds.), *New Directives in Strategic Thinking* (George Allen and Unwin, Sydney, 1981).
8. Robert G. Kaiser, *Russia: The People and the Power* (Atheneum, New York, 1976), pp. 456-7.
9. See for instance, 'Strategic Balance: Trends and Perceptions' in *Washington Report*, Washington (April 1977), WR 77-4. (Speech and questions answered by General George Keegan.)
10. *New York Times*, 6 May 1960, p. 6.
11. Ball, *Politics and Force Levels*, p. 89.
12. All figures cited here are based on Captain John Moore RN (ed.), *Jane's Fighting Ships 1979-80* (London, 1979) or *The Military Balance* (IISS, London, 1980).
13. Captain John Moore (ed.), *Jane's Fighting Ships 1973-74* (London, 1973).
14. *The Military Balance 1980-81*.
15. *The Military Balance 1977-78*.
16. *The Military Balance 1978-79*.
17. Kaiser, *Russia*, pp. 224-5.
18. For example in *Marxism-Leninism on War and Army (A Soviet View)*, translated from the Russian (published under the auspices of the US Air Force, Washington, 1974), pp. 157-61 and V.D. Sokolovsky, *Soviet Military Strategy* (Stanford Research Institute, 1975), pp. 53 ff.

PART TWO:

THE POWER OF THE NEW STATES

4 BRITISH ESTIMATES OF JAPANESE MILITARY POWER, 1900-1914

Philip A. Towle

At the beginning of the twentieth century the European states had, for the first time for many years, to deal with a non-European aspirant to the ranks of the Great Powers. They had become accustomed to the idea that Europe should rule the world and it was inevitable therefore that there should be some resistance to the belief that Japan had become a major military power. Perhaps what is surprising in the circumstances is that the resistance was not greater. The efforts of European statesmen, commentators and military officers to assess correctly the power of Japan are of particular interest today when there are several aspirants to great power status, such as India and Brazil, amongst the non-European nations. Like their predecessors who watched the growth of the Japanese army and navy, the intelligence services and national leaders of the existing Great Powers have to assess the power and efficiency of the new armies and navies spread across the world from Korea to Nigeria. They also have to make these assessments at a time when the established Great Powers are rarely involved in combat.

A Last Resort

In 1902 the British government showed its faith in Japanese military strength in the most direct way by forming an alliance with Japan. However it must be admitted that the 1902 alliance was something of a last resort. Britain's isolation and the hostility of most of the European countries towards the British Empire had been only too clearly demonstrated during the Boer War.[1] In the 1890s there had been considerable friction between Britain and France over colonies; at the same time, Russia appeared to be threatening India by extending its railways to the Afghan frontier and it was also increasing its influence in China. New navies were being built by the United States, Japan and Germany. Britain's strategic position was therefore weakening on both land and sea and the British government attempted to improve its relations with Germany, France and Russia. When these diplomatic efforts failed, Britain turned to Japan.[2]

Early Estimates

The decision to negotiate an alliance with Japan might seem to reflect a consensus of opinion about that country which did not in fact exist in government or military circles. For example, Arthur Balfour, the Prime Minister's deputy opposed the alliance on the grounds that 'if it ends in war, [it] brings us into collision with the same opponents as a German alliance [i.e., Russia and France] but with a much weaker partner'.[3] Balfour was the leading strategist amongst Conservative politicians and his opinions are therefore particularly interesting. Many of the other members of the cabinet simply followed the lead given by the Admiralty and the Foreign Office which were in favour of the alliance with Japan. The War Office does not appear to have consulted the British military attaché in Tokyo and it later became clear that there were fundamental disagreements within the British army about the strength of the Japanese army and therefore about its value in the alliance. The Admiralty was in favour of an alliance with Japan because of the deteriorating naval balance in the Far East which was caused by the build-up in the Russian Pacific Fleet and the improvement of the Russian bases at Port Arthur and Vladivostok.[4] According to the Admiralty's figures, France had one battleship in the area, Britain had four, Russia had five (with three building), and Japan had six (with one building). Because of French, Russian and German strength in Europe, Britain was reluctant to send more ships to the Far East and therefore could only hope to balance the Franco-Russian forces in the area by joining with Japan.

The Admiralty's calculations assumed that a battleship manned by Japanese sailors was approximately equal to one manned by Russians or French. This was a remarkable testimony to Japanese progress since the 1850s, and to the success of the Japanese leaders in modernising their country. In 1868 the few Japanese ships available had only been capable of the simplest manoeuvres.[5] By the middle of the 1880s many of the British doctors and engineers who had founded hospitals and built railways in Japan had returned home and handed over their positions to the Japanese.[6] Roads and railways were being extended and industries started. But it was difficult for outsiders to assess how deep this modernisation went. Moreover few people in Europe took a close interest in Japan.[7] Very often those who did write about Japan concentrated upon the picturesque side of Japanese life — the geishas, chrysanthemums and lacquered ornaments.[8] Certainly few British journals were as prescient as the *Quarterly Review*, which argued in 1880 that Japan was the first amongst the Asiatic states to have 'shown herself capable of

British Estimates of Japanese Military Power

marching in the forefront of civilization'.[9] The Russians believed that the most perceptive books about Japan were written by Germans who also provided a military mission to assist the Japanese army.[10]

One of the most influential of British visitors to Japan during this period was Lord Curzon, who became Viceroy of India in 1899. Curzon visited Japan in 1887 and again in 1892. He commented subsequently,

> ... the modernisation of the country proceeds apace though perhaps with a less headlong rapidity than before ... Aspiring to play a predominant part in the politics of Eastern Asia, she has spared no effort

Figure 4.1: The Far East in 1904-5

and shrunk from no sacrifice to place herself in the matter of armed equipment upon a level with her possible competitors . . . The Japanese Army need not shrink from . . . comparison, in point of efficiency, with the forces of European states.[11]

Curzon went on to quote approvingly the views of a British officer that the 'Japanese infantry are very good, better even than some European infantry I could name; the artillery good or at least fair; and the cavalry indifferent.'

Western appreciation of Japanese military strength rose after the Sino-Japanese War of 1894-5. The Japanese defeated the Chinese at Pingyang and on the Yalu in September 1894. They swept the Chinese ships from the sea and took the port of Wei Hai Wei early in 1895. In April 1895 the Chinese were forced to agree to the Peace of Shimonoseki.[12] Nevertheless, Japan's success had to be assessed in comparison with its adversary and most observers had a low opinion of Chinese military power. Japan might be able to defeat a European country but that conclusion could not necessarily be drawn from the Sino-Japanese War. However, influential organs of opinion were sufficiently impressed to call for closer relations between Britain and Japan. *The Times*, for example, suggested an agreement between Britain, Japan and the United States to preserve the *status quo* in Asia.[13] Individual British political leaders, such as Joseph Chamberlain, also began to consider the possibility. Chamberlain appears to have been influenced by Sir Edward Arnold of the *Daily Telegraph* who had a Japanese wife and who argued that Japan was 'probably a coming Great Power and a friend'.[14] Arnold's opinions seemed to be confirmed by the very rapid increase in the size of the Japanese standing army from 58,440 men in 1894 to 142,412 nine years later.[15]

After the Sino-Japanese War, Russia joined with France and Germany to thwart Japanese ambitions in Manchuria and began to expand its own influence over China. In 1897 the Germans took Kiao-chau and the Russians took Port Arthur. These threats to the *status quo* in China prompted Joseph Chamberlain to write to the Prime Minister, Lord Salisbury, 'have you considered whether we might not draw closer to Japan? It seems to me that they are rapidly increasing their means of offence and defence and in many contingencies they would be valuable allies.'[16] However, Salisbury preferred an agreement with Russia which, he hoped, would preserve the *status quo* in China. Above all he feared an agreement between Russia, Germany and France against Britain, similar to the combination which had formed against Japan after the

Sino-Japanese War.[17] In the event, such a hostile combination did not materialise but neither did the hopes for an agreement between Britain and any of the European powers.[18]

The Boxer Rising

In 1900 the anti-foreign Boxer Rebellion broke out in China. The Boer War was still being waged in South Africa and Lord Roberts, commanding the British forces there, said that he could spare few troops for operations in China. Consequently Salisbury turned to Japan for help but the Germans and Russians were determined that Japan should not be able to strengthen its position in the Celestial Empire by dealing with the situation single-handed.[19] In the end it was a combined force, including British regiments from India, which made its way to Peking to rescue the besieged foreign legations there. Some historians have argued that the experience of working with the Japanese during the expedition raised Britain's estimates of Japanese power.[20] In fact, although Japan's efforts at this time may have increased the appreciation of Japanese strength amongst British statesmen and the public at large, they did not always increase esteem for the Japanese amongst British army officers and particularly those who were attached to the Japanese army.

Of these officers, Colonel A.G. Churchill, the military attaché, was the most important. Churchill was extremely suspicious of all aspects of the Japanese army. When the Japanese authorities estimated that 70,000 troops would be needed to push through to Peking, Churchill argued that the 'estimate was largely political and had in view amongst other things the idea that a low estimate would tend to diminish the performance of the Japanese in the Japan-China war'.[21] Churchill's praise for the Japanese was always grudging; when they refrained from looting Peking, unlike many of the other relieving forces, he commented merely, 'the behaviour of the Japanese in this respect compared favourably with that of the allies'. Of the commander of the Japanese forces, General Fukushima, he noted that he was able and 'different from the majority of his class in being extremely abstemious both in the matter of liquor and women'.[22] The bravery of the Japanese troops was obvious and their ability in bayonet fighting was beyond reproach but Japanese tactics were poor and they appeared indifferent to casualties. Out of the 400 Japanese cavalry who set out on the relief expedition, only 60 survived to reach Peking.

Churchill seems to have resented Japanese pride in their military achievements and their comments about the Indian regiments on the expedition. 'In comparing their own troops with those of the allies', he wrote, 'the Japanese made the mistake of not allowing sufficiently for various difficulties with which every other country had to contend.' Troops from elsewhere were often not suitably equipped for the Chinese climate and they found the food unsatisfactory. If they preferred to use rifle fire, rather than to rush into the attack with bayonets this only showed their prudence. The Japanese commander believed that the Indian soldiers whom Britain sent on the expedition 'were wanting in spirit' and he attributed this to 'their being a subject race'. Churchill thought that Japanese comments were motivated by their chagrin that the cavalry was not put under their control. He also felt that, in so far as their comments had any justification, this was because only inferior Indian regiments had been sent. However this second explanation appears to have been untrue.[23]

Churchill's comments on the relief expedition did not make much impression at the time, despite the fact that an alliance with Japan was being seriously considered in London. His views could perhaps be dismissed as eccentric, had they not been shared by so many of the other British army officers who lived in Japan in the two decades before the First World War. Of course, not all those who knew Japan well took so low a view of Japanese military capabilities. Sir Claude MacDonald, the British Ambassador there, had previously been a serving officer and he was a firm believer in Japanese strength. Subsequently he wrote that he told Lord Salisbury 'one of the assets . . . in favour of the alliance was the splendid courage of our allies (then to be)'.[24]

British strategists who had had no contact with Japan were starting to take the same view. For example, Sir George Clarke, the future Secretary of the Committee of Imperial Defence, wrote in June 1902,

> Japan is a very big fact as her army is ready and Russia alone is not a match for Japan in the Gulf of Pe-Chi-Li. Similarly we alone could not do much against Russia beyond sealing the ports and making sea communications impossible.[25]

At that time Clarke did not think a Russo-Japanese War likely but, by the beginning of 1903, he had changed his mind because 'although Russia wants a very few years more to be more than a match for Japan . . . Japan on the other hand may consider that it is a case of now or never'.[26] As the Intelligence Section of the War Office minuted in March 1902,

British Estimates of Japanese Military Power

Japanese troops are as yet untried against Europeans. Yet if reckless courage combined with perfect discipline and good leading go for anything they should be able to hold their own with the troops of any nation.[27]

The Japanese themselves appear to have been confident that they could defeat the Russians in Manchuria, although, after the Anglo-Japanese alliance was signed, they said that they would welcome British help.[28] As the Intelligence Section noted,

> ... the task proposed by the Japanese army is no light one but having regard to the efficiency and relative strength and to the strategical consideration it seems to be not beyond its powers.[29]

These views were shared by some members of the British cabinet. St John Brodrick, who was successively War Minister and Secretary of State from India, wrote to Lord Curzon in February 1902, 'I believe we shall be great gainers in the Far East' from the Japanese alliance.[30] By early 1904 Brodrick felt that Britain had benefited whether or not there was war between Japan and Russia, because Russia had been forced to spend so much on Port Arthur and other facilities in the Far East by the Anglo-Japanese 'threat', that Russian efforts in other directions had been curtailed. Many of Curzon's other correspondents believed the Japanese could defeat the Russians, as one wrote in February 1904,

> ... of late, it has been difficult not to say impossible to prevent oneself from hoping for [the outbreak of war between Russia and Japan]; it seems obvious that sooner or later it must come, and this being so the sooner it comes the better for Japan and us.[31]

Lord Curzon, however, was less sure about the benefits to Britain of a Russo-Japanese war. But, fortified by his earlier high estimates of Japanese strength, he was not apparently afraid that Japan would be defeated. Nor was this because Curzon had a low estimate of Russian military prowess. On the contrary, for much of the time that he was Viceroy of India, Russian expansion southwards towards Afghanistan was the main worry of the Indian government. Curzon feared that if there were war, 'sooner or later whether it be from ... victory or from anger at defeat Russia will probably feel tempted to exert great pressure on our frontiers'.[32] Before that happened Curzon thought that the war might provide Britain with the opportunity to extend its influence in

Persia or Tibet. However Brodrick warned that Russia was looking for an opportunity to pick a quarrel with Britain and that moves in these areas would probably precipitate Britain into the Russo-Japanese conflict.[33]

It was in the months preceding the Russo-Japanese War that the War Office's intelligence services decided that the time was ripe to ask Colonel Churchill how Japan would fare in such a conflict. Colonel (later Field Marshal) W.G. Robertson told the Director of Military Operations, Sir William Nicholson, that he had asked Churchill for an appreciation of Japanese strength, since 'we are not too well informed on the subject'.[34] It was a curious admission to make a year after the Anglo-Japanese alliance had been signed and the response certainly surprised the War Office. Churchill had not changed his views since the Boxer Rebellion. Looking back to the Sino-Japanese War, Churchill stated, 'I have no hesitation in saying that in my opinion the world at large overestimated what the Japanese then did.'[35] Primarily Churchill believed that this overestimation was caused by an exaggeration of Chinese military power. To defeat the Chinese the Japanese needed 200,000 men but Churchill believed 'from our own experience of campaigning in China' that a British or a French force of 20,000 could have done as much. The Russians were a much more formidable enemy than the Chinese;

> ... the Russians ... are perhaps the hardest troops in the world to turn out of a position they have occupied, e.g., the Crimean War, the Russo-Turkish War of 1877-8 and more recently on a small scale the Tientsin railway station.

The Japanese cavalry was particularly poor and 'there is a real danger therefore that the Japanese divisions may find themselves stifled by ... Cossacks who, man for man, I consider far superior to the Japanese cavalry'. The Japanese artillery was insufficient, the new Japanese field gun was unsafe and there were too few field guns compared with the smaller mountain guns. All in all, Churchill concluded,

> ... if left to themselves 100,000 Russians would be equal to 250,000 Japanese but the addition on the Japanese side of 10,000 British (white) troops would necessitate another 100,000 Russians to preserve equality.[36]

Racial stereotypes therefore played an important part in Churchill's judgement. Nor is this very surprising. Although Asian troops had beaten

British Estimates of Japanese Military Power   119

European troops in the field in Afghanistan and elsewhere, they had done so with decreasing frequency in the second half of the nineteenth century and usually when conditions were peculiarly favourable to them and when the Europeans had been unable to bring modern technology to bear on their enemies. As the *Fortnightly Review* commented, with some exaggeration, during the Russo-Japanese War 'the East for the first time since the Middle Ages has again equality in weapons and equality in the use of weapons'.[37]

Churchill's assessment gradually made its way up the military hierarchy in the War Office to the Commander in Chief, Lord Roberts. On its way its conclusions were severely criticised. Captain Black, AQMG in the Intelligence Section observed,

> ... perhaps the most important conclusion arrived at by Colonel Churchill is that Japan left to herself would be unable successfully to cope with Russia, although possessing a marked numerical superiority in infantry. Japan's great defect both as to quality and numbers is her cavalry while her artillery is little if at all superior to what the Russians could put in the field in Manchuria.[38]

Black admitted that Japanese infantry formations were too dense but argued that this could be changed, once it became obvious how many casualties they produced in the face of modern weapons. Initially the casualties might nevertheless be very great but, 'in discipline, elan, patriotism and absolute callousness towards death the Japanese are well up to European standards'. Captain E.A. Altham, AQMG, agreed with Black 'in thinking that Lt Colonel Churchill has taken too pessimistic a view of the fighting qualities of the Japanese army'. In particular he believed that the Japanese General Staff 'appears to be admirably organised on the German system and to be composed of very capable officers'. Moreover Altham believed that Churchill laid

> ... too great stress ... upon the fact that the Japanese army is at present untried. The Prussian army was in a great measure untried before the 1866 campaign yet it defeated in that war an army of great experience and high reputation.[39]

Altham had nevertheless put his finger on two of the reasons why the British found it so difficult to assess the Japanese army, its Prussian methods and its novelty. A third reason was the exaggerated importance ascribed in some sections of the British army to cavalry and hence to

Japanese deficiencies in this arm.

The Russo-Japanese Balance

Churchill suggested that Britain should lend Japan some military aid in the event of a Russo-Japanese war. However, under the terms of the Franco-Russia alliance, this would have brought Russia's ally, France, into the war on the other side and it had already been discussed and rejected at the Anglo-Japanese military discussions in the summer of 1902.[40] Britain was only bound by the Anglo-Japanese alliance to assist Japan if another country joined Russia in the event of a Russo-Japanese war. Moreover there were doubts about the possibility of giving aid to Japan in such an eventuality. Sir William Nicholson forwarded Churchill's report to Lord Roberts while pointing out that, in the case of a general war, Britain would probably be fully involved with the defence of India.[41] In any case the Commander in Chief seems to have been unimpressed by Churchill's fears for Japan's safety and held to his view that Japan would be victorious in a war with Russia.[42]

This was a marked contrast to the views of the British military experts on Russia. When the war broke out, General Sir Montagu Gerard, Colonel W.H.H. Waters and Major Home were sent by Britain to accompany the Russian armies in the field. Gerard and Waters had both been military attachés in St Petersburg and were therefore familiar with the strengths and weaknesses of the Russian military system.[43] Nevertheless, they both expected Russia to win the war easily. 'God help the Japs if they cross the Yalu' (from Korea into Manchura) Gerard opined.[44] Waters had actually visited Japan and observed the Japanese manoeuvres in 1902 but this proved a positive handicap to assessing the strength of the Japanese army.

> The troops did not impress me, accustomed as I was to Russian stolidity . . . the frequent interruptions by relatively junior officers, when the Minister of War or the Chief of Staff were talking, struck me as evidence of Japanese frivolity and superficiality.[45]

Nor was it just the military experts on Russia who took this view. The leading British civilian expert on Russia at the time, Sir Donald Mackenzie Wallace, confidently predicted the defeat of Japan.[46]

It is hardly surprising that there was some confusion at this stage amongst British ministers about the state of the military balance in the

Far East. At the end of 1903 Balfour (now Prime Minister) wrote to the First Lord of the Admiralty, Lord Selborne and to the War Minister, Arnold Forster,

> I think it is important for us to know in somewhat more detail than we do at present what forecast is made by the intelligence departments of the navy and army with regard to the possible course of hostilities should they break out between Russia and Japan in the early spring ... It seems impossible to suppose that Japan can strike an effective blow at Russia unless by means of a large expeditionary force directed against the Russian lines of communication in Manchuria; and if this be so I should be glad to know whether in the opinion of the experts such operations would be possible in the present balance of sea power in Eastern waters as between Japan and Russia. Suppose the operation is not possible, what is Japan going to do? It may be impossible for Russia to attack her directly but the Russians could easily overrun Corea, and Corea has always been regarded by Japan as a vital interest.[47]

Balfour realised that the Japanese were assessing the military situation carefully but he also noted that they seemed dilatory about buying further warships or preventing the Russians buying them from the Chilean and Argentine governments which were anxious to sell them at this time.

The Foreign Secretary, Lord Lansdowne, was in favour of putting pressure on the Japanese to come to terms with the Russians, although he believed that, at the time, Japan had naval superiority in the Far East. It had six first-class battleships to Russia's seven but it also had three second-class battleships. 'Moreover the fleet is better found [it was mainly built in Britain] and has much greater facilities for coaling and docking.' However, Lansdowne warned, 'a few months hence the balance will incline the other way ... by next autumn Russia might be mistress of the situation and might impose terms on Japan.' Alternatively, if war broke out under those conditions, Russia 'might render her an almost negligible factor in Far Eastern politics instead of, as at present, a potential ally of great importance to us'. Lansdowne therefore feared that Japan might be crushed and Britain drawn into the war by the force of British public opinion despite the 'aggravation of [Britain's] present financial difficulties' which had been caused by the Boer War.[48] Lansdowne was certainly not alone in thinking that the balance of power was changing in the Far East. The First Secretary in the Russian

Legation in Tokyo openly boasted of the rapid build-up in Russian naval power in the area.[49]

Balfour was less pessimistic than Lansdowne about Japan's chances in a war over the next few years,

> Russia even though stronger in battleships cannot crush Japan because such a result can only be achieved by a Russian invasion of Japan itself. This is an impossible military operation and one which would become doubly impossible if we had a large force of ships in the East watching events.

Even if it were neutral such a force would threaten to cut the Russian fleet's communications with its base at Port Arthur. Japan could not be starved into submission because it did not depend on foreign food. On the other hand, the Japanese could not land forces on the mainland because of the strength of the Russian fleet (a view subscribed to by the Commander of the Russian Pacific Fleet, Admiral Vitgeft).[50] Russia would therefore occupy Korea and make a permanent enemy of Japan which would wait until Russia's attention was occupied in some other part of the world before seeking its revenge. 'If any war *could* be conceived as being advantageous to us this is one. Both before, during and after its outbreak it is likely to do wonders in making Russia amenable to sweet reason.'[51]

Clearly the outcome of the war would to a large extent be determined by naval power. Lord Selborne, the First Lord of the Admiralty, correctly believed that Japan would want to forestall a Russian takeover of Korea. He also believed that to do this the Japanese would have to fight a fleet action. Much would depend upon whether Russian naval reinforcements reached the Far East before the outbreak of war but, even if they did, 'the Japanese might still quite likely win by superior efficiency'. Selborne was basing his views on naval advice and this was obviously in marked contrast to Churchill's views on Japanese military efficiency. The Japanese navy was modelled on the Royal Navy, while the Japanese army was modelled on the German army. Consequently the Japanese navy looked much more impressive to the Royal Navy than the Japanese army did to the British army officers who served with it.

Nevertheless, Selborne was not entirely confident that the Japanese would prove victorious. Like Lansdowne, Selborne feared that Britain could not stand by and watch Japanese naval power destroyed by Russia, yet to come to Japan's aid would mean bringing France into the war on the side of its Russian ally. 'What prevents one forming a more clear opinion is ignorance of the real intentions of Japan and her estimates of her own strength and ignorance of the intentions . . . of France', Lord Selborne commented. In fact the Japanese were confident that they could handle the situation; on 15 January 1904 they told the British government that they 'confidently believed from the naval and military point of view they were sufficiently prepared . . . if a conflict becomes inevitable'.[52] In any case, Balfour pointed out to Selborne that Britain was not bound to come to Japan's aid in a conflict with a single power and he felt that a Russian effort to control Korea would overextend the Tsar's financial resources. Finally, Balfour wrote to Selborne,

> . . . even if Japan got the worst of the naval battle which you anticipate, Russia could not come out of it unscathed; indeed my belief is that a war between the two countries would render Russia innocuous for some little time to come.[53]

All such speculations were made redundant in February 1904 when Japan staged a pre-emptive torpedo boat attack on the Russian fleet moored outside Port Arthur, thereby greatly increasing the Japanese navy's chances of winning a fleet action. The torpedo boat attack was not as successful as the Japanese attack on Pearl Harbour 37 years later but it demoralised the Russians. The Russian Pacific Fleet retreated into Port Arthur and allowed the Japanese army to land in Korea and subsequently in Manchuria. Port Arthur was cut off by Japanese forces on land and sea, and the Russian fleet was prevented from escaping from Port Arthur to Vladivostok by the battle of 10 August 1904. Port Arthur itself fell to the Japanese at the beginning of 1905, the Russian land forces were pushed back at the battle of Mukden and the Russian Baltic Fleet, sent from Europe to snatch victory from defeat, was annihilated at the battle of Tsushima in May 1905.

Oddly enough Balfour became most anxious about Japan's prospects in the middle of the war. In September 1904 he wrote to Sir George Clarke, the Secretary of the Committee of Imperial Defence,

> I wish I could be as confident about the course of the war as most military critics appear to be. I fear three things: (1) that the Russian [Baltic] Fleet might get round to Vladivostok (2) that it might occupy some Chinese port as a base (3) that Japan which has now landed every regular soldier it possesses upon the mainland may in 6 or 8 months time find itself in considerable difficulties.[54]

By that time however, Clarke was so confident that the Japanese were superior to the Russians, that he believed the Russians would need 500,000 men to defeat 400,000 Japanese. He also expected the Japanese to defeat the Baltic fleet in a great sea battle.[55]

The course of events vindicated the amateurs rather than the professionals, the politicians rather than the soldiers. Waters and Gerard were shown to have gravely overestimated Russian power and Churchill made an equally grave underestimation of Japanese power. Because they had listened to their professional advisers, Lansdowne, Selborne and Balfour had become a little too pessimistic about Japanese strength as the war approached. St John Brodrick, Sir George Clarke, Sir Claude MacDonald and others probably came out of the situation with the best record for correctly assessing the balance of Russo-Japanese power. They had taken a 'broad' view of Japanese progress and of Russian deficiencies, while Churchill took too narrow a view. The British government had seen the alliance with Japan as a useful prop to the British position in the Far East, they had not expected the alliance to lead to a major Russian collapse. Nor were they always pleased with this result. The defeat of Russia and the subsequent revolution seemed to increase German belligerance and to threaten the European balance of power. Sir George Clarke noted in December 1905 'the European outlook makes me anxious. The position in Russia is appalling.'[56]

The concerns felt by British statesmen only gradually spread to wider circles. The general reaction in Britain to Japan's victories was euphoric. Japan was seen as

> . . . a nation in arms which on land as well as on sea has given countless proofs of heroism and a calm disregard for danger, and shown a fixity of purpose and an unruffled patience that has seldom been equalled and clearly never surpassed in the entire course of the World's history.[57]

The *National Review* reflected the views of other influential periodicals when it said that the war was 'an upheaval as momentous as anything that has occurred since the French revolution'.[58]

Military Evaluation of the War

During the war over 20 British army officers accompanied the Japanese army in the field and four naval officers served at various times on board

Japanese ships. Most of the officers who accompanied the Japanese field force were sent out direct from Britain and India, although a few of the language officers who were already stationed in Japan were attached to the Japanese armies towards the end of the war.[59] In general those who watched the Japanese forces in action formed a much higher estimate of Japanese proficiency than those who only watched manoeuvres. In particular they noted the courage and initiative shown by the Japanese. They also observed how Japanese tactics improved; in the first battles the Japanese used the dense formations which they had employed at manoeuvres but they quickly abandoned these in favour of looser formations which reduced their casualties.[60] If the Japanese cavalry remained second rate, the vaunted Cossacks did no better. If the Russian artillery were sometimes better equipped than the Japanese, the Emperor's soldiers made up for this by the resourcefulness of their tactics and by the full use they made of the mobility of their mountain guns.[61]

Yet the British army did not draw any closer to the Japanese army. Most of the officers sent to Japan were kept waiting for months before they were allowed to go to the front. Sir William Nicholson, who was the senior British army officer, and was to become Chief of the Imperial General Staff in 1908, talked of the 'want of courtesy and consideration' of the Japanese and suggested that the British officers should return to England unless the Japanese became more co-operative.[62] General Sir Ian Hamilton, who had also been sent to Japan, was almost equally critical.[63] Fortunately matters improved when Marshal Oyama went to the front and was replaced as Chief of the General Staff by the more cosmopolitan Yamagata. All the attachés were sent to Manchuria and the atmosphere lightened appreciably.[64]

Once the war was over, the reports written by the language officers in Japan reverted to many of the old criticisms of Japanese military methods and tactics. Colonel Bannattine Allason, for example, visited Manchuria at the end of the war and argued that 'the Japanese would not have done much good against a moderately well-organised and led European army'. Four language officers were sent each year by the home government and three by the Indian government, and they lived there for two years. They remained out of sympathy with their Japanese hosts, criticising Japanese army officers for having nothing else to talk about except their profession.[65] Coming from an army which spent so much time in horse riding and sport they found it difficult to understand the intense professionalism of the Japanese. But such social differences do not wholly explain why the language officers should have talked of the disillusionment they felt after hearing about Japan's great victories in Manchuria and then seeing the army undergoing peacetime training in Japan.

There were criticisms of all arms of the Japanese army, although the cavalry appeared particularly poor to British eyes. In 1907 Major Cheyne of the Indian cavalry reported that,

> ... the training of the Japanese cavalry in its main principles is on the same lines as our own but for many reasons the standard reached is not high ... The Japanese cavalry does not even aspire to the degree of horsemanship to which our men attain.[66]

Captain Steel of the Indian cavalry described the Japanese uniforms and saddlery as 'indescribably filthy'. He found that manoeuvres could not be carried out because the ground was unsuitable and that few Japanese liked horses or were prepared to treat them as other than machines.[67] Reports on the Japanese infantry were much more complimentary, although in peacetime the Japanese forces tended to revert to the dense 'Germanic' formations which they had abandoned in Manchuria; a report on the 1907 manoeuvres stated, 'in the final charge the men were in a confused mob often eight or ten deep with numerous stragglers'.[68] Six years later the British attachés reported, 'attacks were purely frontal . . . there was as usual a complete disregard for the effects of modern rifle fire'. Bayonet practice was excellent but marksmanship was often poor.[69] Practice at the rifle range at Okubo was 'very bad indeed, some of the men making only one hit out of five'. Captain Toke, who tried one of the rifles himself, found that his results were equally bad – 'no two rifles appear to be sighted the same and unless you know the rifle it is next to impossible to hit the target even at 200 metres'.[70] Altogether Colonel Bannattine Allason reported, 'much has been written about the superior training of the Japanese forces, all I can say is that the Russians must have been appallingly bad'. Of the Japanese drill book he added, 'there is nothing new and nothing to learn'.[71]

Apart from criticisms of tactics and marksmanship, the basic difference between the British and Japanese armies stemmed from their disparate approaches to the purpose and form of manoeuvres. The idea of manoeuvres for the Japanese, as for the Germans, was to test staff work and planning, not the initiative of the officer corps. Major Somerville concluded that the Japanese exercises were

> ... far too much of a parade movement. There was no ... individual

enterprise about it at all. [They reflected the] apparent poverty of imagination of the officers in dealing with tactical exercises in the field. They only seemed capable of carrying out the obvious.[72]

The Japanese believed that the 'instructional value to be gained from any experience is proportional to the care and thought which has been expended upon its preparation'.[73] Thus the unwary British officers tended to dismiss the whole Japanese army as lacking in initative and resource. Yet officers who watched the army during the war in Manchuria had reached the opposite conclusion.[74] Kuroki and the other generals interfered in the field to avoid disasters, otherwise they successfully relied on the initiative of their subordinates. Sir Ian Hamilton was to try to do the same thing with a British army in the Dardanelles in 1915 with unfortunate effects.

That the Japanese manoeuvres positively hindered a correct appreciation of Japanese strength is confirmed by the parallel experience in Europe. There British officers greatly overestimated French strength and underestimated German military efficiency as a result of peacetime exercises. After the 1906 German manoeuvres one British observer wrote, 'the German infantryman is still the iron-disciplined, wooden, unthinking, fighting automaton that he has always been'.[75] German staff work was admitted to be superb:

> ... the first thing that struck the onlooker during these operations was the ease and certainty with which this huge body of men was moved and handled without the slightest confusion.[76]

But this was achieved at the expense of initiative. The War Office concluded after the 1912 German manoeuvres,

> The actions of commanders were therefore as usual somewhat cramped, the strategical aspect of the operations having already been determined. Turning movements on a large scale were entirely out of the question.[77]

Conversely the French manoeuvres were designed to test the initiative of the officers and the elan of the troops. From the British point of view the Germans were consequently less impressive than the French, as one observer commented,

> It would seem, though it is very difficult to dogmatize in such a matter,

that the French army is a better fighting machine than the German ...
The French army is the one that would command one's faith in the
event of a war between the two.[78]

In neither the German nor the Japanese army was there any question
of the courage or the endurance of the troops — it was their tactics and
their ability to show initiative which was questioned. One of the British
language officers summed up the Japanese army with the remark,

> ... of the spirit of officers and men it would be impossible to speak
> too highly. Calls were made [during manoeuvres] upon their discipline
> and physical endurance which few if any troops would have withstood with equal philosophy and courage.[79]

Major Somerville, like many other English commentators on Japan,
believed that the Japanese army

> ... has arrived at a pitch of excellence which it is never likely to
> exceed for the reason that the ancient, fighting, feudal spirit still
> flourishes as yet practically untouched by the refinements and
> luxuries of our civilization; and to it is united a highly specialized
> knowledge of the science of modern war. A magnificent fighting
> spirit pervades all ranks with a Spartan-like contempt for money and
> the luxuries of life.[80]

British officers believed that German and Japanese tactics reflected
their national characteristics. The Germans were wrongly believed to be
lacking in initiative and resource. Similarly Japanese culture was thought
to be purely imitative. In part this was not surprising. The Japanese had
set out in the 1860s to copy the best aspects of European culture and
science. But they had carefully selected those aspects which they wished
to imitate — they copied the Royal Navy and the German army because
they were the leading European forces. Moreover the fact that they
copied some aspects of Western civilisation did not, by any means, prove
that they were incapable of going beyond it. As a historian has written
of British attitudes or prejudices in the 1930s, 'there are hints of unsound psychological and cultural depths in British attitudes towards
Japan'.[81]

Naval Estimates

Yet, curiously enough, these mistakes did not have the same effect on British appreciations of the Japanese navy before 1914. At the beginning of 1903 the Commander of the British ships on the China station, Admiral Sir Cyprian Bridge informed Sir George Clarke that he got 'on very well with the Japs' but found them 'very sensitive'.[82] Bridge had represented Britain at a conference with senior Japanese naval officers at Yokosuka. The meeting was attended by the Japanese Minister of Marine, the Chief of Staff of the Japanese navy and other Japanese authorities. According to the British reports, 'the utmost cordiality and good fellowship prevailed'.[83] When the Japanese naval forces were victorious against the Russians, the Royal Navy took a vicarious pride in their successes. The Japanese could have resented the slightly patronising tone which occasionally crept into comments published in Britain but they were prepared to give Britain some credit for their naval successes. In October 1905, the Japanese Minister for Marine, Baron Yamamoto, commented,

> Great Britain has been one of the most powerful amongst all the powerful nations in the world ... our navy ever since its creation has been modelled on that of Great Britain and we owe her much in the education of the personnel as well as the preparation of the material.[84]

The alliance appears to have been popular in Britain and in Japan. On the third anniversary of its signature, a Japanese newspaper, the *Kokumin Shimbun* referred to it as 'a very glorious day in our diplomatic and political annals.'[85]

There was no split amongst Royal Naval officers between those who knew Japan well and those who watched its progress from a distance as there was amongst British army officers. Relations between the British naval attachés and their hosts were excellent throughout the Russo-Japanese War and beyond. Captain E.C. Troubridge, the first attaché, was occasionally critical of the Japanese navy. In particular he believed that the Japanese Commander in Chief, Admiral Togo, could have been more aggressive in his tactics[86] but, as Jellicoe was to find in the North Sea ten years later, when you are the only man who can lose the war in a day, this tends to make your tactics cautious. Captain Pakenham, who succeeded Troubridge after the start of the Russo-Japanese War, commented, 'the Japanese are certainly charming people to be with, unfortunately their navy is so like our own in almost all respects that there are few salient points to attract attention'. No comment could sum up better the dichotomy between Anglo-Japanese naval relations and Anglo-Japanese military relations. It seems possible that the Japanese army had a low opinion of its British counterpart after the Boer War and that it considered the British officers in Japan an unfortunate by-product of the Anglo-Japanese alliance. On the other hand, the Japanese navy had a high appreciation of its British counterpart and genuinely wanted its friendship and assistance.

The British in turn reposed a good deal of confidence in the Japanese. During the war Sir Claude MacDonald asked the Admiralty whether it wanted

> to recall Captains Pakenham and Hutchinson, the Attachés serving with the Japanese fleet in view of the desperate nature of the battle which will doubtless take place the next time the Russian fleet leaves Port Arthur. The battle may result in considerable losses on both sides as the Russians are superior in battleships.[87]

The Admiralty wisely ignored MacDonald's suggestion, which would certainly have left the Japanese feeling betrayed and have given them the impression that the British were excessively concerned about the protection of their personnel. Even more significantly, Troubridge, who knew the Japanese navy perhaps better than any other English officer, suggested that, if Britain and Japan were involved in a war with another power, the British ships in the Far East should be placed under a Japanese commander.[88] This had been considered at the time that the Anglo-Japanese alliance was under negotiation but separate command had been decided upon.[89] Troubridge's proposal was an indication of the rise in esteem for the Japanese forces. 'I am very certain that the time has come when we may with utmost confidence entrust our ships to the control of a Japanese Admiral for the sake of the increased efficiency of concerted action'.[90] The First Sea Lord, Lord Walter Kerr, agreed with Troubridge and wrote to the Commander of the British ships on the China station asking for his opinion. 'I would not mind serving under Togo's leadership', he added.[91]

The suggestions made by Troubridge and Kerr were never put into effect but they are a remarkable testimony to British confidence in the Japanese. The Royal Navy had been the dominant force on the world's oceans for at least a hundred years and yet some British officers were prepared to entrust their ships to the Commander of a fleet which had hardly existed forty years before. Moreover, considering the friction which was to occur during the First World War when there were suggestions that a French General should command the allied armies in Europe, Troubridge's suggestion seems even more surprising and progressive. In so far as the Japanese imitated the Royal Navy, this made the British more appreciative of Japanese seamanship, and British naval officers were prepared to admit the occasions when the Japanese navy was more competent than the British. After watching Japanese naval gunnery practice, a British gunnery expert commented, 'there was very little to choose between the Japanese ships and they all obtained a good percentage of hits. There were no cases of really bad shooting which was a characteristic feature of our gunnery.'[92]

There was evidently a much closer rapport between Royal Naval officers and their Japanese equivalents than there was between officers of the two armies. Some might argue that the army officers who were sent to Japan before 1914 were second-rate men who were misfits in their regiments and were not expected to reach high rank. Consequently their reports should not be taken too seriously. In contrast the naval officers who had been attached to the Japanese navy all reached high rank and held important positions. But too much should not be made of this contrast, which underestimates the military attachés. Colonel C.V. Hume, for example, had been aide-de-camp to the Commander in Chief in India from 1885 to 1892 and had served with distinction in wars in Burma and South Africa. He was also considered an Oriental expert having been adviser to the Crown Prince of Siam from 1896 to 1899. Many of the other language officers, including Berkeley Vincent, J.B. Jardine and Hart Synnot, rose to be Brigadier Generals and served with distinction in the First World War.

It may be that the British army was more deeply imbued with a feeling of superiority over non-Europeans than the Royal Navy was. The army had been fighting against non-Europeans throughout the nineteenth century, the Royal Navy had not been involved so deeply in this process. It was possibly easier therefore for the Royal Navy to assess the Japanese on their merits. Moreover materiel plays a greater part in naval than in military calculations. British officers could see that the Japanese ships were well maintained and skilfully handled in peacetime. British army officers had to hazard a guess about the bearing of the Japanese army in wartime. Unfortunately the Anglo-Japanese naval accord was not to last and, as it declined, so did the quality of British estimates of Japanese naval power. Captain S.W. Roskill, the British naval historian, has written of the period after 1918, where British naval authorities went avoidably wrong was . . . in their under-estimate of Japanese skill and prowess and their ability to produce armaments at least as good as, and in some cases markedly better than those of the western nations. It seems likely that this misjudgement derived from Japan's long period of tutelage under British advisers.[93]

Surprisingly, however, British estimates of Japanese naval power were most accurate when the Japanese navy was nearest to being under British tutelage. Subsequently memories of Japanese victories over the Russians in 1904 and 1905 were dimmed. The Japanese and Americans both came to challenge British naval power after 1918 and in both cases the Royal Navy made up for its declining numerical superiority by claiming that its personnel as well as the quality of its materiel were superior and that it had little to learn from its rivals.

Captain Roskill gives examples of the underestimation of Japanese power contained in the reports of the British naval attaché in Tokyo in the 1930s. Individual British army and naval officers could exert an unfortunate influence over their colleagues' estimates of Japanese power. Colonel Churchill's influence before 1904 was clearly undesirable. But Churchill had been replaced by Colonel C.V. Hume before the Russo-Japanese War began and the war might easily have led to a permanent change in the attitude of the British army towards its Japanese equivalent. That it did not do so suggests that there were a number of permanent factors influencing British estimates and that personalities played a less important part than in the estimates of Japanese power made by some other European armies.

Russian Estimates

It is interesting, for example, to compare Russian estimates of Japanese power with British ones. According to the Russian General Staff, the Russian officers sent to Japan in the 1880s and 1890s had a high estimate of Japanese military prowess.[94] Lt Colonel Boutakov reported in 1883 that Japan's troops were 'in perfect order', while Colonel Vogak reported eleven years later,

> I was positively stupified by what I saw in Japan . . . Japan is definitely from the military point of view the strongest power in the Far East without even excepting Russia. I believe we have in Japan a dangerous

neighbour with which we shall have to pay a great deal of attention.

Colonel Yanjoul, who replaced Vogak as military attaché in Japan, agreed with his estimate of Japanese power, despite his reservations about Japanese artillery and cavalry. But Major Vannovski, who replaced Yanjoul at the end of the 1890s, completely reversed the prevailing Russian view of Japanese power. Vannovski concluded,

> dozens, perhaps hundreds of years will go by before the Japanese army attains the moral principles of the Europeans ... the Japanese only assimilate European tactics with difficulty and even the best officers are considered to incorporate only their form.

Vannovski's views were sent to the Russian War Minister, Kuropatkin, who agreed with them generally. General Ivanov, the Chief of the Staff of the First Siberian Army Corps also agreed with Vannovski after watching the Japanese army's manoeuvres which led him to believe that it was 'an army of babies'. Not all Russians were so mistaken however; General Jillinski, the Quarter Master General, had a much higher estimate of Japanese strength and Major Samoilov, who took over as Russian military attaché in Japan just before the Russo-Japanese War, warned,

> in the seven years since the last Japanese manoeuvres I attended the army had made great progress ... subalterns show great initiative .. [Japan] constitutes a serious adversary with which one must take account.[95]

Russian estimates of Japanese military power therefore varied much more widely with the personal opinion of the military attaché in Japan than was the case with the equivalent British estimates. Generally British army officers believed that the Japanese were purely imitative; a belief which was fostered by the influence which the German army wielded in Japan. There was also a pervasive lack of sympathy between the British and Japanses armies. Amongst the professional reasons for British miscalculations were the misunderstanding of the intentions behind Japanese manoeuvres, the overestimation by the British army of the importance of cavalry and consequently the excessive emphasis on the inadequacy of Japanese cavalry, and finally the excessive emphasis on the importance of tactical formations which could be rapidly altered in wartime.

Conclusions

Emotions also had an important influence on British judgements. In many cases officers who disliked Japan underestimated Japanese power, whilst those who liked Japan also admired Japanese achievements. Moreover, in the years after 1905 Britain and Japan gradually drew apart. There were many reasons for this. British colonists in Australia, Canada and elsewhere had never been enthusiastic about the alliance because they felt threatened by Japan's purported expansionism. British merchants in Asia also resented Japanese commercial competition and particularly the infringement of British trade marks.[96] With so many groups hostile to the Anglo-Japanese alliance, it was not surprising that its popularity gradually declined. Militarily the increasing gap between the two countries was best symbolised by the reversal of the movement begun in 1902 to exchange confidential information. As early as 1906, the Governor of Singapore, Sir John Anderson, was protesting against Japanese efforts to examine the fortresses in the area. The Army Council backed up Anderson's refusal to allow the Japanese to do this and the Foreign office commented,

> the demand could hardly be considered reasonable, the information could only have been of use to the Japanese if they were at war with us ... The Japanese, according to the reports of our Military Attachés, have not allowed our officers to see all they wanted to see by any means. They don't refuse point blank but make out all sorts of excuses.[97]

As the gap between the British and Japanese armies increased and both allies became more secretive, it became even harder for the British armed forces to assess the power of their Japanese ally correctly. Instead of the army coming to have as high an opinion of Japanese military strength as the Royal Navy had, it was the navy which revised its estimates downward.

If there are any 'lessons' to be learned from the British underestimation of Japan they are perhaps that, in cases where materiel is more or less adequate, tactics are usually less important constituents of military power than high morale and national cohesion, and that a narrow 'military' view of a nation's power may put too much emphasis on the obvious external features of an army. Military officers may also be less ready than their civilian counterparts to disgard past images of a nation's strength, yet in estimating the strength of a 'new' nation, the ability to disregard such past images is precisely what is called for. British statesmen and strategists in England looked at Japan with less biased eyes than their military counterparts who lived in Japan itself. Brodrick, Balfour and Curzon took an overall view and assessed the power of their ally, if not correctly, at least more correctly than Churchill or Hume on one side and Waters and Gerard on the other. Lord Palmerston has been quoted as saying that, if he wanted to be misinformed about another country, he asked a man who had lived there thirty years. British statesmen in the years before 1914 had to discount the bias of the soldiers who had lived in Japan and Russia if they wished to reach a correct estimate of the power of these countries.

Notes

1. Balfour papers, British Museum, London, 49775, Balfour to Amery, 14 July 1904.
2. See for example, Julian Amery, *The Life of Joseph Chamberlain*, vol. 4, *1901-1903* (Macmillan, London, 1951), pp. 180-92.
3. George Monger, *The End of Isolation* (Thomas Nelson and Sons, London, 1963), p. 63. See also Kenneth Young, *Arthur James Balfour* (G. Bell and Sons, London, 1963), p. 233 and Amery, *Joseph Chamberlain*, p. 165.
4. Balfour papers, 49707, Selborne to Balfour, 3 November 1902.
5. Foreign Office papers, Public Record Office, London, FO/262/100, report by A. Bertram Mitford, 20 April 1868.
6. Grace Fox, *Britain and Japan 1858-1883* (Clarendon Press, Oxford, 1969), p. 533 passim.
7. Ibid.
8. For exceptions see E.J. Harrison, *Peace or War East of Lake Baikal?* (Kelly and Walsh, Yokohama, 1910) and B.L. Putnam Weale, *The Reshaping of the Far East* (Macmillan and Co., London, 1905).
9. Quoted in Fox, *Britain and Japan*, p. 551.
10. Russian General Staff, *Guerre Russo-Japonaise* (the Russian Official military history of the war) (Paris, 1910), Tome 1, part 1, p. 199.
11. G.N. Curzon, *Problems of the Far East* (Archibald Constable and Co., London, 1894), p. 44 passim.
12. For the British government's attitude to the war, see Ian H. Nish, *The Anglo-Japanese Alliance* (University of London, Athlone Press, 1966), p. 23 passim.
13. L.K. Young, *British Policy in China 1895-1902* (Clarendon Press, Oxford, 1970), p. 18.
14. J.L. Garvin, *The Life of Joseph Chamberlain*, vol. 3, *1895-1900* (Macmillan, London, 1934), p. 96. Many lesser-known writers favoured an alliance with Japan; see Henry Norman, *The People and Politics of the Far East* (T. Fisher Unwin, London, 1900), pp. 399-401.
15. Russian General Staff, p. 505.
16. Garvin, *Life of Joseph Chamberlain*, p. 249.
17. Garvin, ibid., p. 250-2.
18. Monger, *End of Isolation*, chap 1.
19. L.K. Young, *British Policy in China*, p. 141 passim. For Japan's views, see Nish, *Anglo-Japanese Alliance*, pp. 81-2.

20. L.K. Young, *British Policy in China*, p. 295. Nish argued that 'Japan certainly gained a reputation as a military power'. Nish, *Anglo-Japanese Alliance*, p. 99.
21. War Office papers, Public Record Office, London, WO/106/74, Relief of the Pekin Legations by Colonel A.G. Churchill, March 1901. Churchill was military attaché in Tokyo from 1898 to 1903.
22. Ibid. For Russian estimates of Japanese achievements during the Boxer rising see Russian General Staff, *Guerre*, pp. 571-8.
23. WO/106/48, minute by Captain Black, 2 June 1903, the 24 Punjab Infantry who were on the expedition were amongst the best Indian regiments though under strength at this time. For a different view of the Japanese by a British Officer on the expedition, see *The Autobiography of General Sir O'Moore Creagh* (Hutchinson, London, 1924), p. 220. Creagh argued that allied relations on the expedition were good, except for relations with the Germans.
24. MacDonald was educated at Sandhurst and joined the 74 Highlanders in 1872. He was Ambassador in Peking during the Boxer outbreak and in Tokyo from 1900 to 1912. See Foreign Office papers, FO/46/577, MacDonald to the Foreign Office, 18 February 1904.
25. Clarke papers, British Museum, 50831, Clarke to Chirol, 7 June 1902.
26. Clarke papers, Clarke to Chirol, 30 January 1903 relating a conversation with *The Times* Peking correspondent, Morrison.
27. War Office papers, WO/106/48, The Value of Japan as an Ally, by Major Peach, 29 March 1902.
28. War Office papers, Report of a Conference held at Winchester House, 8 July 1902, comments by Major General Fukushima.
29. See note 27 supra.
30. Curzon papers, India Office Library, London, F/111/10B, Brodrick to Curzon, 13 February 1902.
31. Curzon papers, F/111/163, Godley to Curzon, 12 February 1904.
32. Curzon papers, F/111/163, Curzon to Brodrick, 11 February 1904.
33. Curzon papers, F/111/163, Brodrick to Curzon, 26 February 1904. See also my article on 'The Russo-Japanese war and the Defence of India', *Military Affairs* (1980).
34. WO/106/48, minute by W.G. Robertson, 5 June 1903. Robertson was in charge of the Intelligence section of the War Office.
35. War Office papers, report by Colonel A.G. Churchill, 27 May, 1903.
36. Ibid.
37. Calchas, 'The War and the Powers', *Fortnightly Review* (March 1904).
38. See note 23 supra.
39. War Office papers, minute by E.A. Altham AQMG. Altham later became a well-known writer on strategy, see *The Principles of War* (Macmillan, London, 1914).
40. See note 28 supra.
41. War Office papers, minute by Nicholson, 13 June 1903. Nicholson became Director of Military Operations in 1901 controlling the Intelligence and Mobilisation sections.
42. Roberts papers, National Army Museum, London, 7101/23/115/9, Roberts to Sir Ian Hamilton, 15 June 1904.
43. W.H.H. Waters, *Russia Then and Now* (John Murray, London, 1935), p. 188.
44. Roberts papers, 7101/23/53, Dighton Probyn to Roberts, 18 July 1904. For Gerard see *Leaves from the Diary of a Sportsman and Soldier* (John Murray, London, 1903).
45. Waters, *Russia Then and Now*. For a different view of these manoeuvres see O'Moore Creagh, *Autobiography*.

46. See note 42 supra.
47. Balfour papers 49707. See also Nish, *Anglo-Japanese Alliance*, p. 275 passim.
48. Balfour papers, 49729, Lansdowne to Balfour, 24 December 1903. See also the King's fears of war quoted in Kenneth Young, *Arthur James Balfour*, p. 234.
49. FO/46/578, MacDonald's report of 7 May 1904.
50. Russian General Staff, *Guerre*, pp. 300-5.
51. Balfour papers, 49707, Balfour to Selborne, 23 December 1903, and Selborne to Balfour, 25 December 1903.
52. FO/46/576, MacDonald to the Foreign Office, 1 January 1904. See also Russian General Staff, *Guerre*, p. 74, report from the Russian military attaché in Japan.
53. Balfour papers, 49707, Balfour to Selborne, 29 December 1903.
54. Balfour papers, 49700, Balfour to Clarke, 20 September 1904.
55. Balfour papers, Clarke to Balfour, 23 September 1904.
56. Clarke papers, 50832, Chirol to Clarke, 27 December 1905.
57. Putnam Weale, vol. 2, p. 181, vol. 1, p. 388 passim.
58. Episodes of the Month, *National Review* (May 1904).
59. FO/46/592, MacDonald report of 25 April 1905.
60. WO/33/337, report by Major J.M. Home on the Russo-Japanese War and Reports on the Campaign in Manchuria, Colonel W.H.H. Waters. See also WO/106/38, Reports of the Attachés with the Russian Army, General Sir Montagu Gerard.
61. Ibid. See also FO/46/578, Hamilton's report of 13 May 1904 on the Yalu battle.
62. FO/46/578, Nicholson to MacDonald, 5 July 1904.
63. Foreign Office papers, Nicholson to MacDonald, 5 July 1904 and MacDonald's reply to Nicholson.
64. Foreign Office papers, MacDonald report of 20 July 1904.
65. WO/33/432, Extracts from the Diaries of Officers Attached to the Japanese Army, 2nd series, 1907, Major J.A. Somerville commented, 'professional topics are for him (the Japanese officer) the one subject of conversation'. For Bannattine Allason, see FO/371/86. Not all officers believed that the Japanese lacked recreations, see 1906 extracts, first series, WO/33/425, report by Captain W.G.H. Salmond, Royal Field Artillery.
66. WO/33/447, Extracts from the Diaries of Officers Attached to the Japanese Army, 1907, 3rd series, printed by the General Staff, War Office, February 1908.
67. War Office papers, report by Captain A.R. Steel 17 Cavalry Indian Army. Interestingly the Handbook on the Japanese army issued by the War Office in London in 1908 said that the Japanese cavalry had the 'cavalry spirit', see WO/33/473.
68. War Office papers, report by Major R.T. Toke of the Welsh Regiment.
69. For British comments on Japanese bayonet practice, see the 1906 'Extracts' in WO/33/425, report by Captain P.W. North of the Royal Berkshire Regiment. The reports were also very complimentary about the Japanese army's transport system, see the report by Captain Leader of the Bedfordshire Regiment in loc. cit.
70. See note 68 supra. Major Somerville had a slightly higher estimate of Japanese marksmanship, see 1907 extracts, second series.
71. FO/371/86.
72. See note 69 supra, report by Major J.A.C. Somerville, Northumberland Fusiliers.
73. WO/33/618, *Report on Foreign Manoeuvres 1912*.

74. See particularly I. Hamilton, *A Staff Officer's Scrap-book* (Edward Arnold, London, 1905).
75. Howard Hemsman, 'Some Impressions of the German Manoeuvres', *United Service Magazine* (October 1906).
76. Ibid.
77. See note 73 supra.
78. Howard Hemsman, 'The French and German Manoeuvres', *United Service Magazine* (November 1909).
79. See note 73 supra.
80. See note 65 supra.
81. Bradford A. Lee, *Britain and the Sino-Japanese War* (University of California, 1973), p. VIII.
82. Clarke papers, 50831, Clarke to Chirol, 14 February 1903. Bridge was in favour of increasing exchanges of information with the Japanese on military matters, see the letter from Bridge of 20 December 1902 in WO/106/48.
83. WO/106/48, letter from Sir Claude MacDonald, 19 May 1902. For Bridge see *Some Recollections* (John Murray, London, 1918).
84. Noel papers, National Maritime Museum, 15A, copy of a speech given at the Tokyo Naval Club, October 1905.
85. FO/46/673, report on the Japanese press, 12 February 1905.
86. *Naval Attachés Reports on the Russo-Japanese War*, copy in the National Maritime Museum, Greenwich, vol. 1, Troubridge's report of 28 February 1904.
87. FO/46/582, MacDonald report of 19 September 1904.
88. Admiralty papers, Public Record Office, London, ADM/116/1231b, Troubridge's note of 27 May 1904.
89. WO/106/48, letter from E. MacGregor to the Commander in Chief of HM ships on the China Station, 'I would draw your attention to the omission from the report (on the 1902 Anglo-Japanese Conference at Winchester House) of any reference to the command of the allied force in time of war. All such references were omitted advisedly as it is their Lordships' intention that the senior officer of both nations should act in concert and that no officer of one nation should be given authority to control any part of the naval forces of the other'. But see also Nish, *Anglo-Japanese Alliance*, p. 252.
90. See note 88 supra.
91. Sir Gerard Noel's papers, National Maritime Museum, 4b, Lord Walter Kerr to Noel.
92. K.G.B. Dewar, *The Navy From Within* (Victor Gollancz, London, 1921), p. 93.
93. S.W. Roskill, *Naval Policy Between the Wars*, vol. 11 (Collins, London, 1976), p. 188. See also p. 212.
94. Russian General Staff, *Guerre*, p. 543 passim.
95. Ibid.
96. FO/371/472, see particularly the 'Lee and Perrins' case which was concluded in December 1907.
97. FO/371/87, report by Sir John Anderson, 27 November 1906.

5 AUSTRALIAN ESTIMATES OF THE JAPANESE THREAT, 1905-1941

D.M. Horner

Early Fears

The Japanese attack on the British Empire and the United States of America on 7 December 1941 came as no surprise to the Australian defence planners. Not only had they, like their counterparts in Britain and America, been well informed of Japanese intentions throughout 1941, but the threat of Japan had, in fact, formed the focal point of Australian defence planning since federation in 1901.[1]

There may have been little rationality in the early fears. After all, through the latter half of the nineteenth century the colonial governments had imagined themselves to be threatened at various times by the Russians, Germans, French and Chinese.[2] The Australian settlers, thinly populating an isolated outpost of the British Empire, and enjoying freedom and well-being in advance of that in the mother country, imagined themselves as likely prey for a predator nation. Perhaps the Australians during this period had an emotional need for a defence threat. As David Sissons has noted, 'they were a small, largely immigrant community, used to the prestige of being Britishers, with I think the emotional trappings of Empire and arms associated with the ideology of the day'.[3] There were, of course, racial attitudes which attributed the threat to the 'yellow' races to the north.

The Japanese victory over Russia in 1905 sparked off an intense defence debate in Australia which resulted in an increase in naval and military expenditure between 1907 and 1914. This was accompanied by an acute and widespread fear of Japan. The Japanese vice-consul in Sydney wrote of the Australians in 1911 that 'as soon as we were victorious they came to fear that we would invade Australia. They doubt our every deed.'[4]

But the increased emphasis on defence was no longer completely irrational. Both military and defence planners argued that there was the possibility that, in the face of a German threat in European waters, the British fleet might not be strong enough simultaneously to challenge the Japanese in the Pacific. Thus Captain Creswell, the Director of the Commonwealth Naval Forces, wrote in 1908 that the 'possibility of an alliance between Germany and Japan presents one of the greatest dangers to the British Empire that can well be imagined'.[5]

There is no evidence that Japan, at this time, had any interest in Australia, but Australia had no independent means of satisfying herself on this. She had no foreign affairs department and no diplomatic representative (except for a High Commissioner in London). Australia was thus dependent upon British information, and with the outbreak of the First World War Britain was keen to play down the Japanese threat. Britain had a desire to stop the Australians, with their White Australian policy, from rocking the boat of the Anglo-Japanese alliance.

It is true that Japan joined the Allies against Germany, but once the British were fully occupied in Europe, she made far-reaching demands on China. In the hope of securing more help from Japan against Germany, Britain felt that she had to accept the Japanese position in Shantung. Furthermore, as a result of Australia's dilatoriness in occupying the German Pacific colonies in the Mariana, Caroline and Marshall Islands, Japan gained possession of these. The British approach was pragmatic, and although the cabinet put some value on Japanese assistance, evidence of the value of this assistance was not supplied by the Admiralty. Indeed both Rear-Admiral Sir Hubert Brand, the British naval attaché in Tokyo, and Vice-Admiral W.L. Grant, commander of the Far Eastern Fleet from 1915 to 1917, 'were sceptical of the value of Japanese assistance'.[6]

Although British officials might have had some doubt about the value of the Japanese assistance, they were not keen to pass this opinion on to the Australians.[7] Nevertheless the Australians arrived at a similar view that the Japanese naval contribution had been slight and grudging, and the Australian Director of Military Intelligence, Major E.J. Piesse, wrote: 'The view that the Japanese Navy gave any substantial assistance in assuring the safety of Australia during the war is not in accordance with official documents prepared in the Navy Office.'[8]

As early as 1916 the Australian Department of Defence had become concerned at Japanese activity in the islands north of Australia and noted the Japanese aspirations in the South Seas.[9] Hostility towards and fear of Japan increased in Australia during the war, and the Prime Minister, W.M. Hughes, feared that Japan might change sides and join Germany.[10] Thus Britain's lack of frankness about Japan drove Hughes, Piesse and the Minister of Defence, Senator G.F. Pearce, to the conclusion that Whitehall was now so preoccupied with European affairs that it was blind to the immediate danger of Japan.[11]

Nevertheless Piesse, who, as the Director of Military Intelligence since 1916, had been the principal adviser on foreign affairs to the Chief of the General Staff (CGS) and the Minister of Defence, recognised that Australia had embarked on a defence policy based on the Japanese threat without adequate knowledge of Japanese history, politics and economic conditions.[12] In a small way the government had, on Piesse's advice, attempted to rectify this. In March 1916 Australia had offered to pay the translation costs if the British Embassy in Tokyo would supply copies of all important references to Australia in the Japanese press.[13] A year later the Australian government took the initiative in facilitating the introduction of the Japanese language at Sydney University and the Royal Military College, Duntroon, and in securing the services of the distinguished British expert on Japanese history, James Murdoch, to teach it.[14]

The 1920s

On 29 May 1919 the Pacific Branch of the Prime Minister's Department was formed with Piesse as director. The role of the branch was the careful and continuous study of Far Eastern, and particularly Japanese, affairs. Piesse believed that the Japanese imperialists could be grouped into two schools — the Continental School and the Southern (Nanyo) School. The Nanyo School looked towards the countries of the south — the East Indies, the islands of the Pacific and Australia — as sources of raw materials, as a field for Japanese emigration and ultimately as territories for Japanese control. Clearly it was in Australia's interests that Japan should expand on the continent of Asia, rather than to the south.[15]

Although this view was held by many in Australia, Piesse was appalled by Britain's acceptance of Japan's position in China. He thought that there was 'a blight on British policy in the East', and he urged that 'we should supplement by our own arrangements the information we now get from British sources'.[16] This underlined Australia's main problem in estimating Japanese military power. Although Australia could make her own assessments, the basic information came from British sources.

Meanwhile in Paris, Hughes was putting the Australian case strongly, although the case was very different from Piesse's. He told the British that the people of Australia 'were united on two things; firstly their attitude towards Japan and the White Australia policy, and secondly, the retention of these islands [to the north of Australia]'.[17] Hughes' opposition to the Japanese desire for a League of Nations statement on race equality shows his deep distrust of Japanese motives.

What then were the perceptions in the Australian Department of Defence of Japanese military power in the years immediately following the First World War? Admiral Lord Jellicoe in his report to the Australian government in 1919 saw future Japanese planning to include the invasion of Australia and the seizure of the Netherlands East Indies and New Guinea. There would be a decisive sea action with concurrent thrusts at British bases at Hong Kong and Singapore. This would take place when Britain was involved in Europe.[18]

The following year a conference of senior Australian wartime generals, led by Lieutenant-General Sir Harry Chauvel, reiterated some of Jellicoe's views and applied them to the land defence of Australia. They believed that Japan remained, in the immediate future, the only potential and probable enemy. They noted that Japan could, without difficulty, place in the field an army of 600,000 men, and that in peace the field army comprised 25 divisions which in time of war could expand to 42 divisions. Japan had sufficient mercantile shipping to transport an army of 100,000 fully-equipped men in one convoy. Like Jellicoe, the senior officers believed Japan would strike when Britain was involved in Europe.[19]

Neither of these reports suggested that Japan was planning to expand its empire within a few years but they noted her potential to do so, and the Minister for the Navy, in a speech, emphasised that Japan 'was spending [on her navy] more in proportion to her resources than any other power'.[20] Piesse, who visited Japan in late 1919 and early 1920, observed the pressures in Japan which were causing them to display an imperialist policy. But he found that Japan's army was not equipped for modern war, her navy appeared to be for home defence, and that her air force was at a low stage of development. He concluded that 'it is considered by competent judges very unlikely that Japan would provoke a war against a first class power for some years to come'.[21]

The Effect of the Washington Conference

The 1922 Washington treaties limiting the capital ships of USA, Britain and Japan to a ratio of 5:5:3, were seen in Australia to provide security against Japan. The result of this perception was that the Australian defences were reduced drastically. As one historian has observed, 'defence lay defenceless before the political onslaught'.[22]

The Washington Conference also brought to an end the careful and continuous study of Japanese affairs which had begun in the Prime Minister's Department in 1918. In April 1922 Piesse wrote to the Secretary of the Prime Minister's Department that as a result of the Washington Conference, 'the detailed study of Japanese affairs which is contemplated in 1920 is, for the next few years, at least, quite unnecessary'.[23] The two Australian officers, Captain J.R. Broadbent and Captain G.H. Capes, who were attached to the British embassy at Tokyo to learn Japanese, were recalled to Australia. The detailed study of the Japanese vernacular press by the Pacific Branch ceased, and the services of the full-time lecturer in Japanese at Duntroon were terminated.

It did not take long for the politicians to realise that the Washington treaties had provided little real security and instead the Australian government thought that this might be provided by an imperial base at Singapore. In time of emergency the British main fleet, based at Singapore, would act as a deterrent to Japan. Thus Australia became locked into imperial defence, and Australian defence planners took the easy way of relying heavily on British assessments of the Japanese threat. From early 1921 Australia received the reports of the British military attaché in Tokyo. These reports dealt in detail with the organisation of the Japanese army, but there was little assessment of Japanese capabilities.[24]

The inertia in Australian defence activity can be gauged from the fact that when the Council of Defence considered intelligence-gathering at the end of 1923, it used agenda papers most of which had been written in 1917, 1918 and 1919. In November 1918 Captain Thring, of the RAN intelligence staff, had noted that the principal sources of Australian intelligence were:

(i) British embassy reports;
(ii) British official publications;
(iii) Foreign official publications;
(iv) Consular and trade representative reports, etc;
(v) British and foreign unofficial publications;
(vi) Reviews, periodicals and the press; and
(vii) Visitors to and from foreign countries.

In February 1919 Admiral Creswell had recommended the establishment of an Intelligence Bureau, but although the Pacific Branch was established there was no development in the intelligence-gathering area.[25]

The view from London remained optimistic. In 1923 the Foreign Office assured Australia that as far as British-Japanese relations were concerned there was 'not a cloud in the sky'.[26] In 1925 the Committee of Imperial Defence noted that 'in the existing circumstances agressive action on the part of Japan is not a contingency seriously to be considered',[27] and at the 1926 Imperial Conference Austen Chamberlain affirmed that the Japanese undoubtedly 'desired peace'.[28]

Despite this comforting advice, Australian army officers continued to base their plans on the possible Japanese invasion of Australia. In 1923 a report noted that the Japanese army had been reduced slightly to 21 divisions with a total of about 230,000 men, but it was recognised that the army had become more efficient through the 'liberal supply of Lewis guns, machine guns, anti-aircraft guns etc.'. It was noticed that Japan was building up reserves of war-like stores.[29] Similar details appeared again the following year in an intelligence summary, which estimated that recent reforms in organisation would give Japan by 1930 a fully trained army of 4½ million men after the mobilisation of reservists.[30]

Army-Navy Rivalry

Throughout most of the interwar period a fierce debate took place in Australia between the army and the navy over the nature of the Japanese threat. This debate was linked to imperial defence and the efficacy of the Singapore base. Army doubts centred around four premises. First, whether the base would actually be completed. Secondly, whether the British would send their main fleet in time of emergency. Thirdly, if the fleet arrived, whether it could defeat the Japanese navy. Fourthly, whether the Singapore base would hold out against the Japanese until the British fleet arrived. The CGS, General Chauvel, warned repeatedly that Australia could not rely on the Singapore base, and therefore that the army should prepare against invasion.[31] The navy leaders believed that little more than raids could be expected.

In 1928 some attempt was made to reconcile these views, and a combined services appreciation was prepared which concluded that the invasion of Australia, but only on a limited scale, was 'within the bounds of possibility and not so improbable as to allow of it being definitely ruled out'. It was considered that Japan would have sufficient shipping to embark and maintain a maximum of three divisions.[32] The three divisions would be followed by reinforcements 'according to circumstances'.[33] Nevertheless, the army had a vested interest in exaggerating the Japanese threat while the navy tended to play it down. The navy was assisted in this approach by the Committee of Imperial Defence (CID) in London which also tended to play down the Japanese threat.

In late 1923 Piesse resigned as director of the Pacific Branch, now called the Foreign Section, and the detailed study of Jananese affairs appears to have deteriorated further. Piesse had resigned because most of the papers passed on from the British government were distributed no further than the Australian Prime Minister, and, as Piesse observed, 'I am now without even the scanty means of information I had when I came to the department.'[34]

From mid-1926 to early 1928 Major Capes, who had been one of the army officers studying Japanese in Tokyo, produced 'Notes on the Situation in the Far East'. It appears that these notes resulted from a study of Japanese newspapers, and they had a 'confidential' classification. Nevertheless they provided valuable information not available elsewhere. However the publication appeared to lapse after Capes left his posting with the 2nd Military District Intelligence Section.[35] Also during the twenties the navy had two officers and a civilian attached to the British embassy in Tokyo to learn Japanese.[36] Despite these small efforts, it can be assumed that the Australian government knew less about Japanese intentions and capabilities in 1929 than they did seven years earlier. Piesse claimed, in 1924, that the Japanese army and navy officers, who had been accused of spying in Australia, were probably doing so without the sanction of the Japanese Foreign Office.[37] Certainly, during the years after the Washington Conference, there 'was considerably less suspicion of Japan' than during the preceding two decades.[38]

The election in 1929 of the Labor government with a declared policy of reducing defence expenditure, and the onset of the depression sharpened debate within defence circles. With less money to spend, each service sought to maintain or increase its proportion of the defence vote. The army sought, therefore, to reinforce its claims that Japan could invade Australia, while the navy asserted that the main fleet at Singapore would avert the danger.

On the one hand the navy maintained that Australia was so far away from Japan that insuperable logistic difficulties and the exposed lines of communication would deter the Japanese from attacking Australia. On the other hand the navy pointed out that if Japan, with a population of 70 million, decided to attack Australia, with a population of 7 million people, there was no possibility of Australia defending herself. Therefore there was no point in preparing to meet an invasion.

The Chiefs of Staff were agreed on one fact; that Japan was a threat. The Defence Committee minutes for 17 July 1930 observed:

Japan is obviously the only country at present which can seriously threaten Empire or Australian interests in the Far East.

When considering possible causes of discord in the Pacific it would be imitating the ostrich to ignore the fact that the White Australian Policy and the tariff walls, however desirable and necessary for Australia, are possible causes of friction with other countries and with Japan in particular.

The Japanese appear to have carried out a general reconnaissance of Australia, leaving evidence at times of positively impudent curiosity notably in connection with a survey of Wessel Island. That is not to say that they necessarily entertain aggressive designs against Australia but they are certainly making all reasonable preparations for a possible eventuality precisely as we do ourselves. The mobility of the Japanese Fleet is being secured by a war reserve of 3,000,000 tons of oil fuel, now two thirds complete. The mobility of our Fleet should be likewise secured by the works and preparations at Singapore.[39]

The Director of Military Operations and Intelligence, Colonel J.D. Lavarack, put the army's case in an appreciation in March 1930. After repeating the old army assertion that Japan would make war only when she was certain that no more than minor opposition would be encountered at sea, he went on to state that the invasion of Australia was a feasible operation:

> Japanese strategy and tactics are not subject to the limitations of over caution, as their actions, both at sea and on land, during the war of 1904-05 show, the possibility of their accepting a considerable risk in order to achieve a great end must be taken into account.

On the basis of CID advice, Lavarack estimated that a convoy of Japanese transports would take from 26 to 32 days to reach Australia, so that the original landing force would be reinforced in about two months from its disembarkation.[40]

In conjunction with Group Captain S.J. Goble, Lavarack also pointed out that Japan's carrier-borne aircraft could secure air superiority at a landing. The Japanese naval air service was listed as consisting of 225 shore-based aircraft and 153 ship-borne aircraft. This was vastly more than the whole Australian air force.[41]

Captain C.J. Pope, the Assistant CNS and Director of Naval Intelligence, replied on behalf of the navy. He acknowledged that there would be extensive raiding of trade routes, there might be raids on important centres, and an attack on Hong Kong was almost certain. He concluded, however, that, the 'invasion of Australia is so improbable as to allow of it being definitely ruled out when considering preparations for defence'.[42] The important point from Pope's appreciation is that presumably it was made using the same basic information as that used by Lavarack. Furthermore, it was an attempt to repudiate the conclusion of the combined services appreciation of 1928.

Increasing Threats

The Mukden Incident in September 1931 and the Japanese advance into Manchuria in early 1932, appeared to have little effect on the Australian government. Both the government and the opposition agreed that nothing should be done which might involve Australia in military action in Manchuria.[43] Nevertheless the Manchurian Crisis dealt a severe blow to Australian confidence in the League of Nations, and by late 1932 government back-benchers and the press began to agitate for rearmament.[44]

The defence authorities in Britain and Australia immediately saw the signs of danger in the Manchurian Crisis, and in mid-1932 the Committee of Imperial Defence, without public announcement, decided to accelerate work on the Singapore base.[45] Lavarack took the opportunity to revise his appreciation of 1930 and he warned

> that recent events in Manchuria and Shanghai point to the fact that Japan is perfectly ready to take aggressive action in defiance of covenants and pacts . . . Given a favourable opportunity, she would lose no chance of extending Southwards her influence in the Western Pacific.

He estimated that from the outbreak of war it would be four months before Australia was attacked; during this time Hong Kong and Singapore would be reduced.[46] In fact when war came nine years later Japan attacked the Australian islands less than a month after the beginning of the war.

The Australian authorities now received more information about the expansion of the Japanese air force. In December 1931 the British ambassador in Tokyo reported that there had been 'a rapid growth in numbers of aeroplanes during the last few years'. Exact figures for the Japanese Naval Air Service were not available, but the naval attaché,

Captain M.G.B. Legge, reported that in 1930 there were 672 trained pilots. The military attaché, Colonel Simpson, reported that the Army Air Service totalled 6,944 personnel and 838 aircraft (not including school aircraft).[47]

The views of the Australian army were now beginning to take definite shape.[48] In 1933 the Director of Military Operations and Intelligence, Lieutenant-Colonel V.A.H. Sturdee, delivered a lecture to the Senior Officers Course on the form of a possible Japanese invasion. Although the Japanese army was estimated to consist of about 23 divisions, only about 100,000 men (3 divisions and base organisations) could be transported at one time. But for Australia, this would be

> no small nut for us to crack as they would all be regulars fully trained and equipped for the operation, and fanatics who like dying in battle, whilst our troops would consist mainly of civilians hastily thrown together on mobilisation with very little training, short of artillery and possibly of gun ammunition.

Sturdee went on to point out that a further three divisions could be landed in about two months. Japan would not declare war before launching her expedition, but Sturdee said that British intelligence organisations at Shanghai and Hong Kong would watch closely Japanese shipping.[49] There would also be the further warning that Japan would probably attack Hong Kong and might attack Singapore. He estimated, therefore, that Australia would have about seven weeks' warning.[50]

The estimates of Japanese capabilities continued to expand. In 1931 the CID had told Australia that the Japanese could despatch a force of between 60,000 and 100,000 men.[51] Four years later the Chief of the Imperial General Staff (CIGS) told the Australian CGS that 'sufficient tonnage is available in Japanese ports at any one time to convey a force of from 120,000 to 170,000 men and its immediate needs to Australia's shores'. Since the necessary shipping could be collected from within Japan, the CIGS suggested that it was safer to rely on only 31 days' warning.[52]

British and Australian Views

Sufficient evidence was now arriving in Australia to reinforce the attitude that the Japanese threat was increasing. The Foreign Office Report on Japan for 1934 dealt with the topic in detail. According to the report the Japanese army could no 'longer be classed with the pre-war armies of Europe, though it must be some time yet before it can take its place among the most modern'. But expenditure on modernisation was heavy, new types of tanks, arms and aircraft were appearing and new tactical ideas were being tested. The report stated that the 'Japanese military authorities frankly take no interest whatever in disarmament questions'. With regard to the navy, the Foreign Office noticed an increasing propaganda campaign against the Washington and London Naval Limitation Treaties, and that Japan was preparing to man a larger fleet than allowed under the treaties.[53]

The Australian Prime Minister, J.A. Lyons, and R.G. Menzies (then Attorney General), when in London in 1935, received similar advice from the Foreign Office: 'there is no general moderate party in Japan, and she is likely to grasp at as much as she feels capable of reaching at any given moment'. But Neville Chamberlain, the Chancellor of the Exchequer, made every effort to allay Australian fears.[54]

While both Britain and Australia now recognised the magnitude of the Japanese threat, the events of the next few years show that Britain consistently attempted to persuade the Australians of the security of the Singapore base. In doing so they tried to play down Japanese capabilities. Hence at the 1937 Imperial Conference the Australians asked the CID to comment on the Japanese threat up to and after 1942. The British had to admit that until 1942 the position would be 'unsatisfactory',[55] but that there were compensating factors. The Japanese were always 'years behind the other powers in aircraft design',[56] and even if the Royal Navy was inferior in numbers to the Japanese fleet in the Pacific, it was asserted that it would still be 'at least equivalent in fighting value'.[57]

In the view of the Australian government, the situation in Japan was 'by no means wholly satisfactory'.[58] The American Consul-General in Australia noticed that the Minister for External Affairs, Sir George Pearce, was concerned more and more with the Japanese threat, and the Secretary of the Department of External Affairs, Major W.R. Hodgson, talked of Japan's increasing 'megalomania'.[59] The outbreak of war between Japan and China in the latter half of 1937 reinforced these attitudes, and the President of the Chinese League of Nations Union warned Australia that 'recent activities [of the] Japanese Navy along [the] South China coast threaten Australia. Foreshadow [sic] your country will be the next victim of their incessant aggression.'[60] The Australian government was not generally in agreement with this last statement but was concerned by the demonstration of Japanese aggression. Nevertheless, it was felt that a 'further moral censure on Japan or proposal for economic boycott ... would ... probably antagonise and harden feeling in Japan to such an extent as to preclude any possibility of a settlement'.[61]

Following the 'goodwill' mission of Sir John Latham to China and Japan in 1934, Colonel E.E. Longfield Lloyd was appointed as Australian Trade Commissioner in Tokyo.[62] Later this appointment was changed to that of Commonwealth Commissioner.[63] Lloyd, a former intelligence officer, was not as well placed as the British ambassador to report on Japanese activities, but he did report with an Australian eye. Along with the reports of V.G. Bowden, the Trade Commissioner at Shanghai,[64] Lloyd enabled the Australian government to receive its own information about Japan.

Japan and the Pacific Islands

But Lloyd and Bowden were not the only agents reporting to Australia, and from the beginning of 1938 the files of the Department of Defence contain many references to Japanese activities in the islands to the north of Australia. There was not, however, any official intelligence organisation, so far as the Department of Defence was concerned, collecting information on the Japanese activities in the Pacific Islands;[65] the collection of information was in the hands of various government officials and private individuals. Nevertheless, from 1934 there were reports of Japanese naval ships in the Gilbert and Ellice Islands,[66] and there were numerous reports and complaints concerning the Japanese fishing vessels operating along the northern Australian coasts.[67]

The disagreement between the Australian army on the one side, and the navy and the Australian and British governments on the other, as to the magnitude of the Japanese threat and the efficacy of the Singapore strategy, spilled over into the political arena. The leader of the Labor Party, John Curtin, supported the army's view that Singapore was not secure and that Australia should look to her own defences. When Curtin quoted in Parliament a paper by a senior army officer, Colonel Wynter, Archdale Parkhill, the Minister of Defence, had Wynter transferred from army headquarters. The addition of a political element to the controversy meant that the government was less likely to back down from its reliance on the Singapore strategy.

Nevertheless the government was becoming increasingly suspicious of Japan, and at the end of 1938 a Department of External Affairs paper dealt with this problem in detail. It remarked that the Japanese Prime

Minister had declared in the Diet that 'the southward advance is the irrevocable destiny of the Japanese race'. The paper mentioned reports that the Japanese were building up depots of fuel, particularly coal, in the Caroline Islands. Since the Japanese navy was oil-burning, it was suggested that the coal was for transport ships engaged on a long voyage. The construction of submarine bases was also mentioned.[68]

The CGS, General Lavarack, was also worried about Japanese activity in the islands, particularly New Guinea.[69] Japanese agents were detected in New Guinea,[70] and Europeans from New Guinea visiting Japan were questioned closely by Japanese customs officials on the Australian intelligence organisation in New Guinea.[71]

The following February, Lavarack again returned to the Japanese preparations in the Caroline Islands. He pointed out that a study of recent military operations in China indicated that Japan was 'extraordinarily well equipped' to undertake an invasion or raid, and that the Carolines provided a launching base for an attack on Australia. Japan had largely modernised her shipping and had a considerable fleet of fast merchant vessels capable of accompanying a naval escort at high speed. The Japanese army also had been extensively modernised and was 'well equipped and trained in the use of modern armament... its commanders and staff will have had ample war experience in their employment'. The Australian forces had not yet been re-equipped.[72]

The thrust of Lavarack's appreciation was that the army had to be prepared to resist invasion, but, as in past years, the navy could not agree. In their view Australia could not defend herself against Japan: 'To speak therefore of a policy of defence against invasion is in the opinion of the Naval Board to arouse fake hopes and to mislead the public'.[73] This was substantially in line with the declared policy of the Australian government which the Minister of Defence summed up in April 1939:

> If Japanese economic assimilation of China fails, Japan may turn to her 'southward expansion' policy. At a still later date, say fifteen or twenty years hence, she may adopt that policy as the next step in her programme. In either case, it is improbable that the southward expansion policy will be implemented by force in the immediate future without a situation in Europe that favours her and Allies to support her. In addition to Russia, however, she must also think of the United States of America. Even if Japan has sufficient troops available now or in the more distant future, she would not be able to undertake decisive land operations against Australia while the Empire retains sea control of the Western Pacific. As you know, there is

every reason to suppose that the United Kingdom will, under any circumstances, be able to despatch a considerable force to Singapore in the event of a war in the Far East.[74]

Thus, on the eve of the Second World War the Australian defence planners knew considerably more about Japanese capabilities and activities than they had ten years earlier. They did not, however, have an assessment of the Japanese combat effectiveness. The British reports from China were not flattering about Japanese military prowess;[75] nevertheless, Lavarack shows in his appreciation that he expected them to be tough, well-trained and battle experienced. But the main political ingredient of intelligence was lacking; there was no hard evidence of Japanese intentions. All that the Australians could rely on were the reports of the activities in the islands, and information such as the following letter which was received by an Australian youth in response to his advertisement in the Japan *Advertiser* for a Japanese pen-friend:

I am 17 year old. I learn English at school. My brother is an officer in the Imperial Army. China very bad just like English and Communists. After that we will fight the bad English. My father says first take Singapore then Nanho (South Seas) and the Australians will then ask to become Nipponese like Korea.
You will then become Japan subject. That will be very nice for you and we will become great friends.
You must start learn Japanese.[76]

The Outbreak of War in Europe

The outbreak of war in Europe in 1939 provided one of the situations against which the army leaders had warned during the preceding years; Britain was now occupied in Europe. For all that, with Britain's assurance of sending the main fleet to the Far East if Japan entered the war, and with Japan's announcement of non-involvement, Australia decided to send troops to the Middle East. Australian officials still, however, had their doubts about Japan, and a paper prepared by the Department of External Affairs, stated that Japan's

policy in recent years has been essentially opportunist. She has taken every advantage of world economic conditions and international complications in other continents in pursuing her objectives in the

Pacific and Far East. There is no reason to believe that if the development of the war presents a favourable opportunity to Japan she will not seize it.[77]

In December Longfield Lloyd reported from Tokyo of

> Some extraordinary comings and goings of both Naval and Military officers of importance, to and from the office in Tokyo of the South Seas Development Company, that semi-official concern to which reference has already been made as the persistent instrument of Japan's 'Southward Expansion Movement'.[78]

The army too were concerned about Japan. Although the small intelligence staff realised that the 'imperfect facilities available' lessened the value of their assessments, they nevertheless re-examined the possibilities of a Japanese invasion. They anticipated that Japan would ultimately attack Singapore, and that they would have about 20 divisions available for operations outside of China and Manchuria. About ten of these divisions could be transported to and maintained in the South Pacific. It was expected that the Japanese would use carrier-borne aircraft to support landings in the South Pacific, and that the initial divisional landing would include a minimum of 20 light tanks and a maximum of 21 heavy and 54 light tanks. It was observed that a permanent organisation based upon Ujina was held for the purposes of transporting 10,000 men at any time.

The intelligence assessment also carried a chart contrasting a Japanese division with a division of the Australian Military Forces. In most categories of weapons the Japanese division had a larger complement than the Australian division, and the Japanese division contained additional weapons such as 105 mm AA guns, 75 mm infantry regimental guns, 37 mm anti-tank guns and light tanks.[79]

These details are taken from a paper written by Major Gerald Packer of the intelligence branch of the General Staff.[80] The Secretary of the Department of External Affairs, Hodgson, in 1935 described Packer as 'a most brilliant Duntroon graduate',[81] but Packer was no longer a regular soldier. After graduating from Duntroon in 1920 he had joined the RAAF in 1924 and resigned in 1932. In 1937 he had rejoined the army as a militia officer and after the outbreak of war in Europe had become a full-time member of the intelligence staff. Packer went beyond a recital of facts about the Japanese strengths and made a serious attempt to estimate Japanese intentions. In most cases he was fairly close to the truth, but his estimates were refuted by the senior intelligence staff officer, Lieutenant-Colonel James A. Chapman. Thus when Packer wrote in November 1939 that at some time in the future, possibly in 1940, Japan would be in a position to pursue objectives other than in China, Chapman noted in the margin that this was 'very doubtful'.

Packer believed that when there were favourable military circumstances, Japan could pursue objectives in the Soviet maritime province, Malaya, the Pacific Islands including Australia, the Netherlands East Indies and the Philippines. Chapman was adamant that Japan would not act in any of these areas until she had resolved her problem in China. Furthermore, the Dutch would be too strong in the Netherlands East Indies, and if Japan attacked the Philippines, USA and Russia would be brought in. Japan would not have sufficient strength to attack the Philippines until 1944. Packer concluded that it was practically impossible to differentiate between the relative attractions of these possible objectives, but he thought that Japan could make a rapid choice of any one of the objectives. Chapman noted: 'I entirely disagree . . . would sufficient forces be available to follow up and hold and exploit? When calmly worked out I doubt the possibility'.[82]

It is easy to be wise after the event, but Packer was convinced that he was right and soon afterwards he left the army. However his service career was not over; he joined the RAAF, was promoted, and in August 1941 became the Director of RAAF Intelligence. Undoubtedly Packer was a difficult personality, and some wartime intelligence officers still doubt his effectiveness,[83] but others are convinced that it was his drive which revitalised RAAF intelligence. One RAAF intelligence officer recalled that his organisation 'had the whole history' of the Zero. They had obtained the information from American technicians who had been employed in Japanese factories. But Packer had been unable to convince the senior air officers at Singapore of the validity of these reports.[84] For his part, Chapman was relieved as DMI less than a month after the outbreak of war.[85]

The chain of events which followed the fall of France and Holland in mid-1940 through to the Japanese attacks of December 1941 have been recounted in a score or more books. But it is relevant to ask what sort of information was available to Australian defence planners during this period?

From the beginning of the war the Dominions Office cables, supplemented by those from the United Kingdom Prime Minister, kept the Australian government reasonably well informed of events in the Far East. Some of these cables passed on information which came from highly

Australian Estimates of the Japanese Threat   155

secret sources (probably intercepts). For example, on 7 February 1941 the Australian government was informed that evidence was 'accumulating that the Japanese may already have decided to push on southward even if this means war'.[86] The Australian High Commissioner and the External Affairs Officer in London also passed on information which they had received from the British government.

The Far East Combined Bureau in Singapore was the main British intercept organisation in the Far East and, working with the US organisation at Manila, it kept close and effective watch on the Japanese navy. This intercept information was passed to Commander R.B. Long, the Australian Director of Naval Intelligence, by both signal and airmail, and served to keep the Australian authorities almost as well informed on the movement of the Japanese navy as were the British themselves.[87] But it had needed a visit from the Assistant Chief of Naval Staff, Captain J. Burnett, in October 1940 before there was a steady stream of information, and even then Australia never received all the intelligence available at Singapore.[88]

After the Australian legation was opened in Washington in 1940, the Australian Minister, R.J. Casey, developed close ties with members of the American administration. His cables to Australia show that he was, at times, given access to American as well as British intelligence.[89]

Finally, in late 1940 an Australian legation was opened in Tokyo, and the Minister, Sir John Latham, presented his credentials on 24 December 1941. Now Australia could receive first-hand information on Japan seen with the Australian situation in mind. But as Latham noted, 'You will appreciate that it is impossible to check rumours as the High Command keeps its plans extremely secret and naval, military and air information is almost impossible to obtain.'[90] The Australian government had no desire to assign attachés to Tokyo since they received copies of all the British reports, and they resisted vigorously Japanese attempts to assign attachés to their newly-opened legation in Australia.[91]

It will be seen, therefore, that the Australians had little facility for an independent assessment of Japanese strength and intentions. Nevertheless, they could assign their own values to the information they received from friendly sources. Thus the espionage activities of Major Hashida in Australia in January 1941 seemed to confirm suspicions of Japanese interest in Australia.[92] Reports of Japanese espionage in and preparations for the invasion of the Netherlands East Indies appeared more dangerous when viewed from Canberra than from London,[93] and intercepts of signals between Tokyo and the Japanese Consul-General in Sydney, showing that Japan was anticipating war at some time with

Australia, had more immediacy in Canberra than Whitehall.[94]

Inaccurate British Assessments

It was against this background that R.G. Menzies, now Prime Minister, journeyed to London in early 1941 to press the case for the reinforcement of Malaya, and particularly, the strengthening of the air force there. Whilst in England Menzies was told by the British Chiefs of Staff that:

> The majority of the 450 shore-based aircraft which the Japanese can marshal against us are of obsolete types and . . . we have no reason to believe that Japanese standards are even comparable with those of the Italians . . . [Buffaloes] would probably prove more than a match for any Japanese aircraft.[95]

In Australia the War Cabinet also received similarly misleading advice from the British Commander-in-Chief in the Far East, Air Chief Marshal Sir Robert Brooke-Popham who said:

> He was of the opinion that Japanese planes were not highly efficient and that the Malayan Air Force would put up a good show against them . . . he did not look upon the Japanese as being airminded, particularly against determined fighter opposition.[96]

Ten days earlier the Australian Chief of the Air Staff, the British officer, Air Marshal Sir Charles Burnett, had admitted to the War Cabinet that the Australian fighters were obsolescent, but he considered that few Japanese advanced types would be met in Australia, so the Australian Wirraway trainer had some fighting value and should be retained until Australia was able to acquire a more modern fighter.[97] This was cold comfort for the pilots of the eight Wirraways who went up against over 100 Japanese aircraft (including Zeros) at Rabaul on 20 January 1942.[98]

The British were also wrong about the numbers of Japanese shore-based aircraft and the figure of 450 mentioned to Menzies in London was repeated by Brooke-Popham in Australia. At that time the Australian Chiefs of Staff estimated that Japan had 340 carrier-borne aircraft and 650 land-based aircraft. In fact on 7 December 1941 the Japanese army air force had 1,375 aircraft and the navy air force had 1,250, a total of 2,625 planes.[99]

Some idea of the lack of knowledge of Japanese aircraft can be gauged from the fact that in November 1941 the Air Board requested the Australian ministers in Tokyo and Chungking to send photographs of Japanese aircraft 'to augment our portfolios for intelligence purposes and for training in recognition'.[100] By the time Japan entered the war Britain was still advising Australia 'that Japanese designers of aircraft have not reached a standard equal to that of the leading Western European powers. Moreover, they do not seem to have evolved any notably original military types.'[101]

American writers have observed that this tendency to ignore the development of Japanese aircraft was also present in America. The official view was that the Japanese planes were fairly numerous, mostly derivative and emphatically second-rate. In this, 'the US was guilty of complacency; probably of chauvinism; possibly, even of an unconscious racial arrogance'.[102] When Sir Robert Brooke-Popham saw the Australian Ministers in October 1941 he repeated his earlier advice, that 'Japan had superiority in number but not in quality' of aircraft.[103] Yet ten days before this meeting a RAAF intelligence memorandum had noted that the Zero was powerfully armed, had a maximum speed of 345 mph, and a range with maximum fuel load of 1,500 miles – a performance far beyond that of the Buffalo.[104]

Australian knowledge about Japanese tanks was also inadequate. Major-General R.N.L. Hopkins, then at army headquarters, recalled that there was so little information that he obtained photographs from the Melbourne *Herald* which he had magnified and measured to find out the capabilities of the Japanese armoured fighting vehicles.[105]

What was the Australian view of the Japanese army? British observers, whose reports usually found their way to Australia, had closely observed the Japanese army during the Russo-Japanese War, and in the period between the two world wars. Their reports had defined most of the characteristics which were to be displayed in December 1941 and early 1942. The Australian official historian noted, however, that their observations

> had not sunk very deeply into the consciousness of European officer corps accustomed to regard Asian military leaders generally as deficient in first-rate organising and technical ability, and the rank and file as lacking the fibre and initiative of their own men.[106]

It seems that the officers of the Australian 8th Division, which was to be the first Australian force to meet the Japanese, took the Japanese army more seriously than their British counterparts in Malaya. Perhaps it was because the Australians were newcomers to Malaya, and had not been affected by service in the peacetime tropical environment which many observers have commented upon. Perhaps it was the realistic assessment of the Japanese soldier contained in a booklet issued by army headquarters, Melbourne. Perhaps it was Australia's closer proximity to Japan which concentrated the army's attention on Japanese capabilities. Colonel Thyer, who was GSOI of the 8th Division during the Malayan campaign, recalled a long discussion with three of Brooke-Popham's senior officers, representing the navy, army and air force.

> I shall never forget the overall opinion they gave me of the Japanese Army and Air Force. It can be summed up in the expression used by the army man who had been in Shanghai and Hong Kong – 'The Japanese Army is a bubble waiting to be pricked'.[107]

British military commanders have accused the Far East Combined Bureau of underestimating the Japanese, but members of the FECB have refuted these allegations, and it is certain that accurate information on the navy and probably on the capability of the Japanese infantry was available before December 1941. The difficulty was in getting the British commanders and staff to believe it.[108] It does seem that the air intelligence provided by FECB was particularly weak, and the Australian official history claims that RAAF methods were used in the reorganisation of the Malayan intelligence service at the end of 1941.[109]

Within Australia, by the beginning of 1941, even Colonel Chapman was becoming convinced that Japanese intentions might match her growing capabilities. In February 1941 he made a detailed study of the methods Japan would use to invade Australia, and he considered that Japan would need a force of ten to twelve divisions for southward expansion. He concluded that there would be no attack on Australia in the next three to four weeks.[110]

By April 1941 Chapman was convinced that Japan would move south when opportunity permitted, and he noted that Japan could transport four to five divisions in a surprise strategic move.[111] The following month he observed the concentration on Hainan Island of the force which eventually attacked Malaya.[112] During this period a divergence in opinion between the Australian estimates and those of the British War Office was detected in Australia. The War Office estimated that the Japanese had 21 divisions ready for battle but listed none in Manchuria; army headquarters estimated 22 divisions with 5 in Manchuria.[113]

Australian Estimates of the Japanese Threat 159

But what of Japanese battlefield capabilities? Following the Japanese landings on the Chinese coast in 1937 it was realised that the Japanese had developed effective combined operations techniques, and these were the subject of a number of Australian assessments which give an idea of the sort of information available in Australia in 1941. In May 1941 the army staff stated that there were cracks in Japan's 'imposing parade' of air strength. The intelligence summary continued:

(i) The Japanese air staff, unless advised by German experts, is not competent to deal with prolonged or efficient air opposition.
(ii) The majority of Japanese aircraft types in current use are far outclassed by Western types, although their most modern naval fighter-Type 'O' – and naval light bomber-Type 99 – are good.
(iii) Japanese bomber pilots have become accustomed to lack of opposition, both in the air and from the ground.
(iv) The Japanese do not take their defeats very well; and this applies to the Naval Air Service as well as that of the Army.

In addition to the above, it is well-known that Japanese ground defence against air attack is almost non-existent; this applies to most of the cities in Japan itself as well as to the points in occupied China and the bottle-necks at Formosa and Hainan Island. Against an air power which can strike back, the Japanese should lose a considerable number of aircraft on the ground, for the Japanese, after their immunity in China, do not contemplate the possibility of heavy air operations against their own aerodromes.[114]

In July 1941 the army staff dealt with combined operations in more detail. They believed that:

1. The Japanese fully realise the value of amphibious operations in their national strategy and have developed their methods and equipment to a high degree of efficiency. They have had more up-to-date experience in this type of warfare than any other nation since they have carried out at least twelve major combined operations since July, 1937.
2. It is true that in many cases the operation has been light, but in every instance there is clear evidence of careful planning in every detail. In consequence, their operations should be studied carefully ...

5. Fronts of Landings

The wide front on which the Japanese land is notable. At Shanghai the distance between the wings was about 16 miles and at Hangchow and Bias Bay 20. Success at any point is rapidly and fully exploited.

6. Speed

In all the major landings the speed of advance inland was very rapid. The infantry of the first flight push on to the utmost of their ability, using mountain guns for their artillery and apparently dispensing with tanks and M.T. till these can catch up. In most cases tanks appear to have been little used.

7. Material

They have ample material for combined operations which is both cheap to produce and is reliable in use. They have great reserves of suitable crafts, which in peace are employed commercially and which, with their crews, are readily impressed when required ...

11. Naval Air Operations

... In addition the Japanese lag behind the others in the night operation of their carriers. Their bombing operations during the Sino-Japanese hostilities, many of which have been the work of carrier aircraft, have shown that they dislike night flying especially on moonless nights, during which most of their landings have been staged.

Naval air support has hitherto been sufficient to ensure success against the Chinese. On the other hand we know that attack by shipborne aircraft cannot be heavy because of their inferior performance and moreover their attacks can only be intermittent ...

13. Naval and Air Bombardment

In several cases the Japanese have apparently valued surprise more than the preliminary bombardment, which has not started until after the first flight has landed. On one occasion a preliminary bombardment of enemy positions was made at a range of 3,300 yards, and the covering fire was most accurate, the Japanese keeping only a short distance behind the bursting shells. This was done by destroyers, which never fired at more than 2,000 to 2,500 yards, sometimes using howitzer fire on special areas by extreme elevation and a small charge. By this means shells were lobbed accurately for about 1,000 yards.

Aircraft appear to be used mainly to cover the troops when out of range of the guns of the Fleet, and for reconnaissance. During the landing at Shanghai against opposition they flew at 600-700 feet, and may also have been used for spotting. In the advance on Canton they were used against enemy formations in a manner reminiscent of

Australian Estimates of the Japanese Threat   161

German methods.

The first sentence of this conclusion is formulated as the result of Japanese methods against the Chinese. It would be unwise to assume that they will do the same against a fortress such as Hong Kong or Singapore.

14. *Landing Conditions*

It appears to be the Japanese practice to anchor their transports off the point of attack at about 0200, and for the troops to reach the beaches about 0430, depending on the time of sunrise. In general, therefore, embarkation in landing craft is carried out in the dark, and the first troops land in the dark just before the first light of dawn.[115]

The most noticeable feature of these assessments is the underestimation of the power of an attack from ship-borne aircraft.

The Onset of War

The different manner in which Australian and British authorities interpreted Japan's intentions is illustrated by the comments of the Australian DCGS, Major-General S.F. Rowell. In mid-1941 the War Office told the Australian Liaison Officer in London that Australia was tending to overestimate the capacity of the Japanese and to under-estimate the Australian powers of resistance.[116] Rowell replied to this 'ill-informed criticism by the protagonists of the blue-water school' with considerable feeling:

> Rightly or wrongly we are not prepared to gamble on the period which may, or may not, elapse between the commencement of operations in the Far East and the stage when it is 'our turn next' ...
>
> It is difficult to understand the War Office motive in suggesting that we are overdoing the defence of this country. They should appreciate that the AIF, the only force we can legally send out of the country, is a volunteer force and goodness knows we are doing our best to make it as large as possible even though it has had very profound effect on the AMF by draining it of the best personnel.
>
> We certainly have retained a few AIF units, some being for external commitments in the NEI to which they are the only troops we can legally send. It may be noted that despite the serious deterioration of the Far Eastern situation we willingly sent another Brigade Group to Malaya recently even though we were aware that it brought

the strength of infantry there above the figure fixed as adequate by the United Kingdom Chiefs of Staff. Incidentally, we cannot help contrasting the keenness to get AIF troops in Malaya with the general complacency of the place where it is very much a '9 to 5' war with ample time off for sport.

In brief it can be said that even if the blue-water school could reduce us to a state of great complacency vis-a-vis Japan they would not be able to get any more out of us.[117]

To the Australian defence planners the information now coming in from all sources revealed Japan's increasing preparations for war.[118] On 21 July 1941 the joint service Combined Operational Intelligence Centre (COIC) reported that 'it is known that Japanese Naval leaders favour southern expansion'. On 6 October it was reported that Japan's preparations for war were considered to be almost complete. On 27 October it was 'reported that the Japanese Navy is now fully mobilised on a war footing', and on 1 December, 'Japan is now ready to strike in any direction from Indo-China at any moment'.[119]

In November 1941 Colonel Chapman stated that Japan could assemble 13 divisions and 6 independent mixed brigades for operations in theatres outside China.[120] It had assembled a mobile striking force of some ten divisions for operations in new theatres such as Malaya or towards Australia. Transport was available to move approximately 15 divisions immediately. Chapman considered that the Japanese air force was the weakest of the three services, but it was observed that the navy had 1,718 aircraft, 612 of which were sea-borne. Obsolete types were being replaced by more modern aircraft. Chapman calculated that Japan would have to do something within the next three months, but despite the evidence he drew back from anticipating an attack on Malaya. In his opinion their most probable course was further action against China plus a move against Thailand.

General Rowell, however, was convinced that a Japanese attack was imminent, and the fact that the information contained in the COIC summaries was taken seriously is indicated by an army planning directive which began: 'The general situation is such that war between the British Empire and Japan must be regarded as a probability.'[121] The directive anticipated that the possible Japanese courses, in order, would be:

1. Attack on Malaya with the object of seizing Singapore.
2. Attack on the Netherlands East Indies and British North Borneo.
3. Invasion of Australia or New Zealand.

On 29 November Casey in Washington reported that a Japanese task force of five divisions was assembled for a southward advance.[122] On 4 December news was received from Vice-Admiral C.E.L. Helfrich, the C-in-C of the Netherlands East Indies navy, that the Japanese navy had begun to move.[123] The Dutch cryptanalysts had also broken the Japanese codes.[124] On 6 December Casey reported:

> I was told by a secret but reliable source today that the Japanese Government had instructed Japanese Embassy at Washington yesterday afternoon to begin destruction of papers and records. Please regard this information as completely secret.[125]

Clearly this was 'magic' information.[126]

By now the Australian Prime Minister was John Curtin who had anticipated the fall of Singapore before the war and this news therefore would have come as no surprise to him. Indeed in late November, Kawai, the Japanese minister, had told him that the momentum towards war was too great to be stopped. Soon after that Curtin had learnt that Kawai's staff were burning their papers.[127]

Yet to the last some Australians seemed to think that there would be no outbreak of war. General Rowell, the DCGS, recalled that Lieutenant-Colonel W.R. Hodgson, the Secretary of the Department of External Affairs, told him on the evening of 8 December that until two days before the attack they thought that war in the Far East could be averted.[128] Rowell recalled that army headquarters was 'forbidden to issue any instructions to Commands that war with Japan was inevitable', but that he wrote personal letters to the GOCs warning them of approaching war.[129] Furthermore, Evatt, the Minister for External Affairs, would not allow the Japanese representative's quarters in Melbourne to be 'bugged'.[130]

Conclusion

The Japanese operations during the next eight months confirmed most of the appreciations made by Australian military planners during the preceding twenty years. Once Britain was occupied in Europe Japan seized naval command in the Western Pacific, captured Hong Kong and Singapore, overran the Netherlands East Indies, and tried to isolate Australia. Only the long anticipated invasion of Australia remained to complete the forecast.

164   Australian Estimates of the Japanese Threat

It is now known that the Japanese did not intend to invade Australia, but it was, at one stage, urged by the Japanese navy, and considered by the High Command. The plan was opposed by the Japanese army which did not believe it could spare the troops to overcome the estimated 350,000 trained troops in Australia.[131] The Japanese were mistaken because the troops were largely untrained, but the Australian formations had been raised to counter such an invasion, and had they not existed the Japanese invasion might have been debated more strongly in Tokyo.

The part that geographical perspective plays in the assessment of the military power of other states is nowhere better illustrated than in the Australian estimates of Japanese military power in the 1930s. Using very much the same intelligence sources and information as the British military and political authorities, Australia arrived at a quite different perception of the Japanese threat to that held in Whitehall. The Australian Prime Minister, John Curtin, summed up this fact in January 1942 when he told Churchill that, 'Just as you foresaw events in Europe so we feel that we saw the trend of the Pacific situation more clearly than was realised in London. Events have unfortunately justified our views regarding Malaya.'[132] It is now clear that the British overestimated some aspects of the German military machine, which was threatening their shores, and underestimated the distant Japanese threat. However close the British and Australians were in terms of history, sentiment and tradition, georgraphy and perspective sharply differentiated their views of the relative military power of the major states. Theorists might argue that the greater the distance from a potential menace, the more objective the assessment of it might be. But in this case this was clearly not true.

It was not only a case of geographical perspective. The Australian army and navy leaders, squabbling over the division of the defence vote, favoured assessments which would result in greater expenditure on their own service. Thus the Australian army was more ready than the navy to believe that a Japanese invasion was possible. It was this disagreement, plus the lack of ability to make its own assessments, which caused the government to seek advice from London. With a small population and limited industrial capacity it was, perhaps, inevitable that Australia should seek security within the framework of imperial defence, but these events demonstrate that if a nation is to have an independent defence and foreign policy it is essential that it should have its own diplomatic and intelligence services. The differences between Australian and British estimates of the increasing Japanese threat in the early stages of the Second World War provided perhaps the main impetus to the development of these services in Australia.

Capabilities and intentions are very often confused in the minds of those making assessments. If the Japanese were unlikely to attack, their capabilities could be played down; if they were likely to try to expand then they had to be taken seriously. For many years the British and Australians disagreed about Japanese intentions but, even when their views of these intentions drew closer together, they continued to disagree about Japanese power. With enemies enough in Europe and needing Australian help in the Middle East, senior British officials wanted to believe that Japanese power was less than it turned out to be. The British argued that Japanese aircraft and other equipment was backward, the Australians, who would have to bear the brunt of a Japanese attack, were not so sure. Moreover in every estimate of national power, assessments of national characteristics must play their part. Despite the evidence from the Russo-Japanese War and elsewhere, the British did not believe that the Japanese were peculiarly suited to make fighting men. Perhaps their colonial experience in Asia warped their judgement, while the Australians who did not have this experience, could see more clearly. But whatever the reason it is now clear that the British underestimated Japanese power, and the British Empire, of which Australia was an important part, paid the price for this miscalculation at Singapore, in the Java Sea, and in the islands to the north of Australia.

Notes

1. There is some evidence of a fear of Japan developing in Australia following her victory over China in 1895. The most important source for Australian perceptions of Japan for this period is D.C.S. Sissons, 'Attitudes to Japan and Defence, 1890-1923', MA thesis, University of Melbourne, 1956. Mr Sissons kindly offered helpful comments on a draft of this chapter.

2. Many of the forts around the main Australian coastal cities were built during this period.

3. D.C.S. Sissons, in *Senate Standing Committee on Foreign Affairs and Defence*, Hansard, 28 April 1972, p. 453.

4. Quoted in Sissons, ibid., p. 447.

5. Quoted in Sissons, 'Attitudes to Japan and Defence'. For an account of this period see Neville Meaney, *The Search for Security in the Pacific, 1901-14* (Sydney University Press, Sydney, 1976).

6. Quoted in D.K. Dignan, 'Australian and British Relations with Japan 1914-1921', *Australian Outlook*, vol. 21, no. 2 (August 1967), p. 144.

7. Ibid., p. 149.

8. Memorandum, E.L. Piesse to Secretary of the Prime Minister's Department, 1 November 1920, CRS A 981, item Japan 53, Australian Archives, Parkes, ACT. All files from Parkes have the prefix CRS.

9. For example, on 26 September 1916 the NSW Commercial Commissioner at Kobe, J.B. Suttor, reported on Japanese interest in the South Seas. CRS A 981, Japan 38.

10. Letter, Hughes to Pearce, 21 April 1916, cited in Sissons, 'Attitudes to Japan and Defence', vol. 1, p. 79.

11. Notes on the Foreign Office Memoranda on the Anglo-Japanese Alliance, 28 June 1920 (Piesse Papers), cited in Sissons, 'Attitudes to Japand and Defence', vol. 3, p. 53, fn. 27.

12. Letter, Piesse to Pearce, 13 November 1918 (Piesse Papers), quoted in Sissons, 'Attitudes to Japan and Defence', vol. 1, p. 127.

13. Dignan, 'Australian and British Relations', p. 150. Papers in the Hughes Collection, National Library of Australia (NLA), MS 1538/16/29, indicate that these may not have been received in Australia.

14. Sissons, 'Attitudes to Japan and Defence', vol. 3, p. 34, fn. 24.

15. Memorandum, Major E.L. Piesse to CGS, 22 October 1918, CRS A 981, Far East 8.

16. Ibid.

17. Quoted in W.J. Hudson, *Billy Hughes in Paris, The Birth of Australian Diplomacy* (Nelson, Melbourne, 1978), pp. 91, 92.

18. Report of Admiral of the Fleet, Viscount Jellicoe of Scapa, on Naval Mission to the Commonwealth of Australia, May-August 1919, 4 Volumes, Hughes Papers, NLA, MS 1538/19/2-3.

19. Report on the Military Defence of Australia by a Conference of Senior Officers of the Australian Military Forces, 6 February 1920, Pearce Papers, NLA, MS 1827/1.

20. *Argus*, 16 February 1920.

21. Report by E.L. Piesse to Secretary of the Prime Minister's Department, 22 March 1920, Piesse Papers, NLA MSS 882/5. Australia was not, however, a 'first-class power'.

22. A.J. Hill, *Chauvel of the Light Horse* (Melbourne University Press, Melbourne, 1978), p. 203. Of the diminutive regular force of 1,700 men, 100 officers, 188 warrant officers and 179 other ranks were discharged or retired.

23. Quoted in Sissons, 'Attitudes to Japan and Defence', p. 123.

24. Copies of the military attaché reports can be found in CRS A 981, Japan 38, and Japan 46.

25. Council of Defence Agenda No. 7/13, 26 November 1923, CRS A 2030, vol. 1.

26. Quoted in John McCarthy, *Australia and Imperial Defence 1918-1934, A Study in Air and Sea Power* (Queensland University Press, St Lucia, 1976), p. 49.

27. Quoted in ibid., p. 19.

28. Quoted in ibid., p. 49.

29. Appendix 1 to Report on the RAN College, Jervis Bay, and the RMC Duntroon, c. August 1923, CRS A 664, 435/401/23.

30. Military Intelligence Note No. 47, 20 August 1924, CRS A 981, Japan 38.

31. Report for the Inspector-General, 1924, 1926, 1927, 1930, quoted in Hill, *Chauvel*, p. 210.

32. Appreciation, War in the Pacific, 9 August 1928, Australian Archives, Melbourne, MP 1185/8, item 1846/4/363.

33. Memorandum, CGS to AG, QMG, 20 September 1929, Australian War Memorial (AWM) file 243/6/159.

34. Quoted in Sissons, 'Attitudes to Japan and Defence', p. 131.

35. *Notes on the Situation in the Far East*, prepared by Intelligence Section, G.S. 2nd District Base. A. 981, Far East 8.

36. These were T.E. Nave and W.E. McLaughlin from the RAN and Mr R.A. Ball.

37. Japanese Espionage in Australia and its Relation to Japanese Policy, by E.L. Piesse, 17 April 1924, Piesse Papers, NLA MS 882/9/218-236. For an account of Japanese espionage during this early period see CRS A 981, Japan 55.
38. Sissons, evidence to *Senate Standing Committee*, p. 449.
39. Minutes of Defence Committee, 17 July 1930, CRS A 2031, vol. 1.
40. Appreciation, Australia's Position in Case of War in the Pacific, by DMO & I (Australia), 18 March 1930, MP 1217 Box 39. This series, known as the Shedden Papers, is held by Australian Archives, Parkes, ACT, unlike most of the MP series which is held in Melbourne.
41. Review of Defence Committee's appreciation, War in the Pacific, dated 9 August 1928. By Colonel J.D. Lavarack and Group Captain S.J. Goble, 14 March 1930 CRS A 2031 vol. 1.
42. Review of the Appreciation – War in the Pacific dated 7 August 1928, by Captain C.J. Pope, 18 March 1930, CRS A 2031, vol. 1.
43. P. Harrison-Mattley, 'Australia and the Far Eastern Crisis 1931-32', MA thesis, University of Sydney, 1968. See also E.M. Andrews, 'The Australian Government and the Manchurian Crisis', paper presented to the History of Australian Defence and Foreign Policy conference, Sydney, August 1975.
44. Harrison-Mattley, 'Australia and the Far Eastern Crisis'.
45. McCarthy, *Australia and the Imperial Defence*, p. 50.
46. 'Appreciation of Australia's Position in Case of War in the Pacific', by Australian Section IGS, March 1930, revised to 23 March 1932, AWM 910/2/4.
47. Report 613, Sir F. Lindley to Sir John Simon, 26 December 1931, received 27 January 1932, plus enclosures. CRS A 981, Japan Defence 47.
48. This is borne out by the preparation and circulation of mobilisation plans for the army. See N. Gow, 'Australian Army Strategic Planning 1919-1939', *Australian Journal of Politics and History*, vol. xxii, no. 2 (August 1977).
49. On 14 February 1935 the CNS, Vice-Admiral Sir Francis Hyde, told the Minister for Defence: 'The British Naval Intelligence Organisation makes a special study of the movement of Japanese merchant shipping, and it is considered that any considerable departure from the normal will be appreciated within a few days.' MP 1217, Box 1018.
50. Lecture on the Plan of Concentration by Lieutenant-Colonel V.A.H. Sturdee, Senior Officers Course 1933, AWM 243/6/150.
51. CID Paper 358C of March 1931 cited in Defence Committee Minutes, 5 March 1935, CRS A 2031, vol. 3.
52. Letter from Field-Marshal Montgomery-Massingberd to Major-General J.D. Lavarack, 24 April 1935. AWM 243/6/41. The CIGS's letter does not mean that his views diverged from those of the CID, but he was answering a specific question from Lavarack. On 7 October 1935 Lavarack wrote to E.L. Piesse, 'I myself, nor any of the three Chiefs of Staff under whom I have served – Sir Harry Chauvel, Coxen and Bruche – nor I am sure, Sir Brudenell White, have ever believed that 60,000 was the upper limit. Estimates have always varied from about twice to over three times that number – and that is the first flight only.' Piesse Papers, NLA, MS 882/9.
53. Extract from Foreign Office Annual Report on Japan for 1934, CRS A 816, 19/304/121. The Department of Defence received this report in August 1935.
54. McCarthy, *Australia and the Imperial Defence*, p. 134.
55. Quoted in P. Hasluck, *The Government and the People 1939-1941* (Australian War Memorial, Canberra, 1952), p. 65.
56. Quoted in McCarthy, *Australia and the Imperial Defence*, p. 127.
57. Minutes of Meeting to Discuss Defence Questions, 1 June 1937, in R.G. Neale (ed.), *Documents in Australian Foreign Policy*, vol. 1 (Australian Government Publishing Service, Canberra, 1975), (hereafter *DAFP*), p. 110.

58. Quoted in Hasluck, *Government and the People*, p. 57.
59. Diary entries for 6, 7 February, 13 March, 29 May 1936 of J. Pierrepont Moffatt, Moffatt Papers, NLA.
60. Telegram, Chu Chiahua to Prime Minister of Australia, 18 September 1937, CRS A 1606, C 41/1.
61. Memorandum, Hodgson to Prime Minister, 29 October 1937, *loc. cit.*
62. For Lloyd's experiences see Lloyd Papers, NLA, MS 2887.
63. Cabinet Minute 2241, Melbourne, 1 November 1937, *DAFP*, vol. 1, p. 219.
64. These reports are held in CRS A 1606, C 41/1.
65. Defence Committee Minute No. 30, April 1938, CRS A 2031, vol. 4.
66. CRS A 816, 19/304/216.
67. CRS A 816, 19/304/240.
68. Paper entitled 'Southward Advance Policy of Japan', November 1938, CRS A 1606, E 21/1 Part 1.
69. Memorandum CGS to Secretary of the Department of Defence, 9 December 1938, CRS A 816 19/304/188.
70. Memorandum Secretary of Prime Minister's Department to Secretary of the Department of Defence, 9 January 1939; Letter, H. Page, Acting Administrator – Central Administration Rabaul, to Secretary of Prime Minister's Department, 20 January 1939; Letter, J.H.P. Murray, Lieut-Governor, Papua, to Minister in Charge of Territories, 17 January 1939, *loc cit.*
71. CGS Memorandum, 9 December 1937, *loc cit.*
72. Minute, Lavarack to Secretary of the Department of Defence, 28 February 1939, CRS A 816, 14/301/108.
73. Memorandum, Secretary of the Naval Board to Secretary of the Department of Defence for the Minister, 7 March 1939, *loc cit.*
74. Letter, G.A. Street, Minister of Defence, to Prime Minister, 1 April 1939, CRS A 816, 19/304/214.
75. Cable 216, Secretary of State for Dominions Affairs to Prime Minister, 17 February 1942, A 816, 19/304/214.
76. Quoted in memorandum, Lavarack to Secretary of Department of Defence, 29 March 1939, CRS A 816, 19/304/188.
77. Paper entitled 'Future of Japanese Policy', 11 September 1939, given to Prime Minister, 26 September 1939, CRS A 1606, E/12/1.
78. Memorandum 535, Lloyd to Secretary of the Department of External Affairs, 1 December 1939, CRS A 816, 14/304/275.
79. Memorandum by Major G. Packer to GS (MI) 22 December 1939, AWM 243/6/158.
80. At this stage there was no separate Director of Military Intelligence. The senior intelligence staff officer was Lieutenant-Colonel James A. Chapman who, in July 1941 was promoted to colonel and became DMI when the Directorate of Military Operations and Intelligence split into two separate branches. He is always described as James A. Chapman to distinguish him from his brother, the later Major-General John A. Chapman.
81. Letter, Hodgson to Piesse, 8 August 1935, Piesse Papers, NLA, MS 882/9.
82. Notes upon Possible Japanese Courses of Action, 13 November 1939, by Major G. Packer, with marginal notes by Lieutenant-Colonel James A. Chapman, Gavin Long Correspondence – James A. Chapman, AWM.
83. Interview with Air Vice-Marshal J.E. Hewitt, 3 July 1978.
84. Wing-Commander G.R. Allman to Gavin Long, Sydney, 8 June 1946, Gavin Long Notes, No. 87, AWM. Air Marshal Sir John McCauley, the senior RAAF officer at Singapore, recalled Packer's visit, but not the advice about the Zero. He said that the RAF told him that the Buffalo would be superior to the

Zero. Interview, 31 August 1979.

85. He became the Colonel in charge of Administration in Darwin for four months, then the Commander in Tasmania until the beginning of 1944 when he became the Military Liaison Officer in the Middle East.

86. Cable Z38, Secretary of State for Dominion Affairs to Prime Minister, 2 February 1941, CRS A 816, 19/304/426. It is likely that the only recipients of Z cables during this period were the British High Commissioners in Australia, New Zealand, Canada and South Africa, for transmission to their respective host governments. *DAFP*, vol. 1, p. 563.

87. Memorandum, DNI to Secretary of the Department of Defence, 2 April 1941, CRS A 981, Far East 24.

88. G. Hermon Gill, *Royal Australian Navy, 1939-1942* (Australian War Memorial, Canberra, 1957), p. 269.

89. For example, in the files of the Australian mission there is a letter dated 8 May 1941 to Casey from the British Passport Control Office (the cover organisation for British intelligence): 'herewith a copy of a document from a very secret source which may be of interest to the Australian Government'. CRS A 3300, item 98.

90. Cable 37, Latham to Department of External Affairs, 11 January 1941, CRS A 816, 19/304/425.

91. CRS A 816, 19/304/276.

92. Major Hashida was arrested in Batavia, and extracts of his notes containing information on strategic points in Australia, were passed to Australian authorities. FO 371/27788, 2961, Public Record Office; CRS A 816, 19/304/276.

93. See intelligence reports in AWM 254/5/32; also official Dutch document dated March 1941 in CRS A 816, 19/304/313.

94. See cables from the Australian High Commissioner in London to Australian Prime Minister in CRS A 816, 19/304/420, and CRS A 1606, E 13/1, Part 1. On 18 April 1941 the Director of Naval Intelligence informed the Secretary of the Department of External Affairs that information from 'special secret means' indicated that the Japanese Minister for Foreign Affairs had informed the Japanese Consul-General in Sydney that the strengthening of Malayan defences had to be discouraged by all possible means, and the Consul-General was to forward ideas which could be used to make the Australian troops there homesick and their families uneasy. Evatt Papers, Cables Far East 1941. Flinders University Library.

95. COS (41) 230, 11 April 1941, MP 1049/5, 1855/2/394.

96. War Cabinet Meeting, 14 February 1941, CRS A 2673, vol. 5.

97. War Cabinet Meeting, 4 February 1941, *loc cit.* On 17 August 1941 Brooke-Popham cabled the Air Ministry, 'I had some difficulty in explaining to Ministers and others in Australia why Wirraway was able to give effective war service in the Far East.' Yet the previous month (3 July 1941) he had cabled the Chiefs of Staff, 'Wirraways and Wildebeasts must be considered obsolete types for operations. Squadrons will do good work so long as they last but casualties will be heavy in war and reserves insufficient to keep them operationally efficient for long', AIR 8/945.

98. For an account of this unequal battle see Douglas Gillison, *Royal Australian Air Force 1939-1942* (Australian War Memorial, Canberra, 1962), pp. 351-6.

99. Gillison, ibid., p. 152.

100. Letter, Secretary of Air Board to Secretary of Department of Defence, 14 November 1941, CRS A 981, Japan 47.

101. Summary of Enemy Economic Development for week ending 17 December 1941, by United Kingdom Ministry of Economic Warfare, *loc. cit.*

102. John Grayson Kirk, 'Japanese Air Power' in S.L. Mayer (ed.), *The Japanese War Machine* (Bison, Sydney, 1976), p. 118.

103. Advisory War Council Minute 553, 16 October 1941, CRS A 2684, item 552.
104. Gillison, *Royal Australian Air Force*, p. 170N. The British Official Historian has commented on the unwillingness of the British services to heed intelligence when it pointed to possibilities which lay beyond their own experience and ideas. F.H. Hinsley et al., *British Intelligence in the Second World War*, vol. 1 (HMSO, London, 1979), p. 77.
105. R.N.L. Hopkins, *Australian Armour, A History of the Royal Australian Armoured Corps 1927-1972* (Australian War Memorial, Canberra, 1978), p. 28.
106. Lionel Wigmore, *The Japanese Thrust* (Australian War Memorial, Canberra, 1957), p. 113. A British report of January 1938 noted that the German military advisers in China thought that 'the fighting and military qualities of the Japanese officers and men were distinctly below those of the average European Army'. This report was well received in the Admiralty. Report on Military Information obtained at Hankow, 16-20 January 1938, GSO 111(1), ADM 1/9587.
107. Quoted in Wigmore, *Japanese Thrust*, p. 82, fn. 9. The British official history recorded: 'That two views of Japanese military prowess existed is seen in the fact that in 1940 Army Headquarters, Australia, and Malaya Command held almost opposite views on this vital matter.' S. Woodburn Kirby, *The War Against Japan, Volume 1, The Loss of Singapore* (HMSO, London, 1957).
108. Ibid. Wigmore, *Japanes Thrust*, p. 82. Interview with Captain R.E. Nave RN of FECB. See also Brooke-Popham papers at Liddell Hart Centre for Military Archives, Kings College, London. On 8 May 1942 Major General G.E. Grimsdale of British Military Intelligence wrote to General Ismay about the FECB: 'the GHQ staff [at Singapore] never believed us and always called us "alarmists" when we told them how many divisions or aeroplanes the Japs could use. As it happens our estimates were more accurate than ever we had suggested they were.' Ismay Papers, IV/G.
109. Gillison, *Royal Australian Air Force*, p. 160.
110. A General Review by Military Intelligence, AHQ, etc, 8 February 1941, by Information Section (1a), and An Appreciation of the Probable Action and Plans of Japan etc, 8 February 1941, by Lieutenant-Colonel James A. Chapman, Gavin Long Correspondence – James A. Chapman, AWM.
111. An Appreciation of Probable Action of Japan etc., 24 April 1941, by Lieutenant-Colonel James A. Chapman, *loc. cit.*
112. Memorandum, Chapman to DMO & 1, 8 May 1941, *loc. cit.*
113. Memorandum, Major W.M. Gray to DDMI (Chapman), 29 May 1941, *loc cit.* It seems difficult to believe that the British thought that there were no Japanese divisions in Manchuria and indeed the FECB Intelligence Summary for 16 October 1940 and a memorandum dated 30 April 1941 showed eight Japanese divisions in Manchuria, WO 208/855. But the important point is that the Australians were now making independent assessments.
114. Appendix IV to AHQ Intelligence Summary 132, 4 July 1941, CRS A 981, Japan Defence 45B.
115. Appendix II to AHQ Intelligence Summary No. 131, 25 July 1941, *loc. cit.*
116. Letter, Colonel A.W. Wardell to DCGS, 30 July 1941, AWM 425/11/7, Part 2.
117. Letter, Rowell to Wardell, 2 October 1941, AWM, 425/11/7, Part 1.
118. During 1940 and 1941 Australia had established her own intercept organisation under Captain T.E. Nave RN. It will be recalled that Nave was one of the Australian naval officers at Tokyo in the 1920s. Since then he had joined the RN, and before returning to Australia, had headed the intercept component of FECB. As well as breaking some Japanese naval codes, Nave's organisation was

able to intercept the traffic of the Japanese Consul-General in Australia.

119. COIC Weekly Intelligence Summaries, June-December 1941, AWM 423/11/2. The COIC was an organisation, staffed by members of the three services, with the task of preparing intelligence summaries for joint headquarters and for the War Room at Victoria Barracks.

120. Intelligence Appreciation on the Present Japanese Situation, 5 November 1941, by Colonel James A. Chapman, Gavin Long Correspondence – James A. Chapman, AWM.

121. Operation Planning Directive No. 1, possibly written November 1941, by General Rowell, AWM 243/6/5.

122. Cable 1049, Casey to Department of External Affairs, 29 November 1941, CRS A 981, Japan 185, Part III.

123. L. Farago, *The Broken Seal, The Story of 'Operation Magic' and the Pearl Harbor Disaster* (London, 1967), p. 350. The Australian official historian recorded: 'On the 4th December, the day the Japanese Pearl Harbour force reached its south-eastward turning point, Long, the Director of Naval Intelligence, signalled to the Captain on the Intelligence Staff (COIS) Singapore: "Information received 1800 GMT 3rd December 4am 4th December Melbourne time from reliable Dutch source Menado that eight transports twenty warships left Palau proceeding towards NEI". Singapore replied soon after noon, Melbourne time, on the 5th: "No information here" . . . Actually this force did not leave Palau until 6-8 December, and then for the Philippines. But its presence at Palau was correct, and its constitution was approximately as reported.' Gill, *Royal Australian Navy*, p. 474. Farago states (p. 351), although no other evidence has been discovered, that Casey was ordered to take the information to the White House.

124. E.R. Thorpe, *East Wind, Rain* (Gambit, Boston, 1967), p. 51.

125. Cable 1090, Casey to Department of External Affairs, 5 December 1941, received 6 December 1941, CRS A 981, Japan 185, Part VI.

126. 'Magic' was the name given by the Americans to information received by intercepting and breaking the codes of Japanese diplomatic communications.

127. Curtin to Gavin Long, April 1942, in Gavin Long Diary, No. 3, p. 27, AWM.

128. Interview with Lieutenant-General Sir Sydney Rowell, 26 June 1974.

129. S.F. Rowell, *Full Circle* (Melbourne University Press, Melbourne, 1974), p. 100.

130. Rowell interview. However, they were 'bugged', and when this was revealed Evatt said, on 26 November 1941, that it 'was a serious breach of diplomatic privilege'. Advisory War Council Minute 570, Canberra 26 November 1941, CRS A 2684, item 570.

131. T. Hattori, *The Complete History of the Great East Asia War*, (Masu Shobō, Tokyo, 1953), pp. 113-15. Also Sabura Hayashi with Alvin D. Coox, *Kōgun, The Japanese Army in the Pacific War* (The Marine Corps Association, Quantico, Va, 1959), p. 34. N. Ike, *Japan's Decision for War* (Stanford University Press, Stanford, California, 1967), p. 161, states that on 6 September 1941 the Australian army was believed to be '250,000 regular [sic] troops plus an expeditionary force of 120,000'. Obviously the Japanese misunderstood the Australian meaning of Militia. An Australian General Staff paper entitled 'Japanese Preparations for War and Plans for Australia', probably prepared in 1946 (AWM 423/6/1), states that in July 1940 the Japanese believed that there was a Corps in each state.

132. Cable Johcu 20, Curtin to Churchill, 22 January 1942, PREM 3 166/5.

6 PERCEPTIONS OF NAVAL POWER BETWEEN THE WARS: THE BRITISH CASE

Geoffrey Till

On 14 December 1941, convoy HG 76 sailed from Gibraltar for the United Kingdom. It was to be the object of concerted attacks by up to a dozen U-boats at any one time in a vicious and desperate struggle that lasted for more than a week. Five U-boats were sunk, two merchant ships, the destroyer *Stanley* and the escort carrier *Audacity*. Aircraft were heavily involved, even decisive, both in the attack and the defence. The battle for convoy HG 76 in fact was an exemplar of a type and level of war which the Admiralty of pre-war days had simply not anticipated. The disastrous events of the previous week when the Japanese had attacked Malaya and a stream of bomb- and torpedo-dropping aircraft had sunk the *Prince of Wales* and *Repulse* in the Gulf of Siam, would have shocked pre-war naval staff officers even more. In both cases peacetime estimates had shown themselves to be terribly wrong. Ships were far more vulnerable to air attack than had been generally thought; the armed forces of Japan had proved to be more than a match for their Western adversaries; German U-boats were despite everything able once more to attack Britain's maritime communications with devastating effect; the entire fabric of British security in fact had been cruelly revealed as much weaker than most people had thought in the interwar period.

In all these ways, the Royal Navy's pre-war conceptions of what the war would be like were in fundamental error. The British, however, were by no means the only or the worst offenders. All the other belligerents had their failures too and success eventually came at least as much to those who responded better to the unexpected as to those who guessed more accurately in the first place. Misjudgement of the overall effectiveness of the opposition's military forces was evidently the rule rather than the exception, and was also usually the main component in the more general failure to predict strategic futures.

As far as the British were concerned, they had failed to appreciate the extent to which the German navy would be able to threaten their maritime communications, especially by the use of submarines. In 1937, they believed that the 'anti-submarine measures which have been developed since the war would ... greatly lessen the effectiveness of the submarine as a weapon against shipping',[1] and so did not anticipate the recurrence of an effective submarine *guerre de course*. Instead, they expected submarines to be used against surface warships and invariably assumed that aircraft and surface raiders were the main menace to merchant shipping. This misjudgement partly arose through a failure to appreciate the limitations of ASDIC and partly because they did not anticipate that the German navy would resort to the tactics of the wolf-pack or to the idea of submarines attacking convoys on the surface under cover of darkness. For these reasons, the British failed to estimate the scale of the future German threat correctly and, arguably, failed to make the proper preparations.

In the same kind of way, the Royal Navy underestimated the extent to which both friends and enemies would be able to use air power to influence events at sea. Although this argument can easily be overdone, and often is,[2] the Admiralty did not wholly grasp the general attack potential of aircraft at sea and, more particularly, the extent to which the Japanese had developed this new dimension of maritime warfare. They accepted that 'the Japanese Army is incapable of beating any European Army in the field with the exception of the Italian' and believed that the navy's level of general efficiency was 20 per cent lower than their own.[3] Although Japanese morale and fighting spirit was '. . . of the highest order', the British believed 'that the Japanese would be slow to embody the experience gained in war in new designs of ships and aircraft'. A war would see Japanese operational techniques falling further and further behind their Western counterparts.[4] In particular, 'the aircraft of the Japanese Naval Air Service, though much improved during the last four years, are inferior in performance to those of similar types in use in the Royal Air Force, and it appears extremely unlikely that in the event of war, Japan could keep pace with the rapid changes and progress in design brought on by the necessities of war.' Aircraft maintenance was also poor, and their pilots slow-thinking and lacking in initiative.[5]

With the advantage of hindsight, we can see that such faulty assessments as these were the product of three different kinds of misjudgement. First, there was simple error in estimating the technical effectiveness and number of particular weapons available to the other side, as in the case of Japanese naval aircraft. Second, the unexpectedness of German submarine tactics in the war illustrated a failure fully to appreciate the effectiveness of the other side's operational procedure. Assessments of both these kinds were complex matters. Neither, moreover, could be made in a vacuum, for the vulnerabilities and strengths of British forces had to be built into the equation as well. Hence the potential effectiveness of the German submarine arm was a function not only of their operational tactics and of the number and quality of their U-boats, but also of the extent of British reliance on the trade being attacked and the anticipated strength of British defences. This leads on to the third most difficult and most important kind of assessment, that of gauging the wider military implications of the capabilities being analysed. At this level, for instance, few anticipated the extent to which the German navy's *guerre de course* would allow them to dictate the nature of the war at sea.

Having identified in a very general way the kind of errors that beset those seeking to estimate the other side's maritime capabilities at this time, we should now try to identify the reasons for those errors. Sound assessment of the strength of foreign navies depends on intelligence material being effectively collected, collated, interpreted and passed on to the appropriate policy-makers in sufficient time. There were weaknesses at nearly all stages of this process in the case of the Royal Navy's assessment of their future adversaries.

First, there were very evident weaknesses in the navy's machinery for the collection of data. The nature of the intelligence task has been well described by Captain Roskill:

> The common illusion, fostered in the popular press and by imaginative writers, that an intelligence organisation depends on sensational and daring coups, such as the rifling of a safe of a foreign diplomat or the seduction of officers by beautiful but dissolute women, is far from the truth. In fact such coups are extremely rare, and when they are brought off their effects are often exaggerated. Rather does successful intelligence work depend on the painstaking collection of small pieces of information from scores of different sources, on classifying them for reliability by comparative processes, and on fitting the pieces together, as with a giant jig-saw puzzle until a broad and accurate picture finally emerges.[6]

Evidently an intelligence organisation needs a capacity for sustained, systematic and co-ordinated effort, and the obvious bureaucratic attributes that this capacity requires in terms of the number and quality of personnel, institutional importance and so forth. But for most of the interwar period, the navy's data-collection machinery was grossly deficient in these respects.

The Naval Intelligence Division (NID) was a part of the Naval Staff and so shared to a large extent in the peacetime atrophy of that organisation. The Naval Staff was under great pressure from the economisers. By 1927 the number of officers it carried had fallen from a 1918 total of 336 to 60 and the organisation considered itself to be '. . . down to bedrock, and find(s) it very wearisome, having to deal with repeated attacks on the composition of and numbers on the Naval Staff'.[7] Even within the navy the notion of a group of people, specially trained to think, was still regarded with some suspicion. In 1936, for instance, Admiral Chatfield (then First Sea Lord) remarked that naval air policy '. . . must be based on the opinions of those at sea and in command and must not be created by independent thought in the Staff departments of the Admiralty'.[8] This decline in the Naval Staff was important because that organisation had at least a *prima facie* case to be regarded as the main place where foreign capabilities could be assessed and their implications identified. Everywhere else officers were too bound up with day-to-day business to give such matters the sustained consideration their importance justified.

More particularly, NID had suffered badly on its own account too. Anxious that no future Director of Naval Intelligence (DNI) should aspire to the prestige and political influence of the legendary Admiral 'Blinker' Hall of the First World War, the Foreign Office had inspired the transfer of many of NID's orginal functions to agencies within their own control. NID's cypher and cryptanalysis sections were dissipated. Doubtless partly as a consequence of this, none of the crucial German and Japanese naval codes were known to the British in the late 1930s.[9] Furthermore, NID's achievements in the First World War were shrouded in a kind of secrecy which effectively precluded detailed analysis of the requirements, performance and potential contribution of naval intelligence.

In consequence of all this, the prestige of the NID declined and it became something of a backwater. The ambitious and the able did not seek appointments in it which 'were filled instead, more often than not, by those serving out their last two or three years in the Navy before retirement'.[10] The NID was organised into geographical sections which specialised in foreign naval construction and coastal defences but which were not equipped 'to collect or disseminate information about the organisation, dispositions and movements of foreign fleets'. There was also a tiny 'Movements Section' (usually consisting of one part-time officer), whose methods of operation were antiquated in the extreme and whose reports were virtually useless. To a certain extent, the antennae of the formal and central agencies of naval intelligence were the naval attaché network and the coterie of intelligence officers on the ships of the major fleets. The quality of the intelligence relayed back by these means was, however, uneven. One intelligence officer of the Mediterranean Fleet of the mid-1920s for instance recollected: 'I had already decided the whole system of naval intelligence was archaic and useless and sure enough when certain intelligence was essential as a basis for plans of operations against Turkey, there wasn't a damn thing in our files which was of the slightest use.'[11] Things did begin to improve from 1935 with the appointment of Vice-Admirals William James as Deputy Chief of the Naval Staff and James Troup as DNI, but by this time faulty assessments had become dangerously deep-seated.

The decline of the NID was reflected in the low attention paid to it by the rest of the machinery of defence policy-making. Inter-service planning even of something as central to its concerns as the prospects of a maritime trade war with Germany was undertaken in 1936 without NID being consulted at all. The gap this left was only incompletely filled by the Joint Planning Subcommittee (JPC) of the Chiefs of Staff Committee whose maritime expertise was provided by the Admiralty's all-powerful Plans Division. Although NID did of course supply intelligence to the Plans Division as a matter of routine, the JPC's work was nevertheless often based on intelligence evaluations that were either flimsy or completely non-existent.[12]

These institutional weaknesses were particularly noticeable in regard to the collection of information relating to maritime air power. This was because the institutions of naval air suffered not only the consequences of the decline of the Naval Staff as a whole but also languished as a result of the dual control system under which the Fleet Air Arm was jointly administered by the Admiralty and the Air Ministry. This arrangement was politically very sensitive and tended to project complications into many aspects of naval air policy, intelligence-gathering included. Generally speaking the Air and Naval Staffs were supposed to be the main source of information on aeronautical and naval matters respectively; where the object of interest spanned both dimensions, as did maritime air power, the complexities and sensitivities were considerable. Despite intricate arrangements being made to decide who was to be responsible for what kind of intelligence, co-ordination was often poor.[13] Indeed, over some issues, such as the aircraft complement of American aircraft carriers, the two sides flatly disagreed in their assessments. Another unfortunate consequence of the establishment of the Royal Air Force was the loss of the first generation of naval aviators. As a result of this, the number of officers within the Admiralty able to make informed judgements on foreign naval air policy remained dangerously low for some time. For much of the interwar period, for instance, naval attachés relied on air attachés for reports on the air service of foreign navies.

In the summer of 1938 a representative of the Naval Air Division commented in the course of a general paper on foreign torpedo tactics that he had heard reports of the Japanese developing a long-range aircraft torpedo and said that information on this would be 'of special interest'. But when, some time later, he was asked by NID what exactly it was he wanted to know, he replied that the Division 'has at present no special requirement for information but will study with interest all reports of foreign developments of long range air weapons'.[14] And there the matter rested until the British learnt about Japan's celebrated oxygen-fuelled 'Long-Lance' torpedoes the hard way a few years later. This episode well illustrates the peculiar weakness of the navy's machinery for collecting information on maritime air power in the interwar years.

When information-collecting resources are not plentiful, their efficient allocation becomes especially important. This in turn depends on there being clear ideas about what the priorities are, and what the main targets of such investigation should be. For most of the interwar period no such clear ideas existed. As late as 1933, Chatfield could still write: 'I have an important CID meeting next week at which the Chiefs of Staff are pressing for a policy to work on. Are we to be ready or are we not? If so, when and what for?'[15] As we shall see later, war with Germany and/or Japan was considered by no means inevitable even quite late in the 1930s, and this inevitably coloured both the collection and the interpretation of information about their navies.

The failure to pay any particular regard to the task of monitoring the performance of the Japanese navy, for instance, was an obvious factor in the British failure to notice the significant shift in Japanese intentions and capabilities that occured in the mid-1930s. At this time, the Japanese navy embarked on the ambitious Second and Third Replenishment Programmes. The Japanese naval air service moved into top gear and, with the operational appearance of such aircraft as the A5M Claude fighter in the China war in 1937, reached and surpassed contemporary Western standards. But the really remarkable Japanese aircraft of this era was the Mitsubishi A6MI Zero fighter. This aircraft only arrived on the scene in 1940. By this time British naval intelligence had other more immediate things to worry about and their failure to take due note of its significance is perhaps understandable. American deficiencies in this regard are more difficult to explain away, especially as General Claire Chennault's 'Flying Tigers' encountered and reported on the new Japanese fighters shortly after they made their operational debut. All in all the extent of the transformation in the capabilities of Japanese maritime airpower from the mid-1930s was insufficiently appreciated at the time. While Japanese capabilities therefore changed, British perceptions of them did not. Views that derived from the earlier period, which were then quite accurate, extended into the new era and became seriously wrong.

The evolution of the familiar *canard* that Japanese aircraft were inferior copies of their Western counterparts illustrates the point well. Of course, imitation was an inherent part of the whole transformation of the culture of the Japanese from their first contact with the West in the nineteenth century. It found expression in all spheres and for years the Royal Navy was Japan's mentor, a role much reinforced through the Japanese navy's participation in the First World War. As far as naval aviation was concerned, the British in the 1920s sent over a mission headed by the Master of Sempill (against Admiralty wishes[16]) to supervise the effective creation of a naval air service. Subsequently Western observers often attributed Japan's naval air progress to the help this mission had given. Japanese design was eclectic and most Japanese aircraft of the period contained components that were either of foreign manufacture or copies of some sort. The early results of this policy were not particularly happy either. The indifferent 1932 series of aircraft — especially the fighters produced by Mitsubishi and Nakajima — apparently confirmed foreign ideas about the limitations of Japanese aeronautical expertise. The belief that Japanese success depended on their pirating other people's ideas was also reinforced by the hordes of Japanese naval officers armed with cameras and notebooks frequently said to swarm over contemporary Western naval shipyards, aircraft factories and military equipment when the occasion offered. For such reasons, dismissive assumptions about Japan's aeronautical originality through most of the period seem understandable, and in fact largely correct. But what foreign observers did not notice was that by 1936-7, the Japanese aircraft industry stood on its own feet as far as airframe and engine design was concerned and that the navy was developing some distinctively original operational concepts. The Mitsubishi Zero with its unique stress on range and offensive power at the expense of protection demonstrates the point exactly. Towards the end of the period, some British perceptions began to be appropriately amended, despite the distractions caused by the European war. But old assumptions died hard nevertheless. Their over-long survival was unfortunate in that they encouraged the view that no particular attention needed to be paid to Japanese naval aviation.

Some types of information proved to be especially difficult to get anyway. This was certainly the case as far as the broad considerations of strategy which so much influenced calculations of the military significance of the other side's equipment and procedures were concerned. No one imagined, for instance, the extent to which Germany would overrun Continental Europe when war came. German success made their campaign against British maritime communications much more potent than had been anticipated. It also forced the British to concentrate more of their resources on the European theatre than had been anticipated and this made the Japanese threat in the Far East relatively more dangerous than it would otherwise have been. Even though the strategic environment against which threats have to be assessed was of crucial importance, it was, and is, very difficult to predict its future character.

Much the same can be said about a country's general war-making capacities which, as one historian has recently remarked, should have a considerable bearing on estimates of threat. 'The Cabinet's failure', he wrote, 'to do the job of appraising (correct) military judgements against other factors is seen too in its acceptance of the Admiralty view that it would be fatal to get into war with Italy. While the Admiralty's fears may have been justly grounded in naval arithmetic, the Cabinet forgot to ask itself whether the Italian state was, regardless of the state of the Italian Navy, in a position to make war — which it was not.'[17]

It proved equally difficult to give an accurate weighting to such even more intangible factors as a nation's general morale. The ferocious fighting spirit of the Japanese armed forces, in particular, was insufficiently appreciated. This was doubtless mainly because of the cultural differences between observer and observed. It was very hard for the average British or American naval officer of the period really to understand for instance, the significance of the Japanese concept of *Gyokusai* ('it is better to be a gem that is smashed to atoms than a tile that is whole'), whose death rather than dishonour connotations had a considerable impact on Japanese notions of professional dedication, and which made them a particularly formidable foe.[18]

Western information about Japanese naval preparations was scanty for another much more pragmatic reason as well — the extreme secretiveness of the Japanese authorities. As one DNI commented subsequently: 'Japan, behind an impenetrable security wall had built up a fighting machine about whose composition and intentions we knew very little. Both we and the Americans erred, and there is hardly anyone who is entitled to say: "I told you so." '[19] The Japanese built the super-battleships *Yamato* and

Musashi in conditions of absolute secrecy. High fences were built round the slipways, the bases were declared out of bounds to foreigners and even construction personnel were allowed to see only small sections of the ship they were working on. When the ships were launched, the harbours were completely cleared. No information on exercises, ship design and, from the late 1930s, construction programmes and the naval budget was made available. Where necessary, lies were told.

Of course, the fact that the Japanese shrouded their naval preparations in such secrecy was in itself somewhat disquieting. In 1935, for instance, the British air attaché noted:

> The whole trouble is that I have no knowledge of the weapon efficiency of the Fleet and I doubt if anyone else has. It is true that I have to strain my imagination to the utmost to believe that these people are capable of springing a technical surprise of any importance on us in war: but when one does not know in the least how far advanced they are technically it cannot be ruled out of court.[20]

Also, despite the fact that the West did not practise the intrusive surveillance techniques so commonplace today, rumours about Japanese activities did occasionally get out. Nevertheless, Western intelligence-gatherers remained fairly relaxed about both Japanese secretiveness and the occasional worrying rumour. By and large, as the air attaché remarked elsewhere in the same report: 'All the other foreign naval attachés are firmly convinced that the unwillingness of the authorities to show more is due rather to the barrenness of the cupboard than to any secrets it may contain.'[21] Needless to say this was an impression which the Japanese were at pains to reinforce. In 1938, for instance, the British, French and American governments formally asked if the Japanese were still adhering to treaty limits. Japan replied that there was no reason for others to suppose that silence implied that the limits were being broken (which with the laying down of the huge 64,000 ton super-battleship *Yamato* three months before they certainly were); on the contrary, it was Japan's naval inferiority which made such secrecy necessary.[22] Most foreign observers were fairly satisfied that this was in fact the case.

Contemporary British attempts to monitor German naval performance also reveal the problems of collecting and interpreting information on the preparations of a navy consciously trying to deceive foreign observers. With the advantage of hindsight, we can see that the German navy influenced foreign perceptions of its capacity by four main tactics. In some cases, it sought to conceal the activity altogether; in cases where absolute concealment was impossible, it simply told lies; more often, however, it prevaricated over important details; finally, it spread from time to time what would now be called misinformation.

The tactic of absolute concealment was best illustrated by the German navy's covert involvement in submarine construction at a time when this was forbidden by the Treaty of Versailles. This was done by the establishment of firms in Spain, Finland and the Netherlands, which constructed eight very varied submarines for Turkey and Finland. The navy's involvement in this was heavy. In the Netherlands, for instance, a shipbuilding bureau was set up (*Ingenieurskantoor voor Scheepsbouw*). The bureau was dominated by the very gifted German naval architect, Dr Hans Techel, whose activities were supported by the blueprints and expertise of a talented design team from Krupps Germania Yard at Kiel. A secret firm called Mentor Bilanz liaised between the bureau and the navy until 1928 when it was replaced by another larger organisation called Igewit. The purpose of this liaison was to ensure that the German navy kept abreast of current developments in submarine technology and operation. The German navy was effectively able to hold extensive sea trials of most of these submarines before they were handed over to their customers. The speed and efficiency with which Germany was able to construct her own submarines when the time came bears eloquent testimony to the value of these covert arrangements. Also later in the 1930s, the German navy seems to have been able to conceal very effectively the extensive exercises and training conducted by Dönitz in the Baltic from 1935, where night surface-attack and wolf-pack tactics were perfected.

It was obviously impossible completely to conceal the construction of warships, or from 1935 (when it became no longer necessary for them to do so) of submarines. Nevertheless the German naval authorities do seem to have systematically lied about the standard displacement of some of their vessels. Although subsequent alterations certainly increased the weight of many German warships, a good many had a designed displacement considerably in excess of that officially communicated to foreign governments. The three *Deutschland* 'pocket-battleships' launched in 1933-4, for instance, should have been 10,000 tons according to the Treaty of Versailles but were in fact nearer 12,000 tons. Their destroyers also exceeded the individual limit that would need to have been met if the terms of the Anglo-German naval agreement of 1935 were to be strictly observed. In 1938, the *Friedrich Ihn*, for instance, was officially stated to be of 1,625 tons, but her actual standard displacement was 2,200 tons — an excess of 35 per cent.[23]

A more celebrated example was the battleship *Bismarck* whose standard displacement was said in 1936 to be 35,000 tons but which was in fact 41,700 tons. The length and beam of the ship were generally as officially stated but the draught (the only constituent of her dimension *not* verifiable by an external observer) was 34 feet not 26 feet as the *Marineleitung* claimed. These figures were generally accepted by the British. The naval construction department suggested that the large beam ('a striking feature') and the shallow draught were presumably necessitated by the depth of the Kiel canal and the Baltic and the Director of Naval Plans (Captain T.S.V. Phillips) argued that this all fitted in with German traditions 'and appears to show that Germany is looking towards the Baltic (i.e. Russia) more than in the past'. The then DNI later wrote that it had been assumed that the German navy must have accepted lower standards of speed, endurance and armour than was in fact the case in order to keep down to these dimensions. Accordingly, the *King George V* class was thought to be a reasonable match for the *Bismarck* although it was actually quite outclassed.[24]

The German naval authorities seem also to have indulged in patterns of prevarication consciously designed to mislead, notably over the inauguration of their submarine construction programme. They consistently denied that they were building submarines until the spring of 1935. On 12 April that year, the British naval attaché, Captain G.C. Muirhead-Gould, was informed of German plans and specifically told that no such building was in progress or, he inferred, in prospect. Two months later, Admiral Raeder officially admitted that 12 250-ton U-boats were in fact already under construction. Finally U-I was commissioned two months later on 29 June 1935.[25]

This systematic violation of the Treaty of Versailles was partially obscured by a smokescreen of half-truths. It was subsequently claimed, for instance, that the programme announced on 12 April 'was purely provisional and subject to revision at any time'.[26] The order for the submarines had been placed, it was said, after the date of Muirhead-Gould's interview, so no lies had in fact been told him. Admittedly the preparation of designs and estimates had been put in hand 'some months ago' and the manufacture of machinery, instruments, torpedoes and so forth had been initiated 'about Christmas'. Nevertheless these preliminary preparations (which made possible the very speedy construction of U-I) were said not to have constituted orders for submarines. The real 'order' was the last part of the process — the requirement 'to construct hull and assemble the component parts . . . The order was given by the Chancellor to Admiral Raeder. It was a *political* order not a naval one.'[27] Distinctions were also drawn between the manufacture of parts and components in various yards and factories (which did not constitute 'construction') and their ultimate assembly (which did). The speedy appearance of U-I awakened some public apprehension. In dealing with one such anxious enquiry, Captain V.H. Danckwerts (a member of the Admiralty team negotiating the Anglo-German naval agreement) pointed out that 'putting ships in commission' in any case probably meant different things to the British and German navies. He added: 'The question is largely dependent on the terms employed, none of which have any strict definition.'[28] This was true enough; there was certainly an element of natural ambiguity in these matters. Nevertheless, it is hard to resist the conclusion that the *Marineleitung* deliberately exploited these ambiguities for their own ends.

All these examples of concealment and duplicity were evidently designed to show the German navy to be weaker than it was. On occasion, however, the intention was the reverse; this was certainly the case with Hitler's manipulation of foreign estimates of German air power. A naval example of this seems to have occurred shortly before the war, when the German navy inspired false rumours of U-boats operating in the South Atlantic after the time of the Munich agreement − which led to a half-flotilla of British destroyers being detached to Sierra Leone. Partly because of this, but for other reasons as well, the British began the war with the impression that the Germans had 66 U-boats (having broken the terms of the 1935 Agreement) whereas in fact they had only 57, a mistake which caused some confusion until the matter was finally cleared up in the spring of 1940.[29]

Nevertheless, it would be wrong to suppose that the German navy was wholly successful in this campaign of duplicity. Few doubted, for instance, that Germany had engaged in general rearmament despite the Treaty of Versailles. One ex-member of the Allied Control Commission indeed wrote to *The Times* in 1933 arguing that Germany 'was not disarmed, never intended to disarm and ... did everything in her power to obstruct, deceive and counter the control commission'.[30] Contemporary evaluations of official German announcements of their naval programmes were peppered with references to their past 'record of mendacity'. 'I am surprised', wrote Muirhead-Gould in September 1935, 'at the Foreign Office being so concerned over Germany's morality. I should have thought that the Foreign Office would have realised that the German official never tells the truth except when it suits his purpose, and that he considers that his duty to his country entitles him to tell any story that he thinks will be believed.'[31] The British press were also disinclined to take official

German estimates at face value, and were instead prone to publish alarming, even alarmist, stories about German naval preparations.[32]

Despite all this, the British remained generally fairly relaxed about the discrepancies which came to light from time to time about Germany's naval activities. There seem to have been several reasons for this, mostly having nothing to do with the mechanics of the collection of material but with the process of its interpretation, and it is to the general problem of interpretation that we will now turn.

First of all, it remained the conviction of many observers that the Germans were not deliberately lying; rather should discrepancies be seen as a result of the complexity of the preparations being described. Certainly, when the Naval Staff addressed the problem of the information they should be passing across to the German navy in consequence of the 1935 agreement, they found it a difficult and complicated matter. As Captain Phillips wrote in 1936,

> During the period however the policy regarding both our building programmes and the strength we should aim at has been so constantly under review that it has not at any given moment seemed possible to draw up a forecast to which any degree of reliability could be attached.[33]

At a time when it was not altogether clear to the British what they were doing themselves, it was to be expected that a fair amount of latitude and understanding would have to be extended to the Germans. This feeling was reinforced by the generally good relations that existed between the two navies and by the view often taken of Admiral Raeder himself. One British naval attaché to Berlin wrote afterwards

> That Raeder lied to me and also to my predecessor is undeniable. Muirhead-Gould always said he had, but I fear I was lulled to a certain extent by his apparent sincerity, and moreover I found it hard to understand why he found it necessary.[34]

But even if the Germans were detected in deceit, the British felt they could be tolerant because they assumed that German naval preparations implied no threat to them. The supposedly shallow draught of Germany's major warships and their stress on small coastal submarines implied, as we have seen, that the Germans were thinking of naval operations in the Baltic not the Atlantic, and these were presumably to be directed against the Soviet Union.

Moreover it was widely assumed that German naval activities were largely 'political' in any case. Perhaps they were simply bargaining devices? Interestingly, after complaining about German duplicity over the inauguaration of their submarine programme, Muirhead-Gould remarked,

> I have no doubt that what has happened is that someone realised that the Naval Mission were going over to London with a very moderate programme for this year: so moderate in fact that it would give them no bargaining power. It was felt that they would be obliged to make concessions, and it was therefore decided to arm them with a bigger programme than had been announced, so that they could make nice generous gestures in deleting ships from the programme which they never actually intended to build.[35]

There was also the view that the German navy were really mainly interested in a *Gleichberichtigung* — an equality of rights. From this perspective, German naval preparations could be seen as a diplomatic device intended principally to reverse the unfairness of their general treatment since the First World War and to enable them to secure their rightful place among the nations. German plans did not, therefore, imply any particular military threat. In June 1935 for instance, the Naval Staff remarked,

> Should Germany exercise her power to build up to parity with ourselves in submarines, she could produce a formidable force of some 50 to 60 submarines ... This is a situation which must arouse some misgiving but it is quite apparent from the attitude of the German representatives that it is a question of 'Gleichberichtigung' which is really exercising their minds and not the desire to acquire a large sumarine fleet.

The Germans in fact 'are more likely to build up to submarine parity if we object to their theoretical right to do so then if we agree that they have a moral justification'.[36]

Looking back on this period, the then DNI pointed out that no one wanted to believe that these assumptions might be false and that German preparations were indeed a threat to British maritime security. 'The Naval Staff', he wrote, 'were not inclined to accept anything "awkward" from NID ... It was evident that no one wished to accept an extreme view ... No one was probably prepared politically to handle the resultant accusation.'[37] Reinforcing this reluctance to think badly of the German navy was the very strong conviction that the 1935 agreement was a thoroughly good thing from the British point of view. In January 1937, for instance, Admiral Chatfield called it a 'remarkable agreement, unique in world history ... of the greatest benefit not only from a military standpoint but from a political and international one. Its loss would be serious for both reasons.' This was still the view in 1938, when Phillips wrote from the Plans Division

> The Anglo-German Naval Treaty is probably the most valuable factor that we have today in the whole realm of defence, and what our naval problem would be if it did not exist or if it is denounced is difficult to contemplate.[38]

The agreement was seen as a means of limiting the size of the German naval threat and of bringing an element of certainty into an unknowable world. Given such assumptions, the tendency to give the German navy the benefit of the doubt becomes readily understandable; relaxed assessments of German naval preparations had the particular ring of preferred truth.

All these assumptions about the thrust of German foreign and strategic policy had considerable impact on the way in which information about the German navy was interpreted. In this way, assessments of capability could partly derive from assessments of intention. The same process was evident in the way that contemporary information about the Japanese navy was evaluated.

Although Japanese naval preparedness was a principal measure against which the Admiralty set its aspirations through most of the interwar period, this did not imply that the Japanese were necessarily regarded as hostile. In 1933, for instance, the DNI circulated a report about Japanese naval expansion, especially in the air, which contained figures at considerable variance with those recently circulated by the Japanese themselves 'with a view to showing how they have been disarming'. The DNI admitted 'there can be no question that any of these preparations are aimed at ourselves' but thought nevertheless that 'we must be interested in any increase in Japan's military preparations and consider our own strength in relation to hers'. But even this was going too far for some in the Admiralty. The Permanent Secretary, Sir Oswyn Murray, for example argued that a strong and positive Japan was preferable to chaos in China, Communism or the spread of Soviet influence. Britain should try to moderate Japan's methods, but not necessarily her objectives. 'In the meantime', he added, 'for want of a policy, we are required to attach an exaggerated importance, as it seems to me, to such reports as the present one.'[39] Apprehensions about Japan increased after this period, of course, but were still tempered by the view that Japan's expansion would not be primarily directed against the British Empire.

Among other considerations which affected the way in which facts about the undoubted expansion of the Japanese navy were interpreted, must be put prejudices and assumptions about the Japanese as a people. It is not difficult to find assessments of the Japanese which are frankly racialist in tone and erroneous in concept, and which also reflect the gap between western and Japanese cultures. The 1934-5 despatches of Captain G. Vivian, the British naval attaché at Tokyo reveal such attitudes with some candour. In 1934, for instance, Vivian reported on Admiral Yamamoto, the future leader of the Japanese navy,

> He is far from being the best type of naval officer being, as far as I could gather on short acquaintance, a man of little charm and extremely abrupt manner. He is obviously a hard drinker and is apparently well known as an inveterate gambler: in fact, he stated that his greatest interest is gambling in any form and poker in particular. It may be that his skill at this game has earned him his present appointment. (His aide was also addicted to whiskey) . . . Although a great many Japanese naval officers have the attributes which, to Western minds, are indicative of a 'gentleman' neither of these officers appear to be of that type.[40]

In the following year, Vivian extended his analysis to the people as a whole. He reported that 'the Japanese have peculiarly slow brains'. This was apparently due to the strain put on their minds when they were children by their having to learn 6,000 different Chinese characters even before formal education began. The damage this did was permanent and later showed itself in an inability to accept new ideas, and a reluctance to change things. Instead the Japanese stuck firmly to the textbook and specialised to a degree Western navies would find excessive. The Japanese were therefore in a bad position to keep abreast of technological innovation or to react with speed and efficiency to the sort of drastic changes and uncertainties that major war would undoubtedly bring. Captain Vivian was also at great pains to stress how difficult it was actually to get much information about Japanese naval training, exercises and the quality of their equipment. The implication was, however, that whatever their number of materiel the Japanese navy would suffer severe disadvantages simply by virtue of the fact that it was Japanese.[41]

Although the Controller, Admiral Henderson, sounded a note of caution about the extent to which the Japanese could really be said to be 'slow in the up-take', the report was generally well received. This was doubtless a comment not only on what Captain Vivian had said but also on the extent and scope of his investigation, which were plainly considerable. His views on Japanese thought-processes, for example, were not the product of passing speculation but of much discussion with English teachers in the country, especially at the Etajima Naval Academy. The fact that this report, probably the most thorough of the whole period, could get things so wrong was an indication not of the stupidity or carelessness of its author but of the width of the cultural divide which existed between watcher and watched. In all these cases, political and cultural assumptions clearly distorted the way in which information about the German and Japanese navies was interpreted.

There were, finally, several other more pragmatic reasons why evidence of the expansion of Japan's naval air forces or of the German submarine service was not taken as seriously as hindsight suggests it should have been. It was, for example, as difficult for the British as anyone else to test the technical efficiency of their own equipment and operational practices. Not surprisingly, their assessments of their own capabilities were wrong in some particulars and this obviously carried over into assessment of equivalent aspects of the other side's naval potential. Thus the Naval Staff appear to have overrated the efficiency of their anti-submarine measures, especially ASDIC. For this reason, the British were generally convinced that 'the submarine would never again be able to present us with the problems we were faced with in 1917'.[42] Accordingly, they were inclined to underestimate the significance of the expansion of the German submarine force.

The Royal Navy was apt to make its interpretations in the light of the weaknesses of British equipment as well as in that of its supposed strengths. To take one quite specific example, the aircraft-per-ton-of-displacement ratio of British carriers was actually rather low for most of the interwar period. Thus whereas the 22,600 ton *Eagle* could operate only 18 aircraft, and the *Illustrious* (23,000 tons) 36, the Japanese *Kaga* (26,000 tons) operated 60 aircraft and the American *Lexington* (33,000 tons) 84.

There were a number of reasons for this, including the fact that a high proportion of the British carrier force comprised old and inefficient first-generation vessels. Less obviously, the British did not for most of the period put aircraft in deck-parks — partly from choice and partly because they were behind in arrester wire technology. Although the Japanese and the Americans did use this method of increasing their carriers' aircraft complement, the British did not think such practices would be possible in war. The British also pioneered the whole concept of the armoured carrier, which sacrificed aircraft complement for high standards of protection against air attack.

All this tended to make the British very sceptical about the high aircraft-to-displacement-ton ratio of foreign carriers. In their assessments of foreign naval air strength, therefore, they were inclined to make careful distinctions between the aircraft a carrier 'carried' and those it could 'operate'. They accordingly underrated the effectiveness of a carrier like the *Lexington*. In May 1928, for example, Admiral Dudley Pound (then Assistant Chief on the Naval Staff) estimated *Lexington*'s effective complement as only 50 aircraft. In fact it was much more than this and in January of the following year, during the course of the celebrated Panama Canal exercise, *Lexington* flew off 83 aircraft in one morning.[43] Although in this particular case, the gap between reality and the Admiralty's perception of it narrowed thereafter, it had a significant impact on the way in which the British reacted to high declared levels of American sea-borne aircraft.

Finally, the British did not pay sufficient attention to the operational significance of the quality and large numbers of aircraft they knew existed in the Japanese and American fleets — mainly because they had so few aircraft of their own. They were aware of the fact that these two navies had larger air forces than they did, but not of what this fact meant. Accordingly, they did not realise the extent to which such numbers increased the effectiveness of nearly all the functions of air power at sea for these two navies. By virtue of their ability to launch massed attacks for instance, the Japanese and Americans were nearer the position where the role of air power at sea would be transformed from a secondary activity in support of the all-big-gun battle line to a primary, even dominant activity in its own right. In short, the Royal Navy did not grasp the tactical and strategic value of the air services of these two other navies, relative to its own.

Such comparative capacities were fundamentally a matter of emphasis and degree and so were particularly difficult for external observers to measure. Gauging them was not a mechanical process of collating the numbers and performance of the other side's aircraft, but of assessing intangibles, of analysing perhaps unspoken concepts and expectations. These things became apparent only in the context of exercises and operations. But, unfortunately, the Royal Navy was not well informed about foreign naval exercises in this period.

Like all other Western navies, the British knew little, for instance, about what the Japanese actually did in exercises with their naval air service. They knew of course that the Japanese 'seem to rely greatly upon submarines and aircraft to reduce the strength of the enemy . . . especially in the chains of islands in the path of the approach to Japan;'[44] but not much more than this. In 1935, the British naval attaché explained why this was so. 'No officer under the rank of Admiral', he wrote 'dare discuss any naval question with a foreigner', and they would not talk about tactics and practices at all.[45] Given this almost total absence of information, it is perhaps not surprising that the British should have failed to grasp quite the extent of Japanese aspirations in this field, and so failed to draw the right conclusions from the raw figures they had on the Japanese naval air service.

But, rather more unexpectedly, this is partially true of British assessments of American performance as well. The limits of British perception can be seen if we compare the British naval attaché's annual report from Washington for 1926 (actually dated 23 April 1927) with an attempt ten years later to contrast British and American naval air performance.[46] Both analyses were undertaken by air experts; in the first case it was the product of Captain the Hon. Arthur Stopford (a noted air enthusiast) and in the second, of the considered judgement of the Naval Air Division. Stopford's report was 74 pages long and dealt with all aspects of the US navy; it accurately recounted American carrier construction and detailed their plans for aircraft procurement, noted the different types of aircraft available and put proper stress on the administrative and personnel aspects of US Naval Air. None the less, it had virtually nothing to say about the role naval aviation was expected to play in fleet operations and warfare at sea generally. In consequence, it was insufficiently realised that, as the First Sea Lord (Admiral Madden) remarked some years later, 'the United States Navy is more advanced than we are in Naval air matters . . . I find they put a higher value on the Naval Air Arm than do the Admiralty and they are determined to increase it both in numbers and efficiency.'[47]

The story was much the same in 1936. Once again, practical and measurable issues like carrier construction policy, numbers of aircraft, personnel policy and technical progress were accurately described. But, said the report, it was difficult to compare the operational efficiency of the two navies 'when no really first-hand information is available about one of them'. The Assistant Chief of the Naval Staff commented: 'As I was afraid would be the case, our information is too scanty to provide any reliable data upon which to form an opinion . . . and I think it would probably be unwise to use this paper outside the Admiralty.'[48] These two reports make it clear that even when detailed information about naval air materiel was available it was still very difficult for the Naval Staff accurately to gauge how the other side would actually use it. Drawing the right operational inference from known details of the size and quality of the other side's equipment in the end proved beyond the Naval Staff's capacities.

Given the problem of discovering the other side's operational concepts, the tendency was for the Royal Navy to frame its interpretations in the light of its own experience. Thus in December 1937, there was a quite detailed report on ship attack tactics which discussed differing American views on low-level and dive-bombing and torpedo-dropping. But it failed to attract much interest because it was not quantified and so did not seem to imply that American operational practices were significantly different from the British.[49]

Nor in fact were they, in virtually all aspects but that of scale. But this was an important difference. Just over a year later, for instance, some units of the American fleet exercised in the Caribbean for 'Fleet Problem XX'. They divided into two fleets; the Black fleet had 72 carrier-borne aircraft and a further 164 on shore; the White fleet had three carriers with 216 aircraft. One single attack by the Black fleet comprised no less than 70 patrol bombers, 12 torpedo aircraft and 36 fighters.[50] The Royal Navy at this time was simply not in a position to aspire to the kind of tactical power such numbers represented. Its total air component on the eve of war, for instance, was only some 218 front-line aircraft. The British failed to pay sufficient attention to this vital difference, did not realise that tactical performance went up faster than the straight increase in numbers would suggest and so underestimated American and Japanese superiorities.

To summarise, explanations for failures in the Royal Navy's assessment of the capacity of foreign navies can be found in the process by which information was collected and interpreted. These deficiencies led the British to underestimate quite seriously the capacity of the German and Japanese navies to do them significant harm. Of course, the Royal Navy realised that fundamental uncertainties in their assessments remained — as in fact they always do. The military's usual solution to this problem is to frame their assumptions on the basis of the worst case and to make sure they err on the side of safety in their consequent preparations. But the strategic, political and economic environment in which the Royal Navy found itself in the 1930s prevented it from resorting to this normal expedient. As a consequence, it soon found itself in difficulty when the particular capacities that it had underestimated were clearly revealed for the first time in the early years of the Second World War.

Notes

1. Naval Staff notes for the 1937 Naval Estimates, 26 February 1937, ADM/116/3596.
2. This is a major theme in the author's *Air Power and the Royal Navy* (Jane's London, 1979), subsequently referred to as *Air Power*. See particularly chap. 6.
3. Views of General Von Falkenhausen, repeated in Hong Kong report of 5th February 1938, ADM/1/9587.
4. Report of Vice Admiral G.C. Dickens, Director of Naval Intelligence, 20 May 1935, ADM/116/3862.
5. Report of the air attaché to Tokyo, included in the naval attaché's report of 29 April 1936.
6. Captain S.W. Roskill, *Hankey: Man of Secrets*, vol. 1 (Collins, London, 1970), p. 81.
7. Admiralty letter to the Treasury, 17 February 1927, Keyes 8/3, Churchill College, Cambridge Archive Centre.
8. Chatfield, minute of 3 October 1936, ADM 116/4030.
9. A.R. Wells, 'Studies in British Naval Intelligence', unpublished PhD Thesis for the University of London, 1973, p. 349 and F.H. Hinsley *et al.*, *British Intelligence in the Second World War*, vol. 1 (HMSO, London, 1979), pp. 52-3.
10. P. Beesley, *Very Special Intelligence* (Hamish Hamilton, London, 1977), pp. 9-10.
11. Admiral Sir Stephen King-Hall, *My Naval Life* (Faber, London, 1952), p. 223.
12. Wells, 'Studies in British Naval Intelligence', pp. 372-3.
13. For such arrangements in 1919 see Air 2/122/B9685 and more generally *Air Power*, chap. 5.
14. Commander M. Ellis, minute for NAD, 28 June 1938, ADM/1/9649.
15. Chatfield, letter of 3 November 1933 to Admiral W.W. Fisher, CHT/4/5, National Maritime Museum, quoted by permission of the Trustees.
16. *Air Power*, pp. 63-4.
17. Peter Calvocoressi, letter to *The Times*, 1 August 1970.
18. A. Marder, 'Bravery is Not Enough', a lecture delivered to the University of California at Irvine, June 1979, p. 9.
19. Admiral J.H. Godfrey, 'Naval Memoirs' (unpublished), referred to subsequently as Godfrey, vol. V, part 1, p. 77.
20. Air attaché's addition to the naval attaché's report of 18 February 1935, ADM/116/3862.
21. Ibid.
22. S. Pelz, *Race to Pearl Harbour* (Harvard University Press, 1974), pp. 200-1.
23. For official comments on this and other ships see ADM/116/3368.
24. Minutes by S.V. Goodall and Captain T.S.V. Phillips of September 1936, ADM/116/3368. Also Godfrey, vol. V, part II, pp. 243-54.

25. P. Marcelle, 'Naval Rivalry Renewed', unpublished PhD Thesis for the University of Cambridge, July 1970, pp. 113 ff.
26. Raeder, letter of 28 May 1935 in *Documents on British Foreign Policy*, Second Series, vol. 13, subsequently referred to as DBFP (London, HMSO, 1973), p. 211.
27. Ibid.
28. Danckwerts, letter to Mr Gore-Booth of the Foreign Office, 18 July 1935, *DBFP*, p. 535.
29. Godfrey, vol. VIII, p. 113 ff.
30. General J.H. Morgan, letter to *The Times*, 4 November 1933.
31. Muirhead-Gould, letter of 14 September 1935, *DBFP*, p. 642.
32. For instance see Hector C. Bywater, 'Plans for a Navy Second to None', *Daily Telegraph*, 4 April 1934.
33. Phillips, Minute of 19 October 1936, ADM/116/3929.
34. Captain T.H. Troubridge, letter, quoted in Godfrey, vol. V, part 11, p. 248.
35. Muirhead-Gould, letter of 29 May 1935, *DBFP*, p. 313.
36. Ibid., p. 332.
37. Godfrey, vol. V, part II, p. 258.
38. Chatfield, minute of 8 January 1937 and Phillips, minute of 11 January 1938, ADM 116/3929.
39. Minutes by J.S. Barnes, Admiral G.C. Dickens and Sir Oswyn Murray of January-February 1933, ADM 116/3116.
40. Captain G. Vivian, letter of 5 September 1934, *DBFP*, p. 34.
41. Captain G. Vivian, report dated 18 February 1935, ADM 116/3862.
42. Quoted Wells, 'Studies in British Naval Intelligence', p. 376.
43. Pound, minute of 27 May 1928, ADM 116/2550.
   Memo by Vice Adm G.C. Dickens of 20 May 1935, ADM 116/3862.
45. Report by Captain Vivian, 18 February 1935, ibid.
46. Respectively to be found in ADM 116/2430 and as a NAD Memo of 16 September 1936 in ADM 116/3722.
47. Admiral Madden, after a conversation with Admiral William Moffett, Chief of the US Navy's Bureau of Aeronautics, minute of 14 February 1930, ADM 116/3479.
48. Rear-Admiral C.E. Kennedy-Purvis, minute of 15 December 1936, ADM 116/3722.
49. Naval Staff Report of 21 December 1937, ADM 1/9072.
50. P. Abbazia, *Mr Roosevelt's Navy* (US Naval Institute Press, 1975), p. 33 ff.

7 NINE EXAMPLES FROM RECENT INDIAN EXPERIENCE, 1962-1980

Ravi Rikhye

Introduction

Though India is a democracy, in matters of defence-related information it is a closed society. After the 1971 Indo-Pakistan War, thanks largely to the pioneering efforts of the Institute for Defence Studies and Analyses in New Delhi, a great deal more public discussion takes place than was previously the case. None the less, any debate involving the military must still proceed without access to core material which is invariably classified.

Inevitably, therefore, much reliance has to be placed on discussions with people who refuse to be quoted. Using such sources, this study covers nine examples of the way the balance of military power in South Asia was assessed or mis-assessed from 1962 to 1980. These are:

1. The Indian failure to predict the Chinese attack in 1962.
2. The Indian failure to predict post-1962 military expansion would lead to war with Pakistan.
3. The failure of Pakistan to predict the Indian attack south of Kashmir in 1965.
4. The failure of Pakistan to predict Indian strategy in East Pakistan in 1971.
5. The failure of India to predict US intervention in the 1971 war.
6. The failure of India to predict Pakistan would rearm after the 1971 war.
7. The failure of the *Military Balance* (IISS, London) correctly to estimate Pakistani tank strength.
8. The difficulties in estimating reinforcements available to the Pakistan Air Force in wartime.
9. The failure to appreciate that India is stronger than China along the Northern borders.

In five of these nine cases (1, 2, 3, 5 and 9), adequate intelligence information was available, but the assessment procedure failed for various reasons. In one case (4), an entirely correct prediction paradoxically contributed to disaster. In two cases (6 and 8), there are genuine limitations on the intelligence available. In one case (7) the wrong assessment has been made by a foreign agency, and the reasons for this are unknown.

Case 1. Failure to Predict the Chinese Attack in 1962

Background to the Case

The overrunning of the Indian 4 Infantry Division at the Tse La Pass in November 1962, was the greatest defeat of arms suffered by independent India. For ten years that defeat crippled every expression of Indian nationhood; two decades later, though mitigated by the 1971 victory, it still overshadows India's foreign and military policy.

When, on 18 September 1962, the Indian 7 Infantry Brigade was ordered to clear the Chinese from Thagla Ridge, north of the Tse La Pass, the army had deployed a grand total of five brigades against the Chinese: one brigade in Ladak, one in Sikkim, one in the western Northeast Frontier Agency (NEFA, now the State of Arunachal Pradesh), one in eastern NEFA, and one on loan to Nagaland.[1] The Chinese strength on 7 September 1962, was assessed by the Indian Intelligence Bureau at over 7 divisions deployed on India's borders, plus 3 or 4 more in reserve.[2] The estimate was made in great detail: 6 infantry battalions facing north Ladak; 8 facing southern Ladak, Punjab, and Himachal Pradesh, 23 facing Nepal, 9 facing Sikkim, 5 facing Bhutan and 19 facing NEFA. The Chinese reacted to the efforts to recover Thagla Ridge by staging a massive invasion of India's northern borders. Why was the reaction not anticipated, and why did the Indian Army think it could take on the Chinese in NEFA with one brigade of three battalions?

Discussion of the Case

Part of the problem was that the army refused to accept the Intelligence Bureau estimates. The army felt China had a maximum of five divisions in Tibet, and could, at best, sustain two in combat.[3] It is not known how the army arrived at its estimates, since at that time it had no means of independently gathering information about Tibet. It is probable that the army was relying on British and American estimates and that these, for reasons unknown, were off the mark by a factor of two or more. As for the supposed Chinese ability to support no more than two divisions in combat, it is possible the army was using Indian logistic requirements as a yardstick. At that time, these ran at a minimum of 130 tons per day of supplies for an infantry division.[4] The other part of the problem

Figure 7.1: China, Northern India and East Pakistan

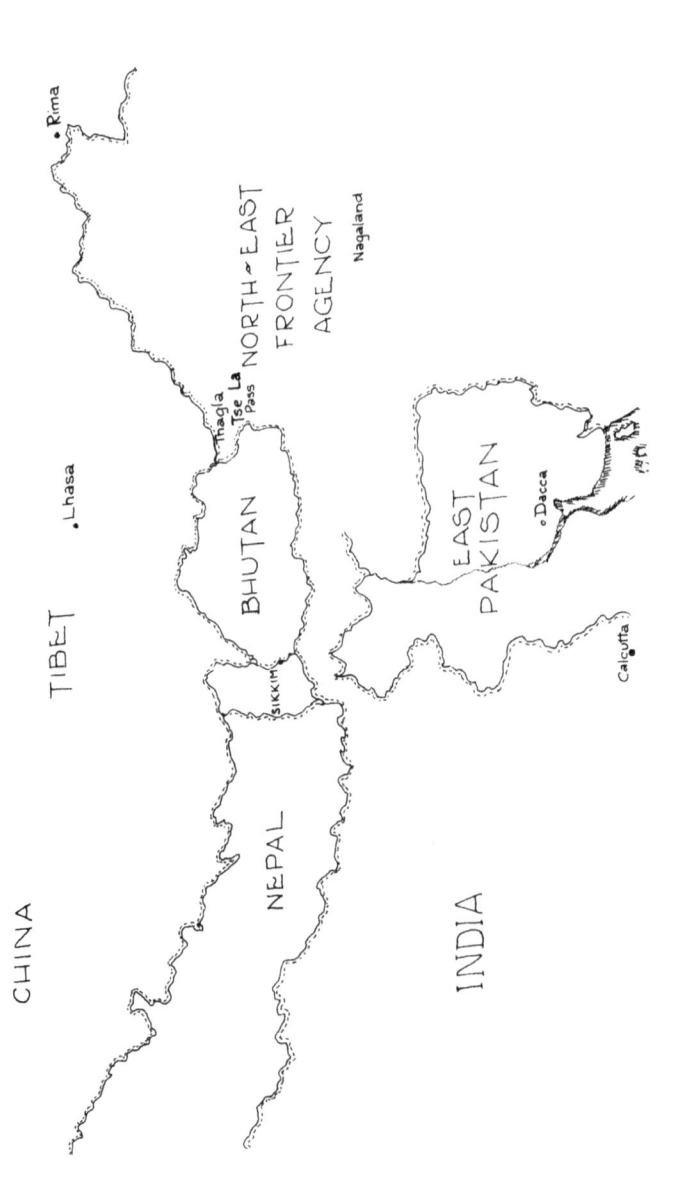

was that the political assessment held that the Chinese were unlikely to do more by way of retaliation than seize a couple of outposts elsewhere.[5] This view was not wholly fantastic: the battle of the checkposts had been going on since 1959 without escalation. Still, this was not a mere extension of the battle of the checkposts. This was a heavily publicised major attack operation. Common sense alone would have allowed for the possibility of Chinese retaliation.

What makes the Indian misjudgement all the harder to justify is that the Intelligence Bureau had been warning of an imminent Chinese attack, expected in at least the Ladak sector, since June of that year. Some think that E.N. Mullick, the Director of the Bureau at that time, was merely justifying himself by saying, after the event, that his department gave repeated warnings to the government. His book, *The Chinese Betrayal*, was written after the establishment of a new intelligence organisation, the Research and Analysis Wing, took over external intelligence and assessment because the Bureau was alleged to have failed in its job. There is, however, also the evidence of Brigadier John Dalvi, Commander of the Indian 7 Infantry Brigade, the formation ordered to clear Thagla Ridge. He has said that though the Chinese had begun their preparations in May 1962,[6] the troops of his parent formation, the Indian 4 Infantry Division, were not on alert: 'they had been told that there was no threat of war till the railway line to Lhasa was completed'.[7] Since it was still incomplete twenty years later, and then must have been only in the planning stage, clearly the army anticipated no attack for several more years.

The author has asked the question of many officials with direct knowledge of the 1962 war: Why were all these intelligence warnings disregarded? The uniform and laconic answer is that the credibility of the Bureau at that time was low. The answer surely begs the question, yet that is about as far as it is possible to go. Even so, why send one brigade to do the job when the army itself felt two divisions could be sustained by the Chinese, and why post 5 brigades on the front against their forces three times larger? The army's position is difficult to comprehend because apparently many senior officers were quite aware of the danger. Two examples suffice.

Neville Maxwell notes in his study of the campaign that the General Officer Commanding, Eastern Command (the seniormost officer responsible for the NEFA sector), had drawn up well thought-out plans for defence of the North-east as early as October 1959.[8] In 1961, the

Chief of the General Staff had estimated that a minimum of two divisions with six brigades were required for the defence of NEFA.[9] Had such a force been in place when the Chinese attacked, instead of just two brigades, the story of the 1962 war would have been different. In the event, India was to rush a total of 25 infantry battalions, the equivalent of almost three divisions, to NEFA;[10] even this proved inadequate because of the initial loss of ground and the resulting panic.

The second example concerns the north-western borders. Here the local commanders did heed the intelligence warnings, and were therefore much better prepared to meet the Chinese onslaught. The normal force of one brigade for Ladak was augmented by two spare brigades from Kashmir.[11] Consequently, though territory was lost, there was no disaster to match Tse La Pass. The enemy held the initiative, and concentrated at will by turns in different sectors, thanks to an excellent lateral road;[12] because of the wide frontage involved, losses were inevitable. Later, India was to modify its strategy to cope with such tactics in the future. The matter is discussed in Case 9.

After Tse La, the army sought to make a case that it was ill-equipped and outnumbered. This, however, was not the case.[13] There were problems with warm clothing and training, but it was a matter of improper organisation and planning, not an absolute shortage. Outnumbered the army most emphatically was not, considering the excellent defensive positions it enjoyed and considering its firepower superiority, which included light tanks. It was more a question of the army being totally unprepared despite three years' warning time. An example of this unpreparedness is the speed with which India raised new divisions, and the alacrity with which it shifted divisions from the Punjab to the North-east, once the Chinese had attacked. In September 1962 only the 4th Division was in the North-east; within three months the army had raised the 2, 3 and 8 Infantry Divisions,[14] and shifted the 5, 17, and 27 Divisions from the Punjab. Thus, very quickly, India increased its deployment on the northern borders to no less than seven divisions. Of course, three divisions came from the Punjab, where they formed the main defence against Pakistan. Yet there were many loose brigades and battalions lying around. If these had been formed into divisions before the crisis, India could easily have had a division in Ladak, one in Sikkim, two in NEFA, and one in reserve deployed in Nagaland, for a total of five.

The thought is inevitable that, had the army displayed such initiative before the crisis, the political assessment might have been proved correct. With less than two Indian divisions facing eleven Chinese divisions or more (the Chinese later moved in other divisions from outside

Tibet to build their force to 14 divisions[15]), the Chinese were taking no risks in teaching India a lesson. But had there been, say, five Indian divisions in place by mid-1962, the Chinese might well have had to restrict their retaliation for Thagla Ridge to seizing a couple of posts elsewhere.

The purely military reasons for India's failure are irrelevant to the discussions. The real failure was one of assessment. Had Chinese intentions, and capabilities, been correctly assessed, the army was professionally experienced enough to respond. This is borne out by the conduct of the campaign in the north-west. The reasons for the failure of assessment were:

(i) Shortage of basic hard intelligence data;
(ii) Absence of proper dissemination of whatever information was available;
(iii) Lack of proper assessment organisation, for both political and military intelligence;
(iv) Excessive reliance on foreign agencies for provision both of hard data and of assessment.

There is some question about the Intelligence Bureau director himself. Despite his lack of credibility with the army, once the crisis was upon India, Mullik appears to have exercised a great and possibly inordinate influence on tactical and strategic matters completely unrelated to the field of intelligence. This is apparent from his own book; Maxwell also comments on it. This influence was probably due to the trust the Prime Minister reposed in him. And oddly, Mullik, despite his prescience was responsible — along with the Ministry of External Affairs — for advising the Prime Minister that China would not react violently to the move at Thagla Ridge.

A last point concerns the decision not to use the Indian Air Force in combat. Because the IAF was very well-equipped and excellently trained, its use could have turned the tide of defeat. Mullik attributes the decision to the advice of 'our foreign friends',[16] who in this case were the CIA. A grossly exaggerated picture of the capability of the Chinese Air Force for retaliation was built up. Many years later one Indian official summed up the worth of the CIA's advice: 'We were taken for a ride.'[17]

Case 2. Failure to Predict the Post-1962 Expansion would lead to War with Pakistan

Background to the Case

Before the Sino-Indian Border War, India had around ten divisions; Pakistan had nine in being or under raising. Though the Indian army had more combat units, Pakistan had an equipment edge. A condition of approximate parity existed. After the 1962 conflict, India embarked on a plan to expand its army to 22 divisions, later modified in 1964 to 25 divisions. This included 10 mountain divisions. Given Indian fears after the 1962 disaster, the large number of mountain divisions was understandable. But how did five extra infantry divisions, plus a major expansion of the air force and navy, find its way into the programme? At no time did India pay the slightest heed to the impact of its build-up on Pakistan.

Pakistan's reaction, as could have been expected, was immediate. It felt that China was being used as an excuse for the build-up, which would ultimately be employed against Pakistan.[18] In the event, Pakistan was proved right, though this could have given it little satisfaction. In 1965 three divisions designated for use against China were deployed against it;[19] in 1971, six of the seven divisions used against East Pakistan were mountain formations. As there was no question of Pakistan matching the Indian build-up, its solution to the problem was to try to recover Kashmir by force before the growing Indian strength made it impossible.

Discussion of the Case

It is difficult to determine what was the exact rationale behind the extra infantry divisions as the decisions are classified. Four guesses are possible:

(a) The 1962 defeat perhaps induced such paranoia in India that the army decided to cater for the worst case, a combined attack by Pakistan and China. While 20 divisions were adequate for this contingency, it is possible an extra margin of safety was added.
(b) The army expected an expansion of the Pakistan army in response to the addition of mountain divisions and wanted to counter this without calling on any northern divisions.
(c) Pakistan's technological superiority was perhaps so worrying that India did not reckon the military balance just in terms of divisions, and wanted to compensate for technological superiority by numbers.

Nine Examples from Recent Indian Experience

(d) No specific threat was visualised, and the extra divisions were provided for an unforeseen contingency. This view can be supported by noting that four of the divisions were intended to be reduced strength formations, expandable in emergency.

To assess how the extra divisions affected Pakistan, it is necessary to see what the line-up was prior to the 1962 war. On Pakistan's side, the following units were in service or under raising:[20]

Figure 7.2: The Indo-Pakistan Frontier

East Pakistan:	14 Infantry Division (possibly raised only in 1965)
West Pakistan:	
Holding	12 Infantry Division (Kashmir)
	15 Infantry Division (Sialkot)
	10 Infantry Division (Lahore)
	11 Infantry Division (Kasur) (possibly raised only in 1964)
Reserve:	1 Armoured Division (probably Multan)
	7 Infantry Division (Peshawar)
	8 Infantry Division (Quetta)
	9 Infantry Division (Kharian)

On India's side the matter is more complicated. To make the assessment a variety of sources has been used.[21] The approximate line-up was:

Eastern India:	4 Infantry Division (NEFA)
	20 Infantry Division (Nagaland) (May have been 23 Division)[22]
Western Front:	
Jammu/Kashmir:	19 Infantry Division (Baramula)
	25 Infantry Division (Poonch-Rajouri Sector)
	26 Infantry Division (Jammu)
Punjab:	5 Infantry Division (Jullunder)
	17 Infantry Division (Ambala)
	27 Infantry Division (Amritsar)
Reserve:	1 Armoured Division (Jhansi)
	10 Infantry Division (probably Bangalore)

Looking at the matter from Pakistan's side, by 1967 it expected a line-up in the West that could have looked like this (this is only illustrative, based on the actual deployment for the 1971 war):

Sector	India	Pakistan
1. Eastern	8 divisions	Jaisalmer & Barmer
2. Kashmir	4 divisions at Baramula, Poonch, Chaamb and Jammu	1 division (14th) 1 large division (12th)
3. Punjab	4 divisions at Samba, Pathankot, Amritsar and Ferozepur	4 divisions at Sialkot, Shakergarh, Lahore & Kasur (9th, 15th, 10th, 11th)
4. Desert	2 divisions at Jaisalmer and Barmer	1 division (18th)

Sector	India	Pakistan
5. Reserves	1 armoured	1 armoured (1st)
	3 infantry	1 infantry (7th) divisions
	2 mountain divisions	
6. Other	1 division at Leh	

Thus, in the east, Pakistan would be outnumbered by 9 divisions to 1; in Kashmir, as the Indian 3 Infantry Division out of Leh could also be used against the Pakistan Sector of the Northern Cease Fire line, Pakistan would be outnumbered by 5 divisions to 1 (though probably 4 to 1 in battalions); in the Punjab it would have parity; in the Desert 2 divisions to 1; and in reserves, 2 to 1. It is then hardly surprising that Pakistan felt threatened. Even if China was to intervene on Pakistan's side, India could hold China off with six divisions, still giving it a three-to-one superiority in the east and a two-to-one superiority in the west, in terms of divisions alone. None of this takes into account India's plans to build up 45 air combat squadrons, a force four-and-a-half times as large as the Pakistan Air Force. The situation was scarcely helped by various Indian moves in 1963-4, which were interpreted by Pakistan as aiming towards an irrevocable integration of Indian-held Kashmir with the Indian Union.[23]

Pakistan's solution to the problem, as mentioned earlier, was to attack and take Kashmir before India became too strong. Now, it is hardly to be expected that top Pakistani decision-makers would blandly admit that this was their plan. In fact, Mr Z.A. Bhutto, then Foreign Minister of Pakistan and later its President, claimed that it was India which attacked Pakistan.[24] None the less, a conversation that Mr Bhutto had with Indian journalist Kuldip Nayar comes as close to an admission as it is possible, perhaps, for a politician:

There was a time when militarily, in terms of the big push, in terms of armour, we were superior to India . . . and that was the position to 1965. Now, the Kashmir dispute was not being resolved, and its resolution was essential for the settlement of our disputes and as it was not being resolved peacefully and we had this military advantage, we were getting blamed for it. So it would, as a patriotic prudence, be better to say, all right, let us finish this problem and come to terms, and come to a settlement.[25]

Air Chief Marshal Asghar Khan's book about the 1965 air war, *The First Round*, also has revealing comments on how Pakistan saw the Indian military build-up.[26] President Ayub Khan (1958-65) has left a detailed account of his worries on the score.[27] Asghar Khan carefully refrains from suggesting war was a solution to the problem. From his comments on President Ayub's reaction to the impending danger, it is clear that in 1963, the President had no answers. Later, however, he obviously did find the answers, because it was under his rule that Pakistan attacked India.

The first thing to appreciate is that India has never subscribed to the idea of a military balance between Pakistan and itself. If, in 1962, there was a rough balance, it was by accident rather than design, due more to emphasis being given to other arms rather than the army. This can be seen in the rapid expansion of the navy and air force since 1953, and the even bigger expansion planned for the air force. For example, in 1962 the IAF had two-and-a-half times as many fighter squadrons as the PAF; by the end of 1961 the expansion to 45 squadrons had been sanctioned.[28] (The 45-squadron target was not a consequence of the 1962 war as commonly believed.) The IAF would soon have been four-and-a-half times larger than the PAF.

This steady air and naval build-up was, incidentally, conducted under the Prime Ministership of Mr Nehru, who also laid the foundations for India's arms production base. It is then ironical to have him accused of ignoring India's defence needs. Anyone who can sanction a 45-squadron air force when the only adversary at that time has 10 squadrons is hardly ignoring defence. And such a person certainly does not subscribe to the theory of parity and arms control. If the army was being ignored in the build-up, it was possibly because of Mr Nehru's distrust of the army, his fear of coups, rather than for any other reason.

Whatever Mr Nehru might have said about the need to avoid force, he understood only too well the virtues of force. He had used it many times to maintain India's territorial integrity (Kashmir, Hyderabad, Goa, China border). The shock of 1962 led the government to agree to whatever the army wanted: and the army, naturally enough, wanted as many divisions as it thought the country could afford. The last thing anyone was worrying about at that time was how Pakistan would react. Not only was there no logical reason for the army to have wanted arms control and balance, the very language, the terminology itself, the concepts, were missing from the vocabulary of the Indian soldier, as in those days it was missing from just about every soldier's. A country bought whatever it could afford, or what it needed. No one bothered about destabilisation. Even if the vocabulary had existed, parity is a concept applicable to equals. Since India and Pakistan were not equals, there could be no parity. It was, and is, as simple as that.

The Indian army has always conducted tactical war-gaming exercises – if we attack here with one corps the enemy will react thus, and so on. Strategic gaming is a much more complex and sophisticated procedure – if we add 10 divisions how will Pakistan react in the next 5, 10, 20 years? The need for strategic gaming is obvious. Had it been conducted from 1963 onwards, it is possible that India could have anticipated that Pakistan, lacking the resources to match the Indian build-up, would have to try to grab Kashmir. If this had been anticipated, the Indian government as a whole would not have looked blank when the Kutch incident came. It would have known exactly how to react. In retrospect, it is clear that had India counter-attacked in the Kutch, Pakistan would not have been emboldened to escalate the conflict to Kashmir.

India could have gained much from working all this out beforehand. Nevertheless, strategic gaming was – and is – a tool that is lacking both in Indian foreign policy and military planning. When the whole concept was unknown, no one can be blamed for failing to utilise it. By 1971 some degree of sophistication had been reached. The Indo-Soviet Treaty was signed because it was realised that China and the US could negate India's plan for East Pakistan. Yet, the thinking was confined to what lay ahead a few months at a time. Comprehensive and long-range strategic gaming for India lies in the future.

Case 3. Pakistan's Failure to Predict India's Attack South of Kashmir in 1965

Background to the Case

In August 1965, Pakistan began sending infiltrators across the cease-fire line into Kashmir. The backbone of the infiltration force was provided by the Pakistani 12 Infantry Division, whose dynamic commander had, in fact, originated the idea.[29] The idea itself was sound. A frontal attack in Kashmir was highly unlikely to succeed. Not only had India fortified its mountain positions for almost 18 years, it also had numerical superiority. If, however, infiltrators were sent to link up with the Pakistani underground operating in Kashmir, the Indians would be faced with fighting guerrillas at the same time as trying to put down a local uprising all across the state. For a variety of reasons the infiltrations alone did not score the desired success. India had so pampered and bribed Kashmir that it is possible the inhabitants decided they were better off under India than Pakistan. It is also possible that the Indian security forces, which were already very large, and which were speedily augmented from other parts of the country, were more effective than

Pakistan had anticipated.

At any rate, on 14 August 1965 (coincidentally Pakistan's Independence Day), Pakistan began to send uniformed regulars across the cease-fire line. India immediately responded: on 15 August (Indian Independence Day), Indian infantry battalions began crossing the cease-fire line to seal off infiltration routes. It is possible that the violence of the Indian reaction was not earlier anticipated. In particular, the occupation of the Haji Pir bulge in western Kashmir, a classic case of a first-rate infantry action, disturbed the Pakistanis as their communication line between North-west and South-west Kashmir was blocked.

Pakistan's response was to launch a brigade of its 7 Infantry Division, on 1 September, supported by two tank regiments at Chaamb in Jammu, with the aim of taking Akhnoor. Though the Indian 10 Infantry Division had begun arriving at Akhnoor towards the end of August to stiffen the defences of the area, there was only a battalion to meet the attack. The Indians were forced back, and for a moment it appeared that Akhnoor would fall. Had this happened, the way to Kashmir would have been exposed. Jammu, in the east, could have been subjected to a two-flank attack (with the second thrust coming from Sialkot); and Naoshera in the north would also have been open to a two-flank attack. Jammu was the gateway to Kashmir; Naoshera protected the entire north-south line of Rajouri-Poonch-Uri-Tithwal, encompassing all of western Kashmir. The loss of Akhnoor would, therefore, have led to the blocking and isolation of all Indian forces in Kashmir.

In view of the gravity of the threat, India crossed the international frontier in the Lahore Sector, its XI Corps attacking along three axes of divisional-strength each. This caused Pakistan to pull out its 7 Division from Chaamb; further to ensure the safety of Akhnoor, the Indian I Corps launched an attack with four divisions from Jammu, towards Sialkot, on 7 September 1965. The Pakistani riposte to the Indian attacks south of Kashmir was to launch its 1 Armoured and 11 Infantry Divisions south of Lahore, through Kasur. The aim was to get behind Amritsar, then seize the bridges over the Beas, have a straight and easy run to Ambala and then to Delhi.

This bold plan could easily have succeeded, for India was fully committed all along the line: there were absolutely no reserves behind XI Corps, and the Punjab lay wide open. It is scarcely surprising that some generals advocated a withdrawal across the Beas before XI Corps was trapped. To have pulled back, however, would have been to give Pakistan certain victory, as it could have occupied the Punjab and traded it off for the whole of Kashmir. The southernmost prong of XI Corps was diverted further south along with Indian 2 Independent Armoured Brigade to meet the Pakistan thrust. This prong happened to be the same Indian 4 Division (now converted to a lighter mountain configuration) that had broken at Tse La in 1962. The Indians stopped the Pakistanis at Khen Karan, and saved the day. Though Pakistan likes to believe that it could have continued fighting and could have won the war,[30] the reality dictated acceptance of the Soviet cease-fire initative. Pakistan was running out of ammunition and India was starting to bring up fresh troops from the east.[31]

Discussion of the Case

Clearly Pakistan failed to anticipate the attack across the international frontier.[32] One retired army officer even goes so far as to say that 25 per cent of the Pakistan army was on leave on the outbreak of war.[33] India had repeatedly made it apparent that any attack on Kashmir was an attack on India itself and the response would be delivered accordingly.[34] After the Kutch incident in April 1965, India began moving additional divisions into the Punjab and Jammu sectors. For example, the 1 Armoured, 4 Mountain and 14 Infantry Divisions, all reserve formations, moved at this time.[35] How is it that Pakistan so totally misread Indian intentions? To give a reply is difficult, if only because this chapter is written without recourse to any except the skimpiest of Pakistani sources.

Part of the reason may lie in the Pakistani perception of the historical precedent. Despite several incidents, major and minor, between the two countries, there had been no escalation.[36] Yet, this was scarcely a reliable precedent; the Indian hold on Kashmir had not been threatened by these incidents as it was by the Pakistani assault in August 1965. Undoubtedly India's failure to respond to the Kutch incident also played a part in shaping Pakistani perceptions.

But again, to draw conclusions from this would be misleading, because the Chief of Army Staff, General J.N. Chaudhri, refused to commit the Indian army to action as communications in the area were bad and the rains were due.[37] Pakistan should have relied, instead, on Indian troop movements, which were a better guide as to its intentions. It is possible that a good deal of wishful thinking was responsible for the faulty Pakistani assessment. If it was accepted that India could retaliate south of Kashmir, then the Pakistani conquest of Kashmir was impossible. Though the forces that India deployed immediately in the area may not have been substantially superior to Pakistan's, it was just a matter of time before divisions from the East arrived to change the balance irrevocably against Pakistan. If it was accepted that the job in

1965 was impossible, that was the end of Pakistan's chance to take Kashmir, because by its own assessment, as recounted earlier, by 1967 India would be too strong.

The question then arises: Why did Pakistan wait till 1965 before taking on India? Why not 1963, or at the very latest, 1964? First, it appears that during the Sino-Indian Border War, the US obtained (or more likely forced) Pakistan to give an undertaking not to attack India.[38] Secondly, the Pakistan army may not have been fully ready for war in 1962.[39] For one thing, it is likely that the Pakistan army wanted another armoured division to give a decisive superiority over India in armoured strike capability; the Pakistani 6 Armoured Division was activated in 1964 using the 106 Independent Armoured Brigade as a nucleus. Thirdly, though there is no evidence available to determine the question one way or the other, Pakistan may initially have been worried about the vulnerability of East Pakistan to Indian attack; though of course, if Pakistan believed India would not attack south of Kashmir then it probably also assumed that no attack in the East was likely.

But then why stage a dress rehearsal in April 1965, giving India ample warning, and why delay the attack at Chaamb till the infiltrators had shown that they alone could not do the job? The reason for the first is probably Pakistan's sense of insecurity and inferiority *vis-à-vis* India's growing strength. Though militarily it threw away the cardinal principle of surprise, it was probably politically necessary, both to convince the doubters in Pakistan, and possibly even to convince the exponents of the scheme themselves. The gradualism in Pakistani escalation was due both to wrong assessments of India's capabilities in hunting down the infiltrators, and to the political need to show the world that the 'uprising' was a genuine revolt by the Kashmiris, thus limiting open use of the army.

In passing, it may be noted that while Indian intelligence assessments had improved between 1962 and 1965, they were still inadequate. For example, the existence of Pakistan's 6 Armoured Division and the strength of the Icchogal Canal obstacle system were known to Indian intelligence. The news, however, either was not properly disseminated to the army, or (as in the case of 6 Armoured Division), the army refused to accept information gathered by civilians.[40] Another nasty surprise for the Indians was the strength of the Pakistani resistance around Lahore, mainly on account of the very tough fight put up by the Pakistani militia (Local Defence Units). Later, of course, the army was to deny that Lahore was an objective.[41] But Lt General Harbaksh Singh, the GOC Western Command, and responsible for operations against Pakistan, did announce publicly 'Gentlemen, we will soon be having dinner in Lahore.'[42]

Possibly, however, the greatest Indian assessment mistake of the war was the failure to realise Pakistan was running out of supplies and could not continue the pace of the war. It had been noted at the front that in the last week, the firing rates of Pakistani artillery regiments began to drop sharply. The US had obviously kept Pakistan on a very tight leash as regards ammunition and reserves.[43] Had the implications of the drop in firing rates been appropriately analysed, India might have decided to continue the war and not to accept a cease-fire and the resulting stalemate.

Assessments about Pakistan's decision-making processes are hampered by the same problems as assessments about India, only to a greater degree. Censorship is more severe. Decision-makers are less inclined to write of their experience. Analysts to evaluate the results produced by the decision-makers are fewer in number. And there is a greater tendency to write for propaganda purposes, to justify or glorify whoever happens to be ruling. As such, discussion on the reasons for Pakistan's failure to anticipate India's attack south of Kashmir must involve much speculation.

The parallels with India in 1962 become immediately apparent in that both sides ended up making incorrect assessments though adequate data was available. Pakistan also lacked an impartial, high-level assessment body to evaluate intelligence information. There appears to have been the same wishful assumptions, made by strong-willed men of action anxious for results regardless of the consequences. Decision-making seems to have been conducted, as with India, on an *ad hoc* basis, with favourites getting the ear of the top leaders. (Asghar Khan is quite revealing on this, but it needs to be kept in mind that he is heavily involved in domestic politics and may not be being entirely fair to President Ayub.)

Many Indian army officers are of the opinion that, up to 1971, the chief failing of the Pakistan army was an overrating of its capabilities. The martial classes which comprise the Pakistan army were the Punjabis, Baluch and Pathans, all with a great belief in the attack, but an attack carried out without thinking. Indian officers are quite familiar with this syndrome, not only because many of them served together with their Pakistani counterparts, but because India also has its equivalents of those martial classes (the Punjabis, Sikhs and Jats). The Pakistanis believed, till 1971, that one of their men was worth three Indians. This kind of thinking is needed to inculcate a high morale, but it can not make up for bad staff-work, poor co-ordination between arms, inept armour handling, indifferent reconnaissance, or similar problems which afflicted the Pakistani forces.

Chiefly because of the superior weapons which Pakistan obtained from the United States, the Indians tended to overestimate the Pakistanis. When every military and governmental official became slightly hysterical on hearing the words 'Patton tank' and 'Sabre fighter', it is possible the Pakistanis started believing what the Indians said. In fact, the Sabre was never really better than the Indian air force's Hunter, and the Patton was never really that much better than the Indian army's Centurion. This is not a retrospective statement; any Indian who had cared to read the literature on weapons should have realised as much.

The Indian defeat at Tse La was so ignominious that it is possible the Pakistanis, already operating under a belief that 'Hindus cannot fight', were further reinforced in their beliefs.

Case 4. Failure of Pakistan to Predict Indian Strategy in East Pakistan in 1971

Background to the Case

By October 1971, the Indian deployment around East Pakistan was complete, Lt General A.A.K. Niazi, the General Officer Commanding, Pakistan Eastern Command, and responsible for the defence of East Pakistan, quite correctly assessed that he could not hold off the Indians with just the three divisions he had in the field (Pakistani 9, 14 and 16 Infantry Divisions); accordingly, he requested two more divisions from the west.[44] These were denied to him and he was told to raise the two divisions from local resources. Whereupon, he had to carry out a wholesale reorganisation of his forces, to produce two new 'divisions', the 36 and 39 Infantry Divisions.

His true state, incidentally, can be gauged by the actual deployment of infantry battalions. The following is gathered from the account given by Eastern Command's Information Officer, who presumably should know what he is talking about:[45]

9 Infantry Division — about 9 infantry battalions
14 Infantry Division — about 6 infantry battalions
16 Infantry Division — about 6 infantry battalions
36 Infantry Division — about 2 infantry battalions
39 Infantry Division — about 7 infantry battalions

This adds up to 30 battalions, the equivalent of three divisions, and includes the last-minute reinforcement of three battalions received by Eastern Command.[46] This figure is supported by the then Indian Deputy Director of Military Operations, who says that the Pakistanis had given designations of battalions in the west to paramilitary and militia units, leading the Indians to believe there were at least 35 battalions in East Pakistan.[47] Against this force, India had massed seven divisions, together with brigades from other divisions and independent brigades. Possibly something like 80 or more infantry battalions were available.

General Niazi had deployed his divisions to hold the frontier. As his forces were so thin on the ground, he had absolutely no reserves besides the odd battalion or so each division might have gathered as local reserves. The Indians broke through by employing mobile warfare tactics; if General Niazi had failed to anticipate this, he can be forgiven, because the Indian army had never used anything except orthodox linear warfare tactics before. In fact, it was using linear tactics in the west all during the while it was using mobile tactics in the east, because of the differing personalities of the various commanders in the two theatres. Once the Indians had broken through the frontier defence, as there were no reserves, Pakistan was as good as defeated.

General Niazi has been severely criticised by both sides for not using an alternative strategy, which was to defend the Dacca Bowl, behind the very broad and fast-flowing East Pakistan rivers.[48] India, it is said, would have found it very difficult to cross those rivers.

Discussion of the Case

General Niazi defended the frontiers, and not the Bowl, because he expected the Indians only to seize strips of territory around East Pakistan, permitting the return of the refugees and the declaration of an independent government of Bangladesh.[49] Today, the General is probably passing around copies of an Indian book to all his critics. This book, by the then Indian Deputy Director of Military Operations, says that the decision to go for Dacca was made well into the war.[50] The implication is, quite clearly, that General Niazi's assessment was right. And that, ironically, is what cost him the war, because, of course, there was no way he could foresee that Indian plans would change to take advantage of the situation as it developed. Incidentally, the Dacca Bowl could not, in any case, have been held. This is clear also only in retrospective. For the first time, the Indian army and air force got together to use helicopters to cross the river lines.[51] No one could have predicted this: in the west, for example, there was no effort to use helicopters despite the very tough obstacles all along the front. India's air supremacy and Pakistani lack of reserves made impossible any counter to the New Indian tactics in the east.

The reasons for Niazi's failure are so apparent, that no further discussion is required. It is instructive, however, to see how Pakistan found itself in such a difficult position in the first place. From the start of the crisis Pakistan knew that since the east could not be directly defended, an attack in the west would have to be launched.[52] The size of the force committed to the east, three divisions, was determined by the need to fight the rebels, not to defend against India. At the same time, Pakistan had failed to build its strength in the west to ensure a reasonable chance of victory there. To let itself be manoeuvred into a two-front war was, then, to sacrifice the three divisions in the east to no purpose.

Both the Indian build-up in the east from May 1973,[53] and the Indo-Soviet Treaty of August 1971,[54] should have made it apparent to Pakistan that a real possibility of war in the east existed. Appropriate measures should have been taken even earlier, when the civil war broke out, giving India a fertile field for intervention. Pakistan had been repeatedly disappointed by the US since 1965.[55] China had failed to intervene for Pakistan in 1965, when its risks in doing so were less than in 1971. Neither side had promised intervention to save Pakistan in the east.[56] It was foolishness, then, to expect that intervention would make up for Pakistani defence shortcomings.

Wisdom after the event is often a singularly pointless attainment; none the less, it is worth noting that Pakistan could have spared the 18 battalions that Niazi wanted to secure the east. India played hundreds of war games over several months to determine its optimum strategy. If Pakistan had been doing the same, it would have been apparent that more troops could have been sent to the east. For example, India had 13 divisions to Pakistan's 12. In 1965, Pakistan had stalemated India's offensives with 9 divisions to India's 11, and the defences after that had been greatly improved. It is possible to show that Pakistan could have spared the whole of the 33 Infantry Division while still maintaining intact its two strike forces, and that six battalions could have been shifted from the Kashmir sector, without affecting Pakistan's defences in any way. It could still have fought the 1971 war exactly as it did. This would have made 15 battalions for the east – 3 had in any case been sent. With a total of 45 battalions in the east, Pakistan would have had ample reserves behind its border defence (30 battalions up at the front and 15 in reserve). The generals in the west not only failed to provide for the east, they mismanaged their resources in the west. Thus, there was neither stalemate in the east, nor victory in the west to offset the loss of the east.

Case 5. Failure of India to Predict US Intervention in 1971 War

Background to the Case

In 1962, the United States sailed an attack carrier task force from the 7th Fleet to help India during the Chinese invasion.[57] It would have required an extraordinary seer to foretell that just 19 years later another US carrier task force would sail from the Pacific, this time to thwart India. On 12 May 1977, Richard Nixon told the television commentator, David Frost, that the USS *Enterprise* had been intended as a signal to India that the US would not tolerate the break-up of West Pakistan as a sequel to the detachment of its eastern wing.[58] Henry Kissinger's memoirs, *The White House Years,* confirms this was the case.[59]

India has maintained that it had no designs on Pakistan, and as such the *Enterprise* was sent for other reasons. What was the reality?

Discussion of the Case

Though at that time it was widely believed that the US intended to intervene on Pakistan's side, later, informed Indians put forward the theory that the purpose of the ship was to evacuate the Pakistani troops in East Pakistan; if necessary, by force. The US ships were to cover the sailing of several Pakistani-owned and chartered merchant ships, which would actually embark Pakistani troops. This theory is advocated both by Admiral S.M. Nanda, then commanding the Indian Navy,[60] and by Vice Admiral N. Krishnan, then commanding the Eastern Fleet and responsible for the naval aspects of the Bangladesh operations.[61]

Evacuation by force can be ruled out, if only because until the advent of the F-14 *Tomcat* fleet interceptor, it was standard US practice to work carriers in pairs if shore-based early warning was unavailable. In the absence of shore-based early warning, a minimum of four standing patrols of two interceptors each are required to be maintained at all times for fleet defence, and a single F-4 *Phantom*-equipped carrier cannot do this. Even the F-14 equipped carriers can conduct this mission only for three days.[62]

Also, the *Enterprise* entered the Indian Ocean only on 15 December 1971, after idling off Singapore for four days.[63] It could not have reached Chittagong before 16 December. Already by 14 December cease-fire terms were being worked out between the Indians and Pakistanis,[64] so that on 15 December all that would remain was the implementation of the cease-fire and the signing, which took place on 16 December. Since evacuation was not the mission, there is little choice but to believe

Nixon and Kissinger when they say the *Enterprise* was sent to prevent an Indian attack on West Pakistan.

The question then becomes: since India has denied it had designs on the west, was US intelligence wrong? No, because while India was quite prepared to reassure the US that it had no designs on the west, as T.N. Kaul, the then Indian Foreign Secretary, has himself related, he told the US ambassador that 'we reserved our right of sovereignty over the whole of Kashmir'.[65] Further confirmation, if any is needed when the evidence of the Foreign Secretary himself is available, comes from Indian journalist Pran Chopra: 'Even according to CIA reports read at WSAG meetings, the Soviet Union was reconciled to India continuing the War for a while to complete the eviction of the Palistani forces from Kashmir'.[66]

The evidence from the field is that India intended to continue the war in the west to regain Kashmir. No fewer than seven divisions were planning major offensives which would start around 19 December;[67] for these offensives to be balanced, it was necessary that at least five other divisions attack simultaneously. In other words, virtually the entire Indian army in the west was girding up for the new offensives.

The Pakistanis had been pushed back during the first series of offensives, between 3 and 10 December approximately. With one exception, they were in no position to launch any attacks against India, being too busy fighting for their lives. The one exception was Pakistan's II Corps, the southern half of the Pakistani Strike Force (the northern half, Pakistan's I Corps, was heavily committed delaying the advance of Indian I Corps into the Shakergarh salient). This could have attacked between Fazilka and Ganganagar, though the odds were unfavourable, even before 11 December onwards, when Indian 9 Infantry Division started arriving from the east, to reinforce further India's armoured division and three brigades.

There was thus no reason to continue planning new offensives, right up to the minute of the cease-fire. This could have been declared on 16 December, instead of a day later. So intent was India on concentrating the maximum possible force in the west that it even started pulling out the tanks committed to the east by 9 December,[68] though it already had total armour superiority in the west and fighting in the east was still underway. Similarly, fighter squadrons were being rapidly shifted to the west[69] though they could have helped the combat in the east, and despite the fact that India had already forced the Pakistan air force to restrict itself to defence of its air bases. If all this is not to be treated as wholly conclusive, the circumstantial evidence, at least, is very strong, that India intended to continue the war in the west.

It it is accepted that India planned to liberate Pakistani-occupied Kashmir, the question arises: how did India so badly misjudge the possibility of US intervention? There is only one answer possible, but unfortunately there is only secondary proof of the matter. The Soviets had assured India that they would deter the US if need be.[70] If this be the case, then India once more made the mistake of relying on a foreign assessment of its adversary's capabilities just as it had accepted CIA estimates of Chinese air power in 1962. If India had only made its own assessment of the US-Soviet military balance, it would quickly have become apparent that the Soviets had no capability to deter the US in the Indian Ocean.

On a tactical level, it is known how completely misleading were the Indian military's assessments about its own capabilities vis-à-vis the *Enterprise*. For example, the Indian air force was prepared to form a volunteer 'suicide squadron' against the ship; the navy considered using a submarine to ambush the task force.[71] Neither service appeared concerned with how it was to detect the task force in the first place. Any reconnaissance aircraft would have been turned aside hundreds of miles from the carrier by its fighter escort. The Soviets were several days behind the task force. The task force would have stayed a minimum of 200 miles away from the coast and covered the evacuation by air. Even had it been detected, there was very little hope for Su-7s, Hunters or Canberras to reach the *Enterprise* through its E-2 Hawkeye/F-4 Phantom screen. And even should some planes have managed to crash its deck, nothing would have happened beyond disrupting air operations for a few hours. Similarly, for a successful ambush a conventional submarine would have to know the exact track of the task force. This was because the force had a cruise speed far above that of the submarine, making interception impossible. And since the task force was travelling without an anti-submarine warfare carrier (this was before the days of mixed attack/ASW air groups), it is probable that one or two attack nuclear submarines were with the force, precisely to take care of underwater opposition.

In all fairness to the Indians, their zeal and 'can do' spirit is commendable. And there was a deliberate element of bravado in the contingency plans, because no one seriously expected to have to go up against the *Enterprise*. But it is to be hoped that Indian military planners are now spending more time reading their *Jane's Fighting Ships* and making more realistic assessments.

Oddly, in the end the Americans gave the Soviets credit for restraining India,[72] possibly because the channel of communications was through the Soviets.

Case 6. Failure to Predict Pakistani Rearmament after 1971

Background of the Case

In the euphoria that followed India's 1971 victory, there was a general consensus that Pakistan would no longer be able to maintain its military establishment as before, on account of the loss of the eastern wing, and therefore the threat to India was greatly reduced.[73] Yet, by the end of 1973 or early 1974, Pakistan had expanded the number of divisions in its army by 50 per cent. Whereas at the time of the cease-fire in 1971 it had 12 divisions, it now had 18. Its expansion continued, so that its tank force had increase to virtual parity with India; its air force had been largely re-equipped; and its navy was stronger than before.

Paradoxically, once Pakistan emerged as being clearly superior compared to its pre-1971 establishment, because of a shift in Indian perceptions, the increased strength was no longer a source of worry. How did Pakistan manage this expansion despite the loss of East Pakistan? It is useful to analyse the matter not only because of the situation *vis-à-vis* India, but because Pakistan now faces a new threat in its west, and the following can provide clues for Pakistan's capability to meet it.

Discussion of the Case

In December 1971, the Pakistan armed forces were probably down to approximately 300,000 men. By 1980, the figure was over 500,000.[74] For a poor, populous nation, adding more infantry manpower is no problem. In 1980-1 terms, Pakistan probably spends around $1,500 per man per year in the army, exclusive of equipment.[75] This is a very low and quite affordable figure for a poor country. Manpower can be no problem when good jobs are hard to come by and a country has a population of 80 million.

Freed of the drag generated by East Pakistan, the rest of the country shot ahead economically in the decade following the 1971 War. The GNP grew from Rs 43 billion in 1969-70 (West Pakistan only) to an estimated Rs 264 billion for 1980-1[76] (economic figures are from *Pakistan Economic Survey 1979-80*, a government document, unless stated otherwise). Meantime, prices, measured in 1969-70 terms, rose by a factor of 3.5. So there has been a real growth in Pakistan's economy, averaging 6.2 per cent between 1972-3 and 1979-80. The real growth impact has been dissipated by the phenomenal increase in Pakistan's population, at an approximate 3 per cent rate annually. So Pakistan remains a very poor country, but thanks to the absolute increase in GNP due both to inflation and real growth, Pakistan has managed to increase its defence spending from the Rs 3 billion in 1970-1 (the combined GNP of both wings is estimated at Rs 77 billion in that year[77]) to Rs 14 billion in 1980-1 (estimated budget — the revised budget is likely to be larger, but figures are unavailable at time of writing).

Thus, though defence spending has increased almost five times, its impact on the GNP has gone up from around 4 per cent in 1970-1 (both wings) to 5.3 per cent in 1980-1, and this is quite manageable. As a percentage of net federal revenues, which are often a more important indicator of the defence burden for a poor nation than GNP, the burden has been coming down sharply in recent years, from a high of 58 per cent of federal revenues spent on defence in 1972-3, the first full year after the war, to 38 per cent in 1980-1. That is still somewhat on the high side, but hardly unbearable.[78]

The real constraint on a poor country's defence effort is, frequently, foreign exchange to buy weapons. After all, the expenditures in local currency are helping the economy, by providing wages and purchases in the local economy. Spending the money on defence may not be as productive as investing the money elsewhere, but it does yield benefits. But buying weapons with foreign exchange does not aid the country's economy, if the country is generally short of foreign exchange in the first place.

Prior to 1965, Pakistan's equipment needs were met entirely by the US on an aid basis, so foreign exchange for weapons was not an issue. After 1971, Pakistan has been dramatically increasing its foreign exchange earnings. Of course, it is running enormous deficits, but the absolute sums of money available to it are much larger, so that is in a position to lay out increasing sums of money for weapons on its own. For example, between 1969-70 and 1979-80[79] its exports increased from US $161 million to US $2,360 million, or a factor of 14. Its trade deficit increased from $168 million to $2,128 million during the same period. Let it be assumed that the Pakistan government feels it can spare, say, 10 per cent of foreign exchange for weapons without ruining the economy.[80] Then, if in 1969-70 $16 million was available, in 1979-80 $236 million would be available. In terms of what weapons cost in 1969-70, $16 million was insignificant. For example, about five Mirage fighters could have been purchased for the money. But the 1979-80 figure would be much more substantial. 1981 delivery Mirages are costing Pakistan $10 million each[81] so that now 26 could be bought with one year's allocation.

Thanks to astute diplomacy, by 1979 Pakistan had obtained something like $800 million worth of arms through the Arabs and Iran and

$2 billion as gifts from China.[82] Its own defence budgets between 1972-3 and 1978-9 totalled somewhat under $5.3 billion. Of course, the figures for arms gifts include Chinese deliveries from 1966 onwards, but allowing two-thirds as post-1971 shipments, that would still imply that Pakistan met 40 per cent of its actual defence spending from gifts of arms. Put another way, its actual defence spending from 1972-3 to 1978-9 was $7.4 billion, not $5.3 billion. This trend is continuing. Though China now wants payment for arms supplied, Saudi Arabia is continuing to give large sums of money to Pakistan for arms purchases. It is very difficult to tell what this figure is, especially now that Pakistan is to station troops in Saudi Arabia[83] and will, presumably, be paid handsomely for this, but figures up to $3 billion have been mentioned.

Thanks to a combination of the four factors discussed above, Pakistan has been able to rearm. In 1971, it had 12 divisions to India's 13 in the west, and India could call on at least 3 more divisions from the east even if there was war with China. The true balance was 12 divisions for Pakistan to 16 for India, or 1.25 in India's favour. Today, however, Pakistan has 21 divisions (including one it calls a 'Force Command'), while India can deploy 22 divisions after leaving adequate defence against China, for a ratio of 1.05. Numerically, at least, India is defineitely worse off. Yet, the Indian military assessment of today no longer considers Pakistan an overriding threat. How has this come about?

It is first necessary to ignore the repeated and strident alarms raised by Indian politicians about this Pakistani threat.[84] The politicians have their own reasons for such statements, but since they do not bear much on reality, they are, for the purpose of this analysis, best ignored.

As late as 1978, a common assessment among army officers was: 'The Pakistanis can come in and take over some of our territory. We have the capacity to retaliate and take over some of their territory.' In other words, the situation was perceived as stalemate. Today, the more common assessment is: 'If Pakistan were to get in a surprise attack, it could cause us problems. But our intelligence today is good enough so that a surprise attack is unlikely. For the rest, we can handle them without trouble.'

First, it is necessary to see that no one is making claims about being able to destroy Pakistan. The realisation exists that the power of modern defence is such that it makes the destruction of Pakistan impossible. International intervention would always occur, preventing a long, drawn-out war which India would win by virtue of its greater resources.

Next, it is necessary to see that there is no improvement in the Indo-Pakistan military balance that justifies the newfound confidence. For example, in 1971 India outnumbers Pakistan by a factor of 1.6 in the number of medium tank regiments; in 1980, India's advantage is down to 1.1. In 1971 the Pakistan air force was outnumbered by a factor of 4 in high-performance aircraft (Mig-21, Mirage 3/5, F-104); today the gap is down to a factor of 3 (Pakistan will soon have 6 Mirage squadrons of its own plus at least the equivalent of two more from the Arabs; India will soon have 24 squadrons of Mig-21s, Jaguars and Mig-23s). In some areas, like submarines, Pakistan has maintained its numerical parity but has qualitative superiority.

Rather than being fuelled by changes in the balance, India's perception has altered because of its growing confidence in itself. The 1971 assessments were wildly exaggerated, due to simple paranoia about Pakistan. Today, because of a number of positive developments, like India's nuclear test of 1974, growing modernisation of the armed forces, a stable polity, increasing intelligence-gathering ability, and enhanced, proven crisis management ability, India knows it can handle the Pakistanis.

At the same time there has been growing awareness of Pakistan's problems. These problems include political disunity, economic shortfalls and slowness of military modernisation; all these are common to India in greater or lesser degree. The major change is that with the Soviet intervention in Afghanistan, Pakistan faces a serious two-front defence problem, so that it can no longer concentrate all its troops against India. So, while Pakistan is growing stronger, India is worrying about it less.

In retrospect, it is clear Indian analysts failed to predict the following: (i) rapid Pakistani growth in GNP and exports after the loss of the east; (ii) Pakistan's successful alliance with the Arab states, particularly Saudi Arabia, as a means of obtaining money. The growth of GNP and exports was not fully foreseeable at the end of the war. In an underdeveloped country, managerial and political constraints are more of a factor in economic growth than the absolute availability of resources. Making estimates based on purely economic considerations is pointless; predicting how managerial and political factors will operate in the future is virtually impossible.

As for the alliance with Arab states, in 1971 the oil states were still to reap their immense bonanza in revenues, and it would have been a brave man who predicted that Bhutto would be overthrown and replaced by a general professing Islamic fundamentalism as a way of getting money out of Saudi Arabia. After this assessment failure, entirely understandable in itself, there is a growing sophistication in the approach to Pakistan. There are a number of reasons for this, not solely an appreciation of the

220 *Nine Examples from Recent Indian Experience*

limits of Indian assessment procedure. A decade later it is rare to find an Indian analyst making snap and superficial judgements about any aspect of Pakistan.

Case 7. Failure of Military Balance to Assess Pakistani Tank Strength Correctly

Background to the Case

An odd aspect of the *Military Balance* (International Institute for Strategic Studies, London) is its repeated mis-estimates of the Pakistani tank force. In 1980-1, the *Balance* gives the number of Pakistani medium tanks as: 700 T-59, 250 M-47/-48, 50 T-54/-55, and an unspecified number of M-4s. This adds up to 1,000 tanks, say 1,500 including the M-4s. India is given 2,120 mediums, which is roughly correct, with 950 Vijayantas, 1,100 T-54/55s, and 70 T-72s. The reader is then quick to assess India as being twice as strong in medium tanks.

Discussion of the Case

Till 1965, Pakistan had maintained a lead in the number of tank regiments of around 16 tank regiments to India's 14. This lead was lost by 1971: India had 27 regiments to Pakistan's 22 or 23, which actually overstated Pakistan's true strength, because only 14 of its regiments were mediums, compared to India's 25 medium regiments. After the war, Pakistan has kept relative parity with India. In 1974, for example, Pakistan had 25 regiments to India's 29; in 1975, 29 regiments to India's 31; and in 1978 (the last year for which the author has specific information), 32 or 33 regiments to India's 34. Since India is today manning around 40 regiments, it is likely that Pakistan has between 36 and 38 regiments.

The 1978 breakdown was as follows:

22 T-59C regiments
 6 M-47/-48 regiments
 2 upgunned Sherman/Bulldog regiments
 2 T-54/-55 regiments

Since Pakistan uses 45 tanks per regiment, allowing for a modest 10 per cent reserve, Pakistan would require something like 1,550 mediums in 1978 (excluding the upgunned Bulldogs). At the lower end of the estimate for 1980, i.e., 36 regiments, some 1,700 mediums are needed; at the upper end, about 1,800 mediums (allowing for two regiments of light tanks).

Pakistan is known to have four regiments on the M-48 upgunned medium, added after 1978, and is acquiring the Chinese T-60 light tank. Thus, it is likely that the T-60 is replacing the Sherman/Bulldog combination, and that the M-48 upgunned mediums are to be added to the above list. Pakistan is awaiting delivery of 500 or so TAM 105 mm gun tanks, and it may acquire 200 Shir 1 tanks from the UK. There are reports that it should have, or is in the process of getting, another 200 M-48 upgunned tanks. Meanwhile, Pakistan has opened a tank rebuild factory with Chinese help. It is likely that the T-59s will be upgunned in the manner Indian T-55s have been modified; possibly the M-47s will also be converted to 105 mm gun configuration. At present, it is impossible to say if Pakistan will use its new tanks to replace older tanks, or whether the older ones will be rebuilt and the new ones used to increase tank strength. It can be assumed that the answer will depend, at least in part, on how fast India expands its tank force.

Another anomaly in the *Military Balance* is that it was only in the 1977-8 edition that Pakistan was finally conceded three armoured brigades, though it had raised them as far back as 1970. In that year a defence review had decided that Pakistan lacked sufficient reserves, so a redeployment of infantry divisions was undertaken, to form two reserve corps with a total of three infantry and two tank divisions. As part of the reorganisation, tank regiments from infantry divisions were withdrawn and two new armoured brigades raised, giving Pakistan the 2, 3 and 8 Independent Armoured Brigades. Now Pakistan has five independent tank brigades.

The *Military Balance* gives Pakistan 550 M-113 armoured personnel carriers in 1980-1 when actually it had around 830 with more on order. In 1971, Pakistan had 300 M-113s. Its losses were minor, and were made up by friends and allies. In 1973 delivery took place of 300 more, ordered in 1970 but delayed for various reasons including the Pakistan War.[85] In 1976, among other items, 230 M-113s were ordered,[86] but delivery was delayed due to US-Pakistan disagreements about the latter's nuclear policy. These APCs are now in the inventory. According to information in India, in 1980 further orders were placed, or were under negotiation.

In this particular case there is a probable explanation of the *Balance's* figure. It is possibly unaware that the 1971 losses were made up, accounting for a shortfall of 50 APCs. Because of delays between receipt of information and publication in the *Balance*, the 230 APCs on order in 1976 were probably not recorded in the 1980-1 issue. As for the 1980 order, the *Balance* is probably waiting to obtain official US or Pakistani confirmation before listing the deal.

It is unclear why the *Military Balance* has consistently underestimated Pakistan's tank force for the last decade. Many Indian analysts and military men suspect it is not ignorance but a deliberate attempt at making Pakistan appear weaker than it is. None the less, that suspicion is not easily provable.

Case 8. Difficulties in Assessing Reinforcements Available to the Pakistan Air Force in Wartime.

Background to the Case

Possibly the greatest single problem facing Indian intelligence regarding the Pakistan air force is assessing its reinforcements available in wartime. During the 1971 war, the PAF received last-minute reinforcements from two Arab nations. Jordan sent 10 F-104A Starfighters, and Saudi Arabia sent some F-86 Sabres, possibly as many as 20. These increments were too small to affect the outcome of the air war. After the 1971 war, Pakistan began posting pilots and technicians to several Arab air forces. The move served both Pakistan and the host nation's needs. Pakistan obtained an opportunity for free flying on other's aircraft, plus an opportunity to tap their stocks during wartime; the host nation obtained training for its own developing air force, plus a degree of operational capability otherwise not possible.

The first such arrangement was made with the United Arab Emirates' air arm (which today consists of 32 Mirage 5s). Then Pakistan went on to station personnel in Libya and Saudi Arabia, and to involve itself in active exchange programmes with Iran and Jordan. Co-operation with Turkey has been a more or less constant feature. Aircraft reinforcements from Arab nations would help Pakistan both to enhance reserves for its own first-line squadrons, and to add to the number of first-line squadrons. In both cases there would be a substantial increment in Pakistani air strength; and it becomes important for India to know how many aircraft will be involved. There are, however, serious problems with making this evaluation.

Discussion of the Case

Relations between Pakistan and its Arab friends keep changing. For example, Pakistan's relations with Iran today are quite unsatisfactory; and with Libya a good deal cooler than was previously the case. Relations with Jordan, Saudi Arabia and the UAE remain very close. But there is no way of knowing what happens if Pakistan is in danger in the event of a war. Will Libya and Iran put aside their differences with Pakistan and supply war materiel? It is impossible to predict their reaction in advance.

How many PAF pilots serving in other countries are on detachment from their squadrons in Pakistan, and how many are actually extra to the PAF manning requirements? This is important to know because from this information can be derived how many planes will come in as reserves, and how many will be added to front-line strength. There is a difference in the outcome depending on which course is taken. For example, if the pilots are on detachment, it can be expected the PAF order of battle will show 6 Mirage squadrons (including units to be formed when the present Mirage 3/5 order of 32 aircraft plus 18 more has been fulfilled), and there may be reserves of, say, 9 aircraft per squadron, permitting endurance in a longer war. But if, on the other hand, the PAF pilots abroad are extrà to the normal order of battle, then India might have to face a line-up of, say, 9 Mirage squadrons, including three coming in from abroad. That would increase combat power by 50 per cent for a short war. There are other permutations and combinations possible, for example, adding a fifth flight of four aircraft to each squadron, bringing the Operational Conversion Unit and the Fighter Leader's Squadron to full strength, increasing maintenance reserves, and so on. It may seem that all India needs to know is how many aircraft will come from abroad. The way they are deployed and used, however, affects the tactical situation in wartime. Because of the great flexibility the Pakistanis have in the matter, it is impossible to foretell the pattern in advance. How many aircraft will come into Pakistan? Will Libya, for example, be generous and tell Pakistan to take every single Mirage 3/5 that is flyable, or will it be miserly? Will the UAE find itself willing to spare 8 aircraft, or 12, or 24? This also cannot be answered in advance.

Fourth, will the US permit Jordan and Saudi Arabia to transfer aircraft, specially the F-5E? Pakistan can, at present, very rapidly activate three F-5E squadrons because it has enough pilots trained on the type, and even technicians to do first-line maintenance. For more serious work, the planes would be flown back to their home bases. But will the US allow transfer? Will Saudi Arabia defy the US because of its oil power in the event the US does not agree? There is no way of knowing the answers; yet, for the IAF, they are quite vital. Fighting the Mig-19 is one thing, fighting the F-5E quite another.

Will the host nations transfer technicians to help maintain these aircraft? Jordan, in particular, maintains its own aircraft and the other countries, especially Iran, Saudi Arabia and the UAE, are steadily becoming more competent. The Iranians, for example, can handle virtually all F-5E systems. If these nations, or some of them, decide to transfer technicians as well as aircraft, the problem of maintaining them at Pakistani bases becomes far simpler than if they have to be returned to their home bases. This will materially affect the sortie rate.

What capability does Pakistan have to maintain aircraft other than the Mirage group and the F-5E? For example, could it operate the Mirage F-1s, which Libya has and Jordan is getting, in combat? The issue is not can it fly the plane, which it can as well as any European air force, but can the aircraft be sustained in combat? Again, there is no way of knowing, and the answer is quite important. The PAF's air defence capability increases manifold with the Mirage F-1 in place of the Mirage 3/5. What about other equipment, like helicopters, SAMs and C-130 transports? What about mobile 3D-radars? What about advanced ordnance? Delivery of these systems could materially affect the balance of air power.

Conclusions

A combination of these factors could completely alter the air balance to India's disadvantage. Previously, in the west, air power has not been decisive in any action except the two Chaamb battles where it made a major contribution to limiting Indian setbacks. In a future war, however, this will not be the case. Both sides have been acquiring aircraft and weapons of far greater capability than previously available. For instance, both sides now have first-rate radar coverage and excellent low-level deep-strike aircraft. When an air force shifts from a F-86 interdiction sortie to a Mirage 3/5 sortie, the result is not just an increase in bomb-tonnage by a factor of two, but increases in accuracy, in penetration capability, and in bomb lethality. Previously neither side had the tools substantially to affect the war on land. Now they will have them, and it is a matter of concern to India that it cannot know in advance what to expect.

In passing, it is worth mentioning that the figure of 74 or so Mirage 3/5s that Pakistan is supposed to have, before the delivery of 50 aircraft planned for the 1981-3 period, is wrong.[87] This is nobody's fault, because this figure is based on the numbers that Dassault has released. The Indian estimate is, however, that there have been closer to 100 deliveries; and that something around 90 aircraft remain after attrition and losses in the 1971 war. A very close perusal of the *Military Aviation News* will confirm that the Indian estimate is reasonable.[88] For example (this is not in MILAVNEWS), the first batch of Mirages contracted for in 1966 had 4 more Mirage 3s than publicly revealed, for a total of 28, not 24. This is how the PAF was able to line up 23 Mirages at the end of the war, claiming the loss of just one, whereas the IAF claimed 5. Next, in 1975 a batch of 8 Mirage 3Es was delivered[89] which was not revealed by Dassault. There is a possibility that even more Mirage 3s were delivered[90] and that some were bought from Lebanon. Then, also in 1975, 10 additional Mirage 5Ds (the trainer version) were delivered[91] to help man an advanced training school for Arab pilots training for March 2 aircraft.

There are no parliamentary hearings in France each time weapons have to be exported, so there is no public disclosure of what France actually sells. Pakistan can surely have no interest in revealing exact figures. A request to Dassault to conceal the real figures would suffice. The problem, for Pakistan, is that Indian Intelligence has adequate contacts in France to find out how many aircraft are being shipped. Once they reach the PAF, of course, the Indian assessment problem is simplified.

Case 9. Failure to Appreciate that India is Stronger than China along the Northern Borders

Background to the Case

India knows that, given the length of the Sino-Indian border, it is impossible to prevent the Chinese from seizing large parts of Indian territory. Accordingly, after 1962, a plan was evolved to deal with Chinese attacks. Units that are attacked are to stand fast in their boxes (these have been constructed as very strong defence positions backed by air supply), both to impede the Chinese advance, and to deny the invader clear title to the territory overrun. Meanwhile, Indian divisions in reserve will attack into Tibet once the Chinese have committed their forces to an offensive, and will seize large tracts of Tibet for future bargaining with China.

The military balance between the two countries is, then, perceived as a stand-off, with certain advantages to the Chinese like lateral mobility and easier maintenance of roads. The issue will not be how many square kilometres each side seizes, but the importance of a particular piece of land. The Chinese may seize more land, but that will not matter at the negotiating table, because India will have taken sufficient ground of importance to give it a strong hand. There are few persons who realise that the above assessment is wrong, and that actually India is superior to China in the north. The author has done a detailed study to prove the point;[92] what follows is a summary.

Discussion of the Case (1)

It has first to be seen that India is actually much stronger on the ground than might appear from simply looking at the published figures. There is a tendency to equate an Indian division with a Chinese division, which is not the case. An Indian mountain division is more than twice as large as a Chinese mountain or Class C division; it has five times the artillery in terms of tubes, and an even greater advantage in terms of shell weight; it has over three times as many vehicles; it has far superior signals and engineer equipment; it has many more infantry battalions; and it is backed by excellent helicopter and air mobility.[93]

In 1962, very lightly equipped Chinese troops used manoeuvres to stampede the Indian army into withdrawing, thus avoiding fixed battles. They were therefore able to offset their disadvantages in firepower, mobility and communications. These disadvantages were not so apparent then, not only because no fixed battle was fought, but because the Indians had arrived rather hurriedly on the scene, and their road and logistic networks were incomplete. Today, the Indians are very well prepared. Manoeuvre alone will not help the Chinese. Firepower, mobility and communications will all count in the event of war; for adequate firepower and mobility, a large logistics base is also needed. This too the Indians have.

India has many more troops available for the mountains than is commonly assumed. A problem arises because of the Indian habit of calling some divisions 'mountain' and others 'infantry'. This implies that all India has available to deploy in its northern front is its 10 mountain divisions. China has 8 divisions in Tibet, and it is generally agreed in the intelligence community that this force could be raised to between 15 and 18 divisions in wartime. So the line-up appears to be 10 Indian divisions against 18 Chinese; since the Indians are located in strong defensive positions, their force is considered adequate to produce the sort of stalemate discussed earlier.

Now, it cannot be denied that there *is* a difference between an infantry and a mountain division, but a close look shows that simply by shedding some troops (for example, the medium regiment in divisional artillery, the tank regiment, the recoilless rifles in the infantry battalions), by changing others (taking on 1-ton vehicles in place of many of the infantry division's 3-ton vehicles), and adding others (for example, augmenting transport and engineer units), an infantry division can, very rapidly, be readied for a mountain operation. For short periods, especially in defensive operations, the process can be one of detaching troops, as the augmentations are not critical. For example, if the infantry division is going into reserve, in all probability, its brigades will be independently deployed to boost the defence in threatened sectors. Since the defence has been previously built up over the years, the heavy transport and engineering capability needed in the mountains can be dispensed with.

If India gives up its option to destroy Pakistan's military potential, it can protect its border with 16 divisions, enough to hold the front (12 divisions), and to have two counter-attack forces of two divisions each, these being augmented by a number of independent tank and infantry brigades. So, India can divert three infantry divisions to the mountains, giving it 14 divisions (one infantry division, 3rd out of Leh, is already deployed on the northern border).

Since, however, most of the mountain divisions are heavily overstrength, it is better to talk in terms of divisional equivalents. Many of the mountain divisions have four brigades, even six is not unheard of. And a three-battalion brigade is considered small for the Indian army in the north. It is better, and more accurate, to assess the Indian strength in the north as equal to 16 nine-battalion divisions, and 19 with the augmentation from the plains.

This is not the end of the story. Many divisions in the west can spare infantry battalions (such as the ones in Kashmir), and there are many extra battalions lying all over the place. Most of the battalions thus withdrawn can be replaced by activated reserve battalions from the Territorial Army. So, if the need arose, the Indian army could deploy the equivalent of 21 divisions in the north. Of course, the artillery would then not have a five-to-one numerical advantage over the Chinese, but as a good many artillery regiments can also be shifted, something like a three-to-one advantage might be achieved. All the other advantages mentioned would still exist.

But is it possible to take troops from the plains and throw them into the mountains? Look what happened in 1962. Today, however, the situation is quite different. Every infantry battalion serves a regular tour in the mountains for three years. Unless the battalion in question happens to be a new raising on its first posting to the plains, it will have served previous tours in the mountains. In fact, at any one time something like 40 infantry battalions assigned to the plains are either in transit to their plains stations or have left the plains less than a year ago. It is no problem for them to return within days. In 1962 the army did not have the needed equipment at the right place, so inductees from the plains went cold, or hungry, or without ammunition. But that is all very long ago. Today, the army could throw an additional 36 battalions into Ladak within as many days, and the supplies would be there to sustain them for 90 days without a single supply convoy from the plains. Of course, most of the battalions would have to go up in stages to reacclimatise themselves, but the point stands.

The line-up of 21 Indian divisions to 18 Chinese overstates Chinese strength. At least four of those Chinese divisions are unsuited for offensive operations, being border formations. Some will have to be used to keep the line of communication open. The actual deployable strength of the Chinese army in Tibet is three divisions at each of three axes. To counter these, the Indian army requires a total of six divisional equivalents. There are sectors in which it is not possible to move Indian defenders, even if no Chinese attack is expected, because terrain makes rapid movement difficult. This takes up another three divisional equivalents. That leaves 12 divisional equivalents free to attack, and facing them will be perhaps six Chinese divisions. It needs more than two Chinese divisions to counter an attack by three Indian division equivalents, because each of the latter has much greater capability than its Chinese counterpart. So India emerges much superior on the ground.

Discussion of the Case (2)

India has one very high card, which it never talks about. This is its air force. If the need arose, India could switch two-thirds of its air force against China, while still providing adequate air defence and a minimal ground-attack capability against Pakistan. This two-thirds can generate a sustained 800 sorties a day. In theory China can put 500 aircraft into Tibet and fly 1,000 sorties a day. The reality is different.

A few simple calculations suffice to show that to deliver one-ton-per-day of supplies from Lhasa to the Chumbi Valley opposite Sikkim requires 5 trucks of 3-tons net-load; from Yarkand in Sinkiang to Rudok in western Tibet requires 8 trucks; and from Chamdo to Rima in eastern Tibet requires 3 trucks. A Chinese Class C division requires around 200-tons-per-day in heavy combat,[94] half that in moderate combat, and possibly 50-tons-per day in light combat. Assuming that half of the Chinese force of 18 divisions is in heavy combat, a quarter in moderate combat, and the rest in light combat, something like 2,500-tons-per-day is required by the divisions. This figure should be doubled to allow for other troops in the theatre (corps, army, line of communication, paramilitary, air defence, etc.), giving the army alone a requirement of 5,000-tons. A Mig-19 sortie requires six tons of supplies,[95] so that to fly the 1,000 sorties a day representing the theoretical capability of the Chinese air force in Tibet 6,000-tons-per-day.

Straightaway it is apparent that nothing like these tonnages can be sustained. Stockpilling over many months can permit a war of, say 2 to 3 weeks. However, to sustain three divisions in western Tibet, six in the Sikkim/Bhutan sector, and nine against Arunachal Pradesh would require 16,000 trucks, 30,000 trucks and 12,000 trucks respectively, for a total of almost 60,000 trucks in the theatre (this assumes the air force is distributed over the fronts in the same proportion as the army). The trucks required to move supplies to Yarkand, Lhasa and Chamdo have not been added on as yet. There is no way that China can operate this many trucks over the sparse mountain roads in Tibet — besides which, the trucks themselves make an interdiction target without match. For a few days China might be able to maintain a high sortie rate; but after stockpiled supplies have been exhausted, the replenishment rate will fall off very sharply even in the absence of Indian interdiction.

It is significant that the Chinese did not use their air force against the little Vietnamese air force in the 1979 Sino-Vietnam War. This was despite the availability of major Chinese bases close to Vietnam, with excellent transport networks. The reason was that the Chinese air force is extremely primitive, and would have run into trouble against the Vietnamese air defence network and its Mig-21s/F-5s, few though these might be. The Indian air force has a total qualitative superiority over China, besides having its bases in the plains. It suffers from no logistic problems at all, and can fly its aircraft with full fuel and bomb-loads. China in Tibet has to use restricted loads, further handicapping the already limited Mig-19s.

India will fly the Mig-21M, Mig-21bis, Mig-23/-27, and the Jaguar against Chinese Mig-19s. It has a first-class radar and communications network. It will use SAM-6 and some SAM-3 (the SAM-2, itself a much more advanced model than the one the Chinese use, will soon be on its way out), for air defence. China has no counter-measures against these missiles. India will have superiority in quality of ordnance, ranging from surface-to-air missiles and guided bombs to advanced air-to-air missiles like the Matra 550. To begin with it is unlikely that the Chinese will be able to get off more than 100-200 sorties a day; after a few days their sortie rate will decline sharply as their air bases are attacked and supply dumps blown up. In short, India can expect air superiority over Tibet.

Quite aside from the ground-support and reconnaissance-support that the IAF will provide, it will cut every major road in Tibet within 72 hours, and that too in many places. Road interdiction in the mountains is a very different proposition than in the plains. In the plains it seldom works because pontoon bridges can be pushed across rivers; bypass roads can be constructed; and the holes in the road filled. Within a day, competent engineers can reactivate any plains road. But in the mountains bridges are many and they cannot be replaced except with great labour. Bypass construction is nearly impossible. The road can be cleared and repaired at only two places at one time, the free ends, greatly limiting the speed of work. When it is considered that 4 Jaguars, with 4-ton bomb-loads could cause landslides over one kilometre of road, it is obvious that to clear the debris caused by one such strike will take weeks.

The IAF will first go for the major ingress routes into Tibet, dropping the big bridges, if necessary with the guided bombs it will soon have. It will then start cutting the roads leading to the front, and the roads connecting sectors. Subsequently it will break the roads on the front. For a while Chinese forces will be able to maintain their offensive using whatever supplies they might have stockpiled well forward. But as these run out, there will be precious little to replace them. And the Chinese will lose their lateral mobility. Certainly, it is possible to move 20, 30 or even 50 tons a day by manpack across a road break. But how many road breaks will the Chinese be able to surmount? Breaking roads in Tibet is one of the simplest of air tasks; in fact, the An-12 medium transport with 24 1,000-pound bombs would be perfect for the job.

The Indians are nowhere near as vulnerable to Chinese interdiction. To begin with, the Chinese air force will be too busy saving itself from Indian attacks to concern itself with interdiction. Indian supply bases are very much nearer to the front. And the Indians have a great abundance of tactical transport and helicopters. For example, six An-32s (these are going to replace many different IAS transport types) could put 100 tons into any number of airfields in Ladak in one day without straining themselves. An Indian division on the offensive requires something like 500 tons of supplies a day. So 100 tons may not keep the full division moving. But it would keep a brigade moving at a time when the enemy will find it difficult to sustain one-third the force. Similarly, 4 Mi-8 helicopters can, within five hours, lift 50 tons of supplies within a 50-mile radius. China has nothing to match this.

Does all this mean that the Indian army can, tomorrow, defeat the Chinese in Tibet? No, because like most other armies, India's moves slowly. There is no substantial requirement for taking the offensive against Tibet. In fact, since 1971, India has scaled down the size of its defending formations in many areas. For example, the western UP border is now protected by a brigade instead of a division. Given six months, however, the army could create the infrastructure to take the war into Tibet. Remember, in March 1971 only one division plus some brigades could be supported on the East Pakistan border; by October India was in a position to support indefinitely 300,000 men in battle.

The question will be asked, if all this is true, why has not the Indian army talked about its capabilities vis-à-vis the Chinese? Why have not discussions taken place about the matter, similar to those about Pakistan?

The reason is that the Indian army is not an organisation that devotes much thought to hypothetical situations. It is the government's policy that force will not be employed to recover parts of India under Chinese occupation. This policy has been in effect for two decades, since the disastrous failure of September 1962 to take back ground China had annexed.

Should, however, the government some day change its policy, the army will get down to planning the job. Doubtless, like all armies, it will carefully explain to the government all the shortcomings requiring remedy before embarking on such an expedition is possible. It will try to extract the maximum possible in resources from the government.

Yet, there should be no doubt: India is stronger than China on its northern borders.

Acknowledgements

Thanks are due to Mr K. Subrahamanyam, Director, Institute for Defence Studies and Analyses, New Delhi, for permission to use the IDSA Library; and to Mrs Uma Chopra, Assistant Librarian. Also to IDSA Fellows Dr K.N. Ramachandran and Dr P.B. Sinha for research advice and to Mr P.K.S. Namboodri and Mr Sreedhar Rao for discussions.

Notes

1. Composite figure obtained from: (a) Lorne J. Kavic, *India's Quest for Security: Defence Policies 1947-1965* (Universith of California Press, Berkeley and Los Angeles, 1967) (reprinted in India by EBD Publishing and Distributing Company, Dehradun), p. 99; (b) Neville Maxwell, *India's China War* (Jaico Publishing House, Bombay, 1970), p. 295.
2. B.B. Mullik, *My Years With Nehru: The Chinese Betrayal* (Allied Publishers, New Delhi, 1970), p. 336.
3. Ibid., pp. 304-5.
4. *History of the Army Service Corps, Volume 5, 1947-1976* (Sterling Publishers, New Delhi, 1977), p. 57. This gives the minimum airlift requirement of Indian 2 and 4 Infantry Division as 260-tons-per-day combined.

5. Mullik, *My Years with Nehru*, p. 345.
6. Brigadier J.P. Dalvi, *Himalayan Blunder* (Tacker and Company, Bombay, 1969), p. 152.
7. Ibid., p. 158.
8. Maxwell, *India's China War*, p. 390.
9. Ibid., p. 391.
10. Ibid., p. 425.
11. Conversations; see also Kavic, *India's Quest*, p. 176, and Maxwell, *India's China War*, p. 371 for some details.
12. Mullik, *My Years with Nehru*, p. 377. The Chinese first concentrated in the Northern sector (20-1 October 1962), then in the Central sector (22-4 October), and last in the Southern sector (27-8 October).
13. See, for example, Lt. Colonel J.R. Saigal, *The Unfought War of 1962* (Allied Publishers, New Delhi, 1979), pp. 64-5. Saigal participated in the 1962 war as a junior officer in Indian 4 Division. Though overstated at times, his thesis is generally regarded as being correct when he discusses the war itself.
14. Details from Kavic, *India's Quest*; and *History of Indian Artillery* (Palit and Dutt, Publishers, Dehra Dun, 1971).
15. Mullik, *My Years with Nehru*, p. 407.
16. Ibid., pp. 350-1. See also Air Marshal M.S. Chaturvedi, *History of the Indian Air Force* (Vikas Publishers House, New Delhi, 1978), pp. 127-8. Air Marshal Chaturvedi notes that 'political reasons' prevented combat units of the IAF from taking an active part in the war.
17. Conversations.
18. Air Marshal M. Asghar Khan, *The First Round: Indo-Pakistan War 1965* (Vikas Publishing House, New Delhi, 1979), pp. 7, 89. See also Brig. A.R. Siddiqi, 'Years of Indo-Pakistan Conflicts', *Defence Journal* (Islamabad) iv(3) (1978), pp. 2-10.
19. These included the 4 mountain division, the newly raised 6 mountain division, and the 23 infantry division (in process of converting to mountain configuration).
20. This is a composite figure obtained from a wide variety of sources, including Lt General P.S. Bhagat, *The Shield And the Sword* (Statesman, Calcutta, 1967).
21. This is a composite figure, obtained from a variety of sources, mainly Kavic, *India's Quest*, and the *History of Indian Artillery*.
22. There is some confusion on this point. Also, while Kavic (p. 97) gives India's strength in October 1962, as being 9 divisions, there are definitely at least 10; and there are other indication it might have been 11 divisions. For example, see Mohammad Ayub Khan, *Friends Not Masters* (Oxford University Press, London, 1967), p. 135. In this case both 20 and 23 Infantry Divisions, would have been in existence in October 1962.
23. For example, see Zulfikar Ali Bhutto, *The Myth of Independence* (Oxford University Press, London, 1969), p. 74.
24. Ibid., p. 75.
25. Quoted in Kuldip Nayar, *Distant Neighbours* (Vikas Publishing House, Delhi, 1972), pp. 111-112.
26. Asghar Khan, *The First Round*, p. 70.
27. Ayub Khan, *Friends*, pp. 133, 134-5.
28. Chaturvedi, *History*, p. 117.
29. Asghar Khan, *First Round*, pp. 76, 80.
30. Ibid., pp. 103-5.
31. Ibid., p. 52, mentions 'the army had been using up ammunition faster than expected'. Indian 23 Division was about to go into action at the time of the

ceasefire, after coming from the East; four additional brigades had been inducted into Kashmir during the fighting. The details are from the *ASC History*.

32. Asghar Khan, *First Round*, pp. 75-6.
33. Brigadier A.R. Siddiqi, '1965 War – Battle For or Against Pakistan', *Defence Journal*, Islamabad (1979), pp. 1-12 and particularly p. 8.
34. For example, refer to the speech made by Prime Minister Nehru in the Lok Sabha, 25 March 1957 (*JawaharLal Nehru's Speeches*, vol. 3, p. 238) and on 7 August 1952 (vol. 2, pp. 105-6) – both volumes by the Publications Division, Government of India.
35. *ASC History*.
36. These included mobilisations by both sides in 1950 and 1951, Nekowal Incident in 1954, Cadbet Incident in 1956, Neelum Valley Incident in 1964, plus numerous others in the east.
37. General J.N. Chaudhuri, *An Autobiography*, as narrated to B.K. Narayan (Vikas Publishing House, New Delhi, 1978), p. 190.
38. See Ayub Khan, *Friends*, pp. 140-7; Maxwell, *India's China War*, pp. 387-8; Mullik, *My Years with Nehru*, p. 334.
39. *Defence Journal*, 1979, implies that Pakistan 11 Infantry Division was newly raised at the time of the 1965 war; it is known that Pakistan 6 Armoured Division was raised in 1964; it is likely also that Pakistan 14 Infantry Division was not combat-ready before 1965. It is possible, then, that in 1963 or 1964 the Pakistan army was not ready for war.
40. Mullik, *My Years with Nehru*, pp. 510-11.
41. Chaudhu, R.I. *Autobiography*, p. 194.
42. Conversations.
43. See Asghar Khan, *First Round*, p. 38; 'The Air Force had never possessed any reserves of aircraft'. He also recounts how Iran and Turkey refused to provide aircraft or other major items because of lack of US approval – see pp. 54, 56.
44. Maj.-Gen. F.M. Khan, *Pakistan Leadership in Crisis* (National Book Foundation, Islamabad, 1973), p. 126.
45. Siddiq Salik, *Witness to Surrender* (Oxford University Press, Delhi, 1979), p. 159.
46. Khan, *Pakistan Leadership*, p. 130. Salik, *Witness to Surrender*, p. 127 says five battalions arrived, but Khan has provided battalion numbers so his statement is more credible. Additionally, it squares better with Indian intelligence estimates made after the war (see note 47).
47. Maj.-Gen. Sukhwant Singh, *The Liberation of Bangladesh* (Vikas Publishing House, New Delhi, 1980), p. 133.
48. For example, see Khan, *Pakistan Leadership*, pp. 108, 112; Salik, *Witness to Surrender*, p. 213; Nayar, *Distant Neighbours*, p. 194, quoting Lt.-Gen. Harbaksh Singh, as saying that Dacca should have been held.
49. For example, see Nayar, *Distant Neighbours*, p. 180, also p. 192 where Nayar gives extensive quotes from Lt.-Gen. Niazi's interrogation by the Indians. Also Salik, *Witness to Surrender*, p. 123.
50. Sukhwant Singh, *Liberation of Bangladesh*, p. 151.
51. Chaturvedi, *History of the Indian Air Force*, p. 167. These operations took place in the Indian IV Corps sector and were five in number. The first was a lift of 254 troops; subsequent ones became steadily larger with the last, on 14 December 1971, involving a lift of 2,019 troops and 61 tons by 12 helicopters.
52. Khan, *Pakistan Leadership*.
53. Khan, *Pakistan Leadership*, p. 140. Maj.-Gen. F.M. Khan says that Indian troops movements began in February 1971, even before the Civil War.
54. Khan, ibid., pp. 139, 143. Shows Pakistan correctly assessed the significance of the Indo-Soviet Treaty.

55. Bhutto, *Myth of Independence*. Chapters 5, 6 and 8 are a catalogue of Pakistan's complaints against the US.
56. That China promised no intervention can be seen by Mr Bhutto's interview to Gavin Young in the *Observer* of 14 November 1971. That the US promised no intervention is shown by the US Consulate in Dacca telling Niazi and Farman Ali that it knew of no intervention being planned. See Nayar, *Distant Neighbours*, pp. 188-9.
57. Maxwell, *India'a China War*, p. 411.
58. *Facts on File*, 37 (1906), 21 May 1977, p. 386.
59. Kissinger, *The White House Years* (Vikas Publishing House, New Delhi, 1979), p. 905.
60. Conversation with Admiral S.M. Nanda.
61. Vice-Admiral N. Krishnan, *No Way But Surrender* (Vikas Publishing House, New Delhi, 1980), pp. 52-65.
62. Conversations with US navy officers.
63. James M. McConnell and Anne M. Kelly, 'Super-Power Naval Diplomacy: Lessons of the Indo-Pakistan Crisis, 1971', *Survival*, November-December 1973, pp. 289-95.
64. See, for example, Salik, *Witness to Surrender*, pp. 206-13.
65. T.N. Kaul, *The Kissinger Years* (Arnold-Heinemann, New Delhi, 1980), p. 95.
66. Pran Chopra, *India's Second Liberation* (Vikas Publishing House, New Delhi, 1973), p. 212. Pran Chopra also says that Mrs Gandhi decided the political gains of a ceasefire outweighed the military gains of continuing the war.
67. Information obtained from officers who participated in the war.
68. Singh, *The Liberation of Bangladesh*, p. 103.
69. Chaturvedi, *History of the Indian Air Force*, No. 30 (Mig-21) and No. 221 (Su-7) Squadrons were shifted before the ceasefire in the east. More squadrons would have been shifted but for the ceasefire in the west a day later.
70. Chopra, *India's Second Liberation*, p. 201; Nayar, *Distant Neighbours*, p. 183.
71. Krishnan, *No Way But Surrender*, p. 65.
72. Kissinger, *White House Years*, p. 913.
73. See for example Mohammed Ayoob and K. Subrahmanyam, *The Liberation War* (S. Chand and Company, New Delhi, 1972), pp. 270-1; B.G. Verghese, *An End to Confrontation* (S. Chand and Company, New Delhi, 1972), pp. 67-8; Dilip Mukherji, *Yahya Khan's Final War* (Times of India, Bombay, 1972) (no page numbers, see article 'Bhutto's Limited Options'); D.R. Mankekar, *Pakistan Cut to Size* (India Book Company, New Delhi, 1972), pp. 164-5.
74. *Military Balance 1971-72* (IISS, London) estimated 392,000 troops before the war; 500,000 is the Indian estimate. In general, the US ACDA estimates are much closer to the Indian figures than are those in the *Military Balance*.
75. The methodology used to derive the figures is from a paper by the author 'Non-nuclear and Non-escalatory solutions to Pakistan's Two-Front Defence Problem' to appear in the *Institute for Defence Studies and Analyses, Journal* (New Delhi).
76. *The Pakistan Economic Survey 1979-1980* (Government of Pakistan Finance Division, Economic Advisers Wing, Islamabad, 1980) contains figures only up to December 1979. The 1980-1 GNP estimate here is an extrapolation based on latest available figures from *Quarterly Economic Review of Afghanistan, Pakistan, and Bangladesh* (Economist Intelligence Unit, London, 1980).
77. GNP for 1970-1 taken from *Military Balance 1971-72* as the Pakistan government now only publishes figures dealing with the western part of pre-1971 Pakistan.

Nine Examples from Recent Indian Experience 235

78. Figures given by the US Arms Control and Disarmament Agency are different because they use total federal revenues whereas here revenues net of transfer to the provinces have been used. See *World Military Expenditure and Arms Transfers 1969-1978* (US ACDA, Washington, D.C., 1980), p. 62. These are, 22.5 per cent of federal revenues spent on defence in 1978 compared to 29.0 per cent in 1969.

79. The 1979-80 figure is from *QER* 'Supplement for 1980' (see above).

80. The US ACDA estimates of arms imports as a percentage of total imports are: 1969 = 7.6 per cent, 1970 = 5.2 per cent, 1978 = 5.1 per cent. *World Military Expenditure*, p. 146.

81. 32 Mirage 3/5s ordered for $330 million for 1981 delivery. *Military Balance 1980-81*.

82. The estimate for Chinese arms to Pakistan 1966-79 is from the Soviet military daily *Sovietsakaya Rossiya*, Moscow, 29 February 1980. While not the most impartial of sources, it appears to be in the right area when it is considered that something like 1,500 AFVs, upwards of 200 fighter aircraft, several small warships, and equipment for several infantry divisions (at least 10) has been given by China. The Arab figure is from a study made by the author, 'Pakistan's Military Equipment Needs 1972-82', *Institute for Defence Studies and Analyses Journal*, X (2) October-December 1977, pages 103-30, and includes money from Saudi Arabia and the UAE, plus transfers from Iran. As it is based on published figures, it may be somewhat low.

83. *Indian Express*, New Delhi, 22 December 1980.

84. See, for example, *The Hindu*, Madras, 17 December 1980 and 24 December 1980.

85. See, for example, *Hindustan Standard* (Reuters agency report) for 16 December 1973, also *Institute for Defence Studies and Analyses News Review*, New Delhi, January 1974, pp. 44.-5.

86. *International Defence Business*, Washington, 8(593) 4 October 1976, p. 3101; also *Times of India*, New Delhi, 15 January 1980.

87. *Military Balance 1980-81* gives 70 Mirages of different versions; its various editions list a total of 74 procured since 1966 (24 in 1966 order, 30 in 1970 order, 10 in 1973 order, and 10 in 1977 order); 50 more are under delivery from 1981 onwards but not of relevance to the calculation here.

88. *Military Aviations News* (Milavnews) is a monthly publication of Aviation Advisory Services (England). It is not always accurate, at least about India. In the case of the Pakistan Mirages, however, the Indian air force has fairly detailed information; the *Milavnews* reports are presented merely as a published source whose figures add up to roughly the same totals as the IAF estimates.

89. *Military Aviations News*, April 1975.

90. The report about Lebanese Mirage 3s being sold to Pakistan is from Indian intelligence sources. Lebanon ordered 12 of these aircraft but they have been out of service for many years.

91. *Military Aviation News*, April 1976.

92. 'India versus China: The Northern Frontier Balance', by the author, to be shortly published as part of a book.

93. An Indian mountain division normally has around 72 guns and heavy mortars, but can have more. An Indian corps has two artillery brigades which can contain upwards of 144 guns. There are no figures available on what a Chinese Class C (mountain and jungle warfare) division has by way of guns, but based on figures given in *Handbook on the Chinese Armed Forces* (Defense Intelligence Agency, Washington, D.C., 1976) (kindly provided by Mr Sreedhar Rao, Fellow, Institute for Defense Analyses), for other types of divisions, a figure of 18 tubes for a Class C division has been used, plus 48 total in army artillery.

94. This is an extrapolation from figures given for a Class A division in the *Handbook* (see above).

8 ASSESSING THE ARAB-ISRAELI MILITARY BALANCE

K.R. Singh

While evaluating the Arab-Israeli military balance, one has to take into account several interlocking variables such as their respective economic, industrial and military capabilities, intra-Arab political relations, linkages with foreign powers and the international environment at a given time.

This environment was governed in the past largely by the Cold War. At least for two decades, from 1955 to 1975, the Arab-Israeli conflict reflected superpower rivalry in the region. The USSR supported the confrontation Arab states and the Palestine Liberation Organisation (PLO), while the USA and some West European states supported Israel. That equation is no longer valid. While the change in Egyptian policy is partly responsible for this difference, it is also important to note that countries such as Saudi Arabia, Jordan, Kuwait and the United Arab Emirates (UAE), which are now active among the confrontation states, maintain firm links with the West. The USSR continues to support Syria and Libya but it appears that Iraq, which was dependent upon the USSR until 1978, has now started searching for new options. This is especially true after the recent war between Iran and Iraq. Thus, the Arab-Israeli conflict is no longer influenced mainly by superpower rivalry in the region.

The USSR, at the moment, is isolated except for its links with Syria and Libya. Even there, it is possible that a change of regime might alter the *status quo*. It is, therefore, doubtful whether the USSR will be capable of or even willing to play the same active role that it has played in support of the Arabs before and during the October War. Undoubtedly the Arabs are searching for new friends in the USA and Europe. But it is unlikely that the USA, which is fully committed to Israel, and Western Europe, which still remains within the overall orbit of the Western alliance system dominated by the USA, can tilt the strategic balance in favour of the Arabs and fill the gap left by the USSR. This will naturally effect the Arab position in the broader international strategic balance.

Not only has the global strategic balance tilted against the Arabs since 1976, and more particularly after 1979-80, but the Arab front too has weakened due to enhanced intra-Arab rivalries. Under the Egypt-

Figure 8.1: The Middle East

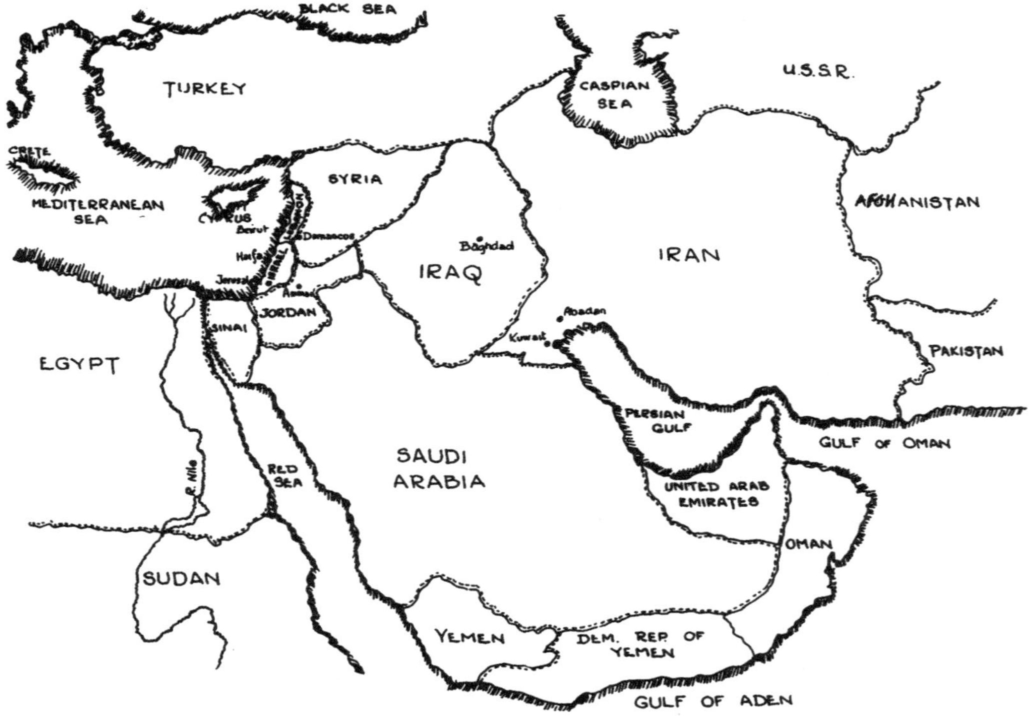

Israel peace treaty the present Egyptian leadership has, for all practical purposes, given up the option of using military force to pressurise Israel to concede to the overall Arab demands. This has not only considerably weakened the Arab political front but has also broken the earlier encirclement of Israel; a matter of some strategic importance when evaluating the Arab-Israeli military balance.

Also, the rift between Iraq and Syria, which has further widened due to the Syrian and Libyan support for Iran after the Iraq-Iran War, has weakened the so-called eastern front. The net result is that, unlike 1973, Israel is today no longer encircled by a united, hostile Arab bloc. It is theoretically possible, at least it is what Arabs dream and Israelis dread, that all the Arab states will ultimately unite but such an eventuality does not seem feasible at least in the near future. Hence it is essential to analyse the Arab-Israeli military balance with different combinations of Arab forces and to see how Israel plans to counter such combinations.

Israel

Israel's main strength lies not so much in its own domestic powerbase as in its strong linkages with the USA, which has provided it with political, economic and military strength *vis-à-vis* the Arabs since the partition of Palestine.

The US commitment to maintain Israeli security, which has become almost an article of faith in US foreign policy, was given concrete shape after the Egypt-Israeli peace treaty on 26 March 1979. Two hours after that treaty was signed, Secretary of State, Cyrus Vance, and the Israeli Foreign Minister, Moshe Dayan, signed a memorandum of understanding between the two countries. It not only reiterated earlier US commitments to Israel but also said that the USA would consider a series of measures — naval and military — to protect Israel if the treaty broke down. This almost amounts to an informal defence pact between the two countries.

Some argue that the near total dependence of Israel on the USA gives the USA a degree of coercive leverage to mould Israeli policies on a desired line especially *vis-à-vis* the Arab-Israeli dispute. But this is not so. The powerful pro-Israel lobby in the USA sees to it that this does not happen. Instead, the pro-Israel lobby has been able to exert a coercive leverage *vis-à-vis* the US administration. In March 1975 the administration was dragging its feet on the transfer of Lance surface-to-surface missiles (SSM) to Israel. Secretary of Defense Schlesinger stated that the USA would be reluctant to enter into any new commitment to Israel during that period of reassessment, pending the second disengagement between Egypt and Israel.[1] Earlier President Ford had sent a telegram to Premier Rabin stating that US policy would be reassessed if Israel were not more flexible.[2] Israel, instead of bowing to this pressure, became more intransigent. The pro-Israel lobby in the USA swung into action and, on 21 May 1975, 76 US Senators told President Ford that they expected the US administration to submit a foreign aid request to Congress that would be responsive to Israel's urgent military and economic needs.[3]

Subsequently, the administration went out of its way to assure all concerned that it was not applying any coercive leverage. In June 1977, Vice President Mondale said that the USA did not intend to use military aid to put pressure on Israel.[4] Similarly, Secretary Christopher, while discussing the sale of US arms to Israel, said, 'I think it would be an improper coercion on our part if we were to condition the sale of planes to the Israelis on their willingness to make concessions on the West Bank.'[5]

The total US commitment to Israel is reflected in its economic and military aid programme. Israel on its own can never survive as a state if it wishes to confront its Arab neighbours. Despite the massive aid that Israel has received from all quarters, its foreign debts are mounting. By 1977 it owed 9.6 billion dollars, the highest per capita debt in the world.[6] Between 1947 and 1977 Israel obtained 11 billion dollars in aid from the USA alone. Almost half of that was in the form of grants.

US military aid to Israel is justified on the grounds that it maintains Israeli security. Alfred L. Atherton, Assistant Secretary of State for Near Eastern and South Asian affairs in his statement at a congressional hearing in 1977 said,

> Our policy, I think, clearly is to maintain Israel's ability to defend itself, which means maintaining military sales. Israel is outnumbered from the population point of view, grossly outnumbered. I would say that this would have to be compensated for by maintaining a clear ability to defend itself should it be attacked and to be successful in countering any attack.[7]

In short, US policy is to ensure an absolute and overwhelming military superiority for Israel which is possible only by a preponderance of superior weapons to balance Israel's smaller population.

Israel is not only receiving new and sophisticated weapons but also advanced, defence-orientated technology. Since it has the necessary infrastructure to absorb this, it has been able to launch into an ambitious plan not only for manufacturing arms but also for introducing innovations that provide it with the technological edge over the Arabs. This has given a new boost to the defence-orientated industries in Israel. The basis of Israeli military technology is the Technion, the Massachusetts Institute of Technology of the Middle East. This fifty-year old institution has produced thousands of highly qualified graduates who have contributed to the Israeli defence programme. Less than a decade ago the Israeli avionics and defence-orientated industry was primarily a manufacturer, under licence, of equipment developed by American and French companies. Today it is producing airborne and ground radars, digital computers, radio communications and equipment for electronic counter-measures (ECM) that are designed and developed in Israel. They are reportedly designed and built to US Defense Department military standards, unless more rigorous Israeli defence force requirements are applied.

This Israeli capability to produce military equipment under licence and also to improve upon the old model is reflected in the development of the multi-role Kfir fighter. Its airframe is based essentially on plans of the French Mirage V, allegedly stolen in Switzerland, while its main engine is a General Electric model built under licence in Israel.

Apart from the transfer of technology, Israel has also acquired new weapons direct from the USA. Besides the newly acquired air-superiority fighter, F-15, it is also to receive F-16 planes. Four E-2C Hawkeye — small airborne warning and control aircraft — have also been transferred to the Israeli forces along with remotely piloted aircraft (RPV) for reconnaissance and ECM. Assorted precision guided munitions (PGMs) and surface-to-surface missiles (SSM) have added strength to its stand-off weapons capability. The army has also been strengthened with heavy self-propelled artillery, tanks and assault helicopters. The result is that Israel is far stronger today than it was in 1973. According to the former Israeli Minister of Defence, Shimon Peres, Israeli military capability in mid-1976 had risen by 30 per cent in comparison with the pre-October 1973 level.[8] That percentage must have increased substantially since then because of the new arms transferred from the USA and those produced locally.

Israel has also built up a larger stockpile of spares. It is reported that it can fight an intense war for 30 days without seeking external support.[9] According to CIA and Pentagon calculations, Israel remains superior to the Arab nations. In a worst case scenario, that is a war breaking out simultaneously on several fronts, with a Soviet airlift to resupply the Arabs in the absence of an American airlift, the Israelis would be able to defeat the combination of Arab armies in a period of one to three weeks, sustaining higher casualties the longer hostilities continued.[10] According to Senator Stone, Israel lost 3,000 men in October 1973. In a future war on two fronts, CIA estimates point to losses of 9,000 killed and 36,000 wounded.

This could influence Israeli strategy in future. Before 1973 Israeli strategy was geared to the concept of 'economy of force', based upon the combination of aircraft and armour. This was useful only when wars were fought on Israeli terms as in 1956 and 1967, but not in 1973. Now, Israel might have to switch over to the strategy of maximum deployable force to compensate for growing Arab military capability and to overcome the problems presented by Arab PGMs. Thus, unless Israel launches a pre-emptive strike, it will have to commit many more soldiers in a future war. Hence, it will have to rely heavily upon the USA, expand its military-industrial complex and opt for a pre-emptive strategy unless it is prepared for a protracted and costly conventional war or to escalate the confrontation to the nuclear level with all its regional and international consequences.

The Arab States

Those who seek to work out an Arab-Israeli military balance often pool the resources of all the Arab states and then compare these with those possessed by Israel. This does not take into account the internal rifts among the Arabs states, nor their low-level links with several great powers which have conflicting interests in the region.

There is also a tendency nowadays to ascribe greater power to the Arabs because of the so-called Islamic solidarity. Undoubtedly, the Islamic countries through their own conferences and also through their votes in the United Nations and other international bodies and conferences, tend to support the Arabs economically and politically against Israel. But it is doubtful whether this political support adds much weight to the military capability of the Arabs. Not only are some of the Moslem states geographically distant, and economically and militarily weak, but their political, economic and military resources are committed, because of regional issues, to their own area. Iran after 1979 did show greater involvement in the Arab-Israeli dispute because of the Islamic tone of the new revolutionary regime and because of the links between

Assessing the Arab-Israel Military Balance 243

the PLO and some elements in the new regime in Iran. But it is doubtful whether Iran under present conditions could or would help the Arabs fruitfully in their military struggle against Israel.

There are two other reasons why Arab-Islamic solidarity cannot be very effective against Israel. Few Arab-Islamic regimes today can push the Islamic option to its logical conclusion because of their own fears of Islamic fundamentalism. The experience of the Iranian revolution is still fresh. Secondly, the Arab-Islamic bloc, despite its alleged leverage with the north because of its oil resources, is as yet a part of the south. Transfer of military technology is one of several issues that plague north-south relations. The Arab-Islamic bloc, despite its advantages in votes, oil power and petrodollars, has not succeeded in making the north concede on that issue. Thus, while Israel is able to obtain, without much constraint, the latest in military technology from the north, the Arab-Islamic bloc has either to beg, borrow or steal whatever it can, or to pay a disproportionately heavy political and economic price for its armaments.

When evaluating the military balance between Israel and the Arabs, it is also necessary to give due importance to various regional factors like the political relations among the Arabs themselves, the actual capability of individual confrontation states to contribute to the anti-Israeli front while keeping in view their other military commitments, the question of logistics and the task of co-ordinating armies with divergent training systems and weapons. For example, the Syrian armed forces operate Soviet equipment and are trained by the Russians. On the other hand, the armed forces of Jordan and Saudi Arabia operate American, French and British equipment and are trained by Western experts. Undoubtedly some efforts have been made by the Arabs to conduct joint exercises on a small scale but it remains to be seen whether the armed forces of these states have integrated themselves enough to act as a collective and co-ordinated Arab force against Israel. Thus, an Arab-Israeli military balance is not a simple matter of pooling the resources of all the Arab states.

Attempts are also often made to equate weapons without evaluating their respective capabilities. Thus, when assessing air power, Mig 21s and 23s are often equated with Phantoms and F-15 Eagles respectively, despite the fact that in terms of electronics, weapons-load and range the American planes operated by Israel are far superior to the Soviet planes operated by the Arabs. The same is true with regard to armour. While the bulk of tanks operated by the Arabs have a 100 mm gun (T-54 and T-55), the Israeli tank mounts a superior 105 mm gun and carries a more sophisticated ranging device, thereby ensuring a better first-hit capability.

Another factor that is often overlooked while assessing the military balance is the weapons mix. For example, the Israeli armoury includes diverse but complementary systems like ground-based radar and communications systems supported by Hawk surface-to-air missiles (SAM), E-2 Hawkeye planes, F-15 interceptors, F-4s, Kfirs and Mirage interceptor-fighters, Skyhawk ground attack planes and attack helicopters. These aircraft are equipped with appropriate PGMs, such as the radar-guided air-to-air Sparrow missiles, infrared guided missiles such as Sidewinder and Shafrir, air-to-surface missiles such as the anti-radar Shrike missile and the television-guided Maverick. The army also uses new anti-tank guided weapons and short- and medium-range surface-to-surface missiles.

This combination is not only capable of ensuring effective control over the air space but also provides a more balanced co-ordination between the air force and the army. The Israelis must have learnt the lessons of the October War and the new weapons are the answer to the Arab strategy of operating behind a screen of surface-to-air missiles and anti-tank guided weapons. Thus the present Israeli weapons mix, attained by the addition of a few selected weapons systems, increases by several times the military capability of the country. Conversely, the Arabs lack some crucial systems, especially in the fields of missiles and electronic equipment to neutralise the Israeli weapons mix. They lack planes of the Hawkeye type, together with superior anti-aircraft missiles, air-to-surface missiles and ECM pods on aircraft. This gives a qualitative edge to Israel and neutralises the effect of any adverse quantitative Arab-Israeli military balance.

Besides variables like the force-levels that can be committed at a given time, the quantity and quality of weapons and the possible weapons mix, as well as the strategy of the parties to the dispute, there are other vital inputs that have to be taken into account. These are the training of the respective armed forces, efficiency of the high command, the morale of the armed forces and of the people, as well as the degree of effective and assured support, both political and military, from outside. Many of these variables are difficult to evaluate but, though judgement about them is bound to be subjective, it is none the less essential to take them into account if one seeks a reasonably accurate military assessment.

Military Training

Military training is very closely connected with the arms trade. Thus, the Arabs and Israelis have not only obtained their arms from several states but have also received military training from them. Except for Syria, both the Arabs and Israelis were trained by the British before the Second World War. The Syrian military training programme during the French Mandate was inadequate to have left much impact by the time the Syrians switched to the USSR for their armaments in 1955. The Egyptians and the Iraqis also depended to a large extent on Soviet weapons after 1955 and 1958 respectively. Libya, which depended upon the West till 1973, began to acquire large quantities of arms from the USSR after 1974. Jordan and Saudi Arabia continue to maintain their links with the West, and, besides British and American personnel, also use Pakistanis in their military programmes.

Soviet military training has had a considerable impact upon the military prepardness of several major Arab confrontation states. Not only have thousands of Arab military personnel been trained in the USSR but an equally large number of Soviet military personnel were sent to their countries to train the armies.

Arab Military Personnel Trained in the USSR to 1975[11]

Egypt	5,675
Syria	3,325
Iraq	2,950
Libya	900

The Soviet training programme would have stopped in Egypt when it broke off its military links with the USSR in 1976 but more military personnel from Syria, Libya and Iraq must have been sent to the USSR for training since then and the number would have gone up considerably.

The number of Soviet military experts in the Arab states has also been fairly substantial. Some of these were involved in the maintenance of Soviet equipment supplied to the Arabs. In the case of Egypt, between 1971 and 1972, they even operated Soviet equipment there. However these technicians were removed after August 1972 on Egypt's request. The Soviet military training programme for the Arabs is closely based on the Soviet pre-nuclear war doctrine and the Syrian forces reportedly followed this during the October War.[12]

Soviet Military Technicians in the Arab World[13]

	1971	1973	1975
Egypt	5,500*	750	200
Syria	800	1,650	3,000
Iraq	400	750	1,000
Libya	0	0	50

* Excludes those attached to Soviet operational units

Saudi training has been intensified since 1972 when the Saudis decided to rebuild their armed forces and their National Guard with the help of the Americans. Though the total number of official American personnel is limited by Congress, private firms have hired thousands of American and foreign nationals for the purpose.

The Israelis, who received some military training from the British during the Second World War, developed their indigenous military training programme subsequently. Their training was conditioned by their small territory and relatively small population. They sent their personnel for training to France and the USA, which supplied them with advanced weapons and weapons technology, but the role of official foreign military personnel in their training programme was limited. Israelis have visited various combat theatres, such as Vietnam, but it is doubtful if they borrowed wholesale military doctrines from the West. This independence gives them a degree of flexibility to improvise a suitable strategy that is a point in their favour when one attempts to evaluate the Arab-Israeli military balance.

Soviet training has been moderately effective in improving the combat capabilities of the Arab armed forces in Egypt, Syria and Iraq. In Egypt this was apparent especially among the junior and middle-grade officers. Syrian combat effectiveness in 1973 was greatly improved over their incredibly inept performance in 1967. Since 1973, the Syrians have been working assiduously, under Soviet guidance, on correcting many of the deficiencies evident during the October War. Iraqi performance in 1973 was also generally regarded as poor and reports on Iraqi military training since 1973 are too scarce to permit judgement as to their post-war training activity.[14] However, the Iraq-Iran war does not point to a marked improvement in the Iraqi military performance.

In contrast to the Arabs, the Israelis have performed much better as a fighting force. There were always criticisms of lack of 'discipline' in the Israeli armed forces. According to one writer, the Israelis displayed battlefield indiscipline during their operations against South Lebanon.

His charges included lack of proper maintenance to equipment, not following orders and not wearing helmets in the battle zone.[15] Probably these criticisms were partly responsible for the change in command in which General Gur was replaced by General Rafael Eytan, a tough paratrooper.

However, the question of 'indiscipline' in the Israeli armed forces has to be viewed from an angle different from that of a conventional army in the West or the East. It is basically a citizen army where class distinctions are blunted to a degree unheard of in other armies. But, if commitment and will to fight is taken as the criterion of discipline, the Israeli armed forces have proved to be well-enough organised. Their survival as a nation depends upon it. Also, Israeli battlefield commanders, even at lower ranks, are trained to take the initiative, to exploit tactical advantages and hence are not 'disciplined' in that sense. But that is supposed to be the strength of the Israeli armed forces. The Arabs, on the contrary, allegedly fight a battle by the book and are trained in setpiece tactics along agreed lines that do not allow for the intervening variables that always occur in combat.[16]

Arab performance in the October War has been studied extensively. Undoubtedly, the Arabs gave a much better performance in 1973 than in 1967. But during that period the Israeli performance also improved. Hence, according to one writer, it was not clear whether Arab combat performance, relative to the Israeli Defence Force, improved more than marginally between 1967 and 1973.[17]

Some experts, however, disagree with this analysis. According to them the Israelis fear that, while they are nearing a plateau, the Arabs are climbing fast and would, given the time, improve their capability.[18] This argument is advanced to support the Israeli demand for more weapons to match Arab weapons in quantity. The Israeli Ambassador to Washington, Simcha Dimitz, and the Israeli Defence Minister, Shimon Peres, were quoted as saying that the one to three quantitative arms ratio was the minimum defence posture that Israel must have to maintain a balance.[19]

In this context one must take note of a very serious shortcoming in some of the Arab armed forces especially at the senior officer level. While some countries like the United Arab Emirates (UAE), Kuwait and even Saudi Arabia lack adequate numbers of senior officers trained in the practical aspects of conducting a conventional military campaign, the efficiency of senior officers in some other Arab states suffers due to frequent *coups d'état* and changes at the top echelon. This not only adversely affects the training at the lower levels but also reduces the efficiency of the officers at the top. Such a politicised army is often a poor fighting force as is clear from the recent experiences in several of the Afro-Asian states.

While evaluating the possible outcome of an armed conflict, another major variable, the willingness of the parties to fight to the last, has to be taken into account. Despite propaganda to the contrary, war is basically a conscious and rational effort to obtain by force what cannot be acquired through economic, political and diplomatic means. Therefore, not only the threat to use force, and the relative military capability, but also the willingness to fight a war becomes an important variable in inter-state relations. The possibility of war is, therefore, directly proportional to the price not only the ruling elite but also the common man in a given state is prepared to pay to obtain what they consider to be their just national demands.

In contrast to the single-mindedness of the supporters of Israel, the Arab-Islamic attitude towards Israel is conditioned by four major variables: the Palestinian question *per se;* the territorial disputes between Israel and some front-line Arab states; the ideology of Pan-Arabism; and finally, pan-Islamism. Thus, in contrast to the cohesive linkage and close identity of interest between the state of Israel and its motive force, international Zionism, Arabs are hopelessly divided not only because of their internal disputes but also because of the varying perceptions, among the Arabs and their supporters, of the Arab-Israeli conflict. While this hinders the emergence of a cohesive Arab-Islamic front against Israel, the wide spectrum of the ineffective anti-Israeli front provides the Zionists with sufficient propaganda material to project an 'overwhelming' Arab-Islamic threat which is out of all proportion to reality.

Possible Arab-Israeli Military Equations

While working out the possible force-levels that might be deployed in a potential Arab-Israeli war one will have to take into account three main factors: the geographical constraints of some Arab states; the political alignments among the Arab states at a given time; and the chances of a possible last-minute decision by an Arab state not to participate in the war. It must be noted that Jordan, a major confrontation state, did not actively participate in the October War and Libya, a very vocal anti-Israeli state, put serious constraints on the use of its war materiel by Egypt against Israel.

Thus, while preparing a realistic Arab-Israeli military balance, one will have to rule out, by and large, the possibility of an effective military participation by distant Arab states like Morocco, Algeria, Tunisia, Sudan, Yemen, Oman, UAE and Kuwait. Despite their willingness to fight against Israel, they can, at best, send only token forces which might reflect solidarity but cannot turn the scales against Israel.

The remaining Arab states will also have to be grouped in terms of their political alignments and possible reasons for not participating in the war. Hence an Arab-Israeli military balance has to be worked out at least on a five-tier system. In the first tier, Israel balances all its neighbouring states; Egypt, Libya, Syria, Iraq, Jordan and Saudi Arabia. In the second, Egypt is excluded because of its peace treaty with Israel. In the third, the countries of the Eastern front alone are taken into account. In the fourth, because of the current isolation of Syria, only Jordan, Saudi Arabia and Iraq are grouped together. Finally, only Syrian military capability is evaluated. Widely used sources like the *Military Balance*, published by the International Institute for Strategic Studies, London and the *SIPRI Year Book*, Stockholm, have been used to evaluate the military capabilities of the Arabs and the Israelis.

While calculating the present Arab-Israeli military balance, stress has been given to their respective capability for a land-air confrontation. The naval balance is not discussed in detail for two reasons. First, naval battles will have only a marginal effect upon the war on the Eastern front. Secondly, Israel during the last decade has acquired an overwhelming naval superiority over the Arabs because of the large number of missile boats of indigenous design that Israel possesses.

As far as the land-air confrontation is concerned, both sides have been enhancing their military strength since the October War. Today Israel can muster a 375,000-strong army after mobilisation. The stress is on armour and mechanised infantry bridges. Self-propelled (SP) artillery has been greatly strengthened. The Israeli army operates 3,050 tanks, 4,000 APCs and armoured cars, 328 SP medium and heavy guns and howitzers, several SP mortars and 950 guns (towed). Its anti-armour capability is buttressed by different types of ATGWs like the TOW, Dragon, SS-11 and Cobra missiles. Many of them are mounted on APCs and helicopters. Its ground-based air-defence depends upon manportable Redeye SAMs and the SP Vulcan-Chaparral system consisting of radar-controlled 20 mm guns and short-range SAMs. It also operates short-range Zeev and medium-range Lance and Jericho SSMs.

The Israeli air force operates 25 F-15 Eagle, 130 F-4 Phantom, 30 Mirage III, 130 Kfir and 200 A-4 Skyhawk planes. These are supported by 12 RE-4E reconnaissance planes and 4 E-2E Hawkeye as well as by several remotely piloted vehicles (RPVs) used for reconnaissance as well as for the ground-attack role. Of these weapons, Hawkeye deserves special notice. These are virtually command posts high in the air which are not only capable of keeping a large area under radar and electronic surveillance but are also capable of directing aircraft to their targets hundreds of miles away. These four planes contribute to a manifold increase in the effectiveness of the Israeli air force as was demonstrated in recent Syrian-Israeli air battles over the Southern Lebanon. The Israelis also operate about 150 helicopters. The ground-based anti-aircraft defence is entrusted to conventional radar-controlled guns as well as 15 batteries of Hawk SAMs. The Israeli air capability will be further strengthened when it receives, in the near future, advanced aircraft like the F-16 and the Hughes-500 helicopter gunships.

It is very difficult to compute the military strength of the Arab states. As seen earlier, the combined strength of all the Arab states is of only theoretical interest because in no foreseeable future would Israel be confronted with that force. Hence only the likely war scenarios are taken into account while computing various Arab forces that can confront Israel.

In the maximum threat when the armed forces (minus the navy) of the immediate Arab neighbours of Israel, Egypt, Libya, Syria, Jordan and Saudi Arabia, are taken into account, their combined armed strength totals 876,000. They have 10,849 tanks, about 9,540 APCs and other armoured fighting vehicles, more than 567 SP guns and howitzers, besides thousands of mortars and towed guns. They also operate Russian, American, British and French anti-tank missiles. The land-based anti-aircraft defence is taken care of by AMX-30 (30 mm), ZSU-23-4 and Z54-57-2 radar-controlled SP anti-aircraft guns, man-portable Redeye and SA-7 SAMs, and self-propelled SA-6/9 SAMs, and fixed SA-2/3 SAMs and radar-controlled guns. They also operate medium-range SSMs like FROG and Scud.

The air forces of these states operate different types of aircraft. In all, they have 29 Tu-22, 23 Tu-16 and 10 Il-28 bombers, 60 Mig-25, 260 Mig-23, 525 Mig-21, 190 Mig-17, 133 Su-20, 180 Su-7, 35 F-4, 40 F-6 (Chinese version of Mig-19), 157 F-5E/F, 170 Mirage III/5, 27 Lightning and 15 Hunter fighter-bombers. They also operate 706 helicopters, some of them being configured as attack helicopters.

It should be noted that Egypt accounts for a high percentage of this total. There are reports that a large number of Egyptian arms of Soviet origin have been rendered ineffective because of lack of spares and

Egyptian efforts to diversify their sources have not succeeded fully. Hence this balance appears to be highly inflated in favour of the Arabs.

If Egypt is deducted from the list of the confrontation states, then the strength of the remaining Arab states — Libya, Syria, Iraq, Jordan and Saudi Arabia — is further reduced. The total strength of the combined army comes down to 616,000. There is also a corresponding decrease in armour and aircraft. The armour is reduced to 9,169 tanks, about 6,540 AFVs and more than 367 SP and 1,600 towed guns and howitzers. The numbers of ATGWs, SP anti-aircraft guns, SAMs and SSMs are also reduced. The air strength is reduced to 29 Tu-22, 10 Il-28 bombers, 60 Mig-25, 250 Mig-23, 335 Mig-21, 60 Mig-17, 90 Su-22, 60 Su-7, 157 F-5E/F, 27 Lightning and 15 Hunter fighter-bombers, and about 538 helicopters.

If one combines the military strength of all Eastern-front states only — Syria, Jordan, Saudi Arabia and Iraq — the total armed strength is reduced to about 570,000. They have 6,769 tanks, about 4,650 AFVs, about 367 SP and 1,600 towed guns and howitzers. The figure of ATGWs, SAMs and anti-aircraft guns is also reduced. As far as their air forces are concerned, they operate 12 Tu-22 and 10 Il-28 bombers, 25 Mig-25, 140 Mig-23, 315 Mig-21, 60 Mig-17, 90 Su-20, 60 Su-7 and 15 Hunter fighter-bombers. They have 450 helicopters. Iraqi losses during the Iraq-Iran war might have further reduced this strength.

It should be noted that, though the military strength of Iraq has been combined for the sake of statistics, these figures give a wrong impression of the forces that can be pitted against Israel in actual combat. Even if the present political differences between Iraq and Syria are resolved, Iraq can never deploy its full military strength against Israel for three main reasons. First, Iraq will have to station sufficient forces on the Iranian border to counter the possible military threat from the Iranian side. Secondly, part of the Iraqi forces will be tied up in Iraqi Kurdistan. Lastly, the long distances involved would put a heavy strain on the logistics which would be stretched to the limit to support even the deployment of small Iraqi forces on the Israeli front. If the experience of the Iraq-Iran war is any guide, it will be a good performance if Iraq is able to deploy even two armoured divisions and half its air force on the Israeli front.

Since 1980 Syria has been increasingly isolated on the Eastern front and a new combination, composed of Iraq, Saudi Arabia and Jordan, is taking shape. This is also a fairly powerful combination on paper. Its army totals 311,000. Its armour is composed of 3,849 tanks, about 3,000 AFVs, about 300 SP guns and a large number of towed guns and mortars.

Its air strength consists of 12 Tu-22 and 10 Il-28 bombers, 80 Mig-23, 115 Mig-21, 60 Su-20, 40 Su-7, 157 F-5, 27 Lightning and 15 Hunter fighter-bombers. The helicopter fleet totals 327. Though this is theoretically a powerful combination, its effective strength lies in Iraq and, as we have seen, the logistics, the long distances and also the new confrontation with Iran will adversely influence the effective deployment of these resources against Israel.

Thus, today Syria alone remains the most important single confrontation state *vis-à-vis* Israel. Its military strength is 200,000. It operates 2,920 tanks, 1,600 AFVs, some SP guns and a large number of towed guns and mortars. Its air force consists of 25 Mig-25, 60 Mig-23, 200 Mig-21, 60 Mig-17, 30 Su-20 and 20 Su-7 fighter bombers. This is far weaker than the Israeli military strength.

Though the Arab military potential, at least on paper, appears to be very large, when reduced to its deployable size, keeping in view the intra-Arab rivalries, one realises that much of it vanishes into thin air and, on balance, Israel does not emerge, as is often suggested, inferior even in terms of quantity of manpower and equipment.

There is also some speculation about the possible military support that Libya can extend to the front-line Arab states. This has gained added strength following the so-called union between Syria and Libya in September 1980. It is known that Libya has acquired large quantities of sophisticated military equipment from the USSR which are of the type used by Syria also. But active Libya-Syrian military co-operation against Israel is constrained by two major factors. First, Libya and Israel are separated by Egypt and the Libyan-Egyptian relations at present do not encourage the emergence of a viable Libyan front on the Western frontier of Israel. Secondly, the Mediterranean is dominated by the Israeli navy and it will be almost impossible for Libya to transfer Libyan troops or even arms to Syria during or on the eve of an Arab-Israeli war. It is claimed by some that Libya is a storehouse of Syrian arms but at the moment the store house is beyond the effective reach of the Syrian armed forces. Thus the total force that the Arabs can bring to bear against Israel in the present juncture is further reduced.

The fact that the real military potential of the Arabs is not what is generally projected does not mean that the Arabs are totally powerless to use force to compel Israel to come to the negotiating table. But their comparative military disadvantages will influence Arab military strategy. The Arabs cannot repeat the 1967 war scenario; the display of Arab military might and a simultaneous aggressive political posture enabled Israel not only to make a pre-emptive strike but also to legitimise its consequences. This time the Arabs will be compelled to evolve a new strategy based upon an effective military surprise and a greater reliance on an aggressive rather than a defensive strategy.

During the October War, the Arabs succeeded in achieving a near total surprise and gained tactical advantages from it. During the first two days, the Syrian armour almost succeeded in over-running the Israeli defences in the Golan Heights. The Egyptians also succeeded in crossing the Suez Canal and neutralising the limited defences at the Bar-Lev line.

Syrian and Egyptian strategies, however, differed on fundamentals. While the Syrians adopted an aggressive and offensive-oriented strategy, based upon an armoured dash, the Egyptian strategy was primarily defensive. It was governed by the experience of the seven years of land-air confrontation in the Suez Canal zone as well as by the fact that the Suez Canal itself put serious constraints upon the armoured dash into the Sinai from the western bank. Thus the primary objective of the Egyptian strategy was the crossing of the Suez Canal and the occupation of a strip of about ten kilometres on the other bank, and conditions permitting, the further exploitation of this advantage.

This strategy was also based upon the type of weapons-mix that Egypt had evolved during the Suez confrontation. The Suez Canal zone was protected by a heavy air-defence system based upon ground-defences on the western bank including the radar network, integrated command structure and fixed SAMs and anti-aircraft guns. The effectiveness of this air-umbrella extended to some extent to the eastern bank of the Suez Canal also. Heavy and medium artillery on the western bank and armour, infantry and ATGW team on the eastern bank came under that protective umbrella. This combination of weapons-mix and the strategy based upon it ensured the successful crossing of the Suez Canal as well as the holding of the bridgeheads across it.

This basically defensive strategy, however, proved inadequate when these bridgeheads were used as a launching pad for further penetration into the Sinai. Despite the fact that Egypt had SP ZSU-23-4 radar-controlled anti-aircraft guns, and SP SA-6 and man-portable SA-7 SAMs, it lacked adequate air power based upon manned aircraft to neutralise the Israeli air force. The result was that the Egyptian armour, when it attacked the passes in the Sinai, was at the mercy of the Israeli air force, armour and the fixed defences in Sinai. The destruction of the Egyptian armour at the passes and the subsequent Israeli counter-offensive demonstrated the inadequacy of a defensive strategy which relied primarily on ground-based anti-aircraft and anti-tank defence systems.

The Israelis, caught unawares, suffered heavy losses in armour and aircraft in the beginning. But they soon made use of counter-measures such as long-range air-to-surface missiles and ECMs which neutralised the SAMs. Subsequently, the ATGWs proved vulnerable to air attacks and high explosive shells from tanks, guns and conventional artillery. Both the ATGWs and SAMs being soft targets, were vulnerable to high explosives fired from a distance.

Israel and the Arab states must have drawn their own conclusions from the lessons learnt in the October War. Some of these lessons were that the missile defences could be penetrated and that the time factor was of crucial importance. Hence one can expect that in the next round, if it is fought, the stress on both sides would be on a determined and aggressive surge in which the armoured force composed of tanks, AFVs and SP guns, SP anti-aircraft guns and SAMs, helicopter-borne commando troops and ATGW teams would seek to cover the maximum distance in as short a time as possible. The control of the air space or denying it to the other side would be of crucial importance for the success of the offensive as well as for an effective reconnaissance and counter-offensive.

Both the Arabs and the Israelis seem to be preparing for that objective. The Israeli weapons-mix for land-air confrontation has been discussed before. The Syrian-Iraqi armour mix, at least on paper, appears to be fairly effective. Moreover their aircraft, like Mig-25, Mig-23, Mig-21, Su-20 and Su-7, in co-ordination with fixed and SP SAMs and SP anti-aircraft guns, are capable of providing adequate air support to their armoured offensive. The Arabs are much better prepared today than they were in October 1973. They have better weapons. The old air force made up of Mig-17 and Su-7s has been upgraded by the addition of Mig-25, Mig-23 and Su-20. Also, some of their old T-54/55 tanks have been replaced by new T-62/72 tanks. There are further reports that the Arabs have been supplied with better ECM equipment. All these give an added edge to the Arab military capability. This could, however, be effective only if all the states of the Eastern front were to unite.

The Arab-Israeli Nuclear Balance

As the theoretical prospects of Arab-Israeli strategic parity, on the level of conventional weapons, become sharper the possibility of their confrontation involving nuclear weapons assumes increasing relevance. Such a development has been agitating the Arabs and the Israelis since the sixties, if not earlier, when both sides began to search for nuclear weapons. According to the journalist, Mohamed Heikal, President Nasser asked the Chinese to transfer that technology but they refused.[20] The Israelis, on their part, also worked on nuclear weapons because of their sense of insecurity. Their more advanced technology as well as Western support has enabled them to attain a higher level of nuclear technology than the Arabs, with the result that they have been recognised as one of the few near-nuclear powers who can, if they so desire, effectively use their nuclear weapon options.

The Israelis started their search for nuclear options as early as 1948 when they made a mineral survey and discovered considerable amounts of uranium in the Negev. Their programme to train nuclear scientists also began soon afterwards when they were sent to France and the USA. Israel got its first research reactor from the USA, which is under International Atomic Energy Agency (IAEA) safeguards. The Israeli nuclear-weapon programme is, however, allegedly based on the Dimona reactor which is unsafeguarded. Since the late sixties, off and on, calculated reports about the projected Israeli nuclear-weapon capability have been leaked so that even informed public opinion is prepared to acknowledge the existence of an Israeli nuclear-weapon capability.

The Israeli nuclear-weapon option is rationalised on several grounds. It has been argued that the Arabs would one day acquire their own nuclear weapons and Israel must be prepared for this.[21] It is also argued that Arabs would, in the near future, bridge the gap in terms of conventional weapons and hence Israel must be ready with an alternative strategy. Also, since no stable balance of force is possible in terms of conventional military capability, 'it seems reasonable to conclude that Israel may eventually turn to a policy of nuclear deterrence to convince the Arab population and their governments of the futility of continuing their confrontation with the Jewish state'.[22]

Israel's nuclear-weapon option is also rationalised in the situation when the Israelis are threatened with overwhelming massed conventional forces penetrating the so-called green-line and threatening the heartland of the Jewish state.[23] It is reported that Israel was planning to use nuclear weapons in the Golan Heights when the Syrian armed forces were on the verge of pushing back the Israelis from there. Ultimately, the Syrians were halted and pushed back by conventional weapons alone and the nuclear weapon was not used. Furthermore, the use of nuclear weapons is envisaged during a long-drawn-out war of attrition which will drain Israeli resources and ultimately cripple it economically and militarily.[24] It is also suggested that the Israelis might even launch a nuclear offensive against nearby Soviet targets in Southern Russia, 'to act as a moderating influence on Russian policy in this region'.[25]

The Israeli nuclear-weapon option is used to blackmail the USA into providing security guarantees to Israel. That policy became effective after 1968 when the USA began to transfer A-4 and F-4 planes to Israel to lessen the chances of a defeat and a desperate resort to the ultimate weapon.[26] Transfer of large quantities of sophisticated military equipment as well as huge economic aid during and after the October War can be explained by the same logic. This nuclear blackmail might also have been designed to pre-empt any change in the US policy as a result of the effective use of the oil weapon by the Arabs.

While the Israeli nuclear weapon programme is accepted as practical there are serious doubts whether the Arabs can develop nuclear weapons in the near future. Till recently, the threat to Israel from that angle was projected as coming from Egypt. It had ambitions of developing a nuclear programme and was also working on missiles. Both have proved abortive so far because of the poor technological base. But the Israelis treat the Egyptians with great seriousness. That is one reason why they have fears about the long-term consequences of the transfer of nuclear technology to Egypt by the USA.

Among other Arab states, Iraq and Libya are said to be searching for nuclear weapon options. Libya was reported to be willing to buy a finished product and had allegedly sought Pakistani help in that direction. Iraq is also planning to develop its nuclear technology with the help of France. It was, however, rumoured that the Israeli agents sabotaged the Osiris nuclear reactor that was going to be shipped to Iraq from Toulon in April 1979. Iraq is reported to be obtaining a duplicate facility from France.[27]

The Arabs are in no position to produce weapons-grade plutonium at the present time. It is doubtful if Pakistan would be in a position to transfer nuclear weapons to them in the near future. Also the idea of the Soviet Union giving warheads to Arab states with their fragile political stability does not sound very plausible.

Conclusion

There is no simple way to evaluate the Arab-Israeli military balance. Though there are two main parties to the dispute, the balance of forces, especially on the side of the Arabs, fluctuates so widely that it is almost impossible to compute its over-all strength at a given time. At the maximum, the strength of the Arabs lies in their large population, area, economic resources, especially oil, and the resulting political, economic, diplomatic and military pressures that they are able to exercise *vis-à-vis* the great powers and also the non-aligned and the Islamic states. But their strength is frittered away due to the intra-Arab rivalries, their asymmetrical linkages with great powers, the qualitative inferiority of their strategic weapons systems, including the nuclear weapon option, and the low level of their technology. Hence, the resulting strategic balance tilts heavily in favour of Israel. This has been the case since the formation of the state of Israel. Yet, despite this imbalance, the Arabs have often tried to obtain by military force what they thought they could not gain by other means.

Today, the Arab-Israeli strategic situation reflects the military imbalance between the two sides and the confrontation Arab states are the weaker party. There are, however, some powerful undercurrents that work for Arab unity. Efforts are underway to resolve differences between Syria and Iraq and to forge a unity among the Arab states of the Eastern front. If these differences were reduced, these states, even without the direct involvement of Egypt or Libya, would be in a position to challenge Israel militarily. The oil weapon can be used once again to reduce the degree of Western support to Israel. It is possible that the Arabs might not be able to achieve the total destruction of Israel because such a threat might not only lead to an active American involvement on the side of Israel but also unleash the Israeli nuclear option which has been talked about so openly. But the Arabs have sufficient military leverage to force Israel to come to the negotiating table provided they were able to sink their differences, evolve a common front, and above all, were prepared to risk a war with all its consequences. Would the Arabs risk it?

Notes

1. *New York Times*, 1 April 1975.
2. Ibid., 25 March 1975.
3. Ibid., 22 May 1975.
4. Ibid., 18 June 1977.
5. *Middle East Arms Sales Proposals*, Hearings before the Committee on Foreign Relations, Senate, (US Government Printing Office, May, 1978), p. 93.
6. *Review of Recent Developments in the Middle East*, Hearing before the subcommittee on Europe and the Middle East, Committee on International Relations, House of Representatives (US Government Printing Office, Washington D.C., 1977), p. 39.

7. *Proposed Sale of Military Equipment and Services to Egypt*, Hearing before the subcommittee on Europe and the Middle East, Committee on International Relations, House of Representatives, 15 September 1977 (US Government Printing Office, Washington D.C., 1977), p. 18.

8. Yair Evron, 'Arms and Security in the Middle East', *Bulletin of Atomic Scientists* (February 1978), p. 45.

9. Carus, W. Seth, *Current History* (January 1978), p. 30.

10. *Middle East Problems*, Hearings before the subcommittee on Near Eastern and South Asian Affairs, Committee on Foreign Relations, Senate, May 1977 (US Government Printing Office, Washington D.C., 1977), p. 76.

11. Data supplied in R.D. McLaurin, 'Soviet Military in the Middle East', *Institute for Defence Studies and Analyses Journal* (IDSA), New Delhi, July-September 1978, p. 19.

12. Chaim Herzog, *The War of Atonement: October 1973* (Little Brown, Boston, 1975), pp. 34-5.

13. McLaurin, 'Soviet Military in the Middle East', p. 13.

14. Ibid., p. 20 and *Middle East Problems* (1977), p. 46.

15. Edgar O'Ballance, 'Goliath's War: Israeli Operation Litani, 15-21 March 1978', *Marine Corps Gazette* (December 1978), p. 38.

16. Herzog, *War of Atonement*, pp. 34-5.

17. T.N. Dupuy et al., *Comparative Analysis, Arab and Israeli Combat Performance 1967 and 1973 Wars*, Paper before the Historical Evolution and Research Organization, June 1976, quoted in McLaurin, 'Soviet Military in the Middle East', p. 17.

18. *Middle East Problems* (1977), pp. 69-70.

19. Steven J. Rosen, 'Nuclearization and Stability in the Middle East' in O. Marwah and A. Schulz (eds.), *Nuclear Proliferation and the Near-Nuclear Countries* (Ballinger, Cambridge, Massachusetts, 1975), p. 160.

20. Mohamed Hassanein Heikal, *Cairo Documents* (Doubleday, New York, 1973), p. 313.

21. Yigal Allon, *The Making of the Israeli Army* (Weidenfeld and Nicolson, London, 1970), pp. 69-70.

22. Rosen, 'Nuclearization', p. 161.

23. Ibid., p. 164.

24. Tod Friedman, 'Israel's Nuclear Option', *Bulletin of the Atomic Scientists* (September 1974), pp. 34-5.

25. S. Jaishankar, 'The Israeli Nuclear Option', *India Quarterly*, New Delhi (January-March 1978), p. 49 and Rosen, 'Nuclearization', p. 164.

26. Friedman, 'Israel's Nuclear Option', p. 34-5.

27. Christopher Sam Raj, *Strategic Analysis* (August-September 1980), p. 261.

PART THREE

9 THE FORGOTTEN DIMENSIONS OF STRATEGY*

M.E. Howard

The term 'strategy' needs continual definition. For most people, Clausewitz's formulation, 'the use of engagements for the object of the war',[1] or, as Liddell Hart paraphrased it, 'the art of distributing and applying military means to fulfil the ends of policy', is clear enough. Strategy concerns the deployment and use of armed forces to attain a given political objective. Histories of strategy, including Liddell Hart's own *Strategy of Indirect Approach*,[2] usually consist of case studies, from Alexander the Great to MacArthur, of the way in which this was done. Nevertheless, the experience of the past century has shown this approach to be inadequate to the point of triviality. In the West the concept of 'grand strategy' was introduced to cover those industrial, financial, demographic and societal aspects of war that have become so salient in the twentieth century; in Communist states all strategic thought has to be validated by the holistic doctrines of Marxism-Leninism. Without discarding such established concepts, I shall offer here a somewhat different and perhaps slightly simpler framework for analysis, based on a study of the way in which both strategic docrine and warfare itself have developed over the past 200 years. I shall also say something about the implications of this mode of analysis for the present strategic posture of the West.

The Dominance of Clausewitz

Clausewitz's definition of strategy was deliberately and defiantly simplistic. It swept away virtually everything that had been written about war (which was a very great deal) over the previous 300 years. Earlier writers had concerned themselves almost exclusively with the enormous problems of raising, arming, equipping, moving and maintaining armed forces in the field — an approach which Clausewitz dismissed as being as relevant to fighting as the skills of the swordmaker were to the art of fencing. None of this, he insisted, was significant for the actual conduct of war, and the inability of all previous writers to formulate an adequate theory had been due to their failure to distinguish between the *maintenance* of armed forces and their *use*.

By making the distinction between what I shall term the *logistical* and the *operational* dimensions in warfare, Clausewitz performed a major service to strategic thinking; but the conclusions he drew from that distinction were questionable and the consequences of those conclusions have been unfortunate. In the first place, even in his own day, the commanders he so much admired – Napoleon, Frederick the Great – could never have achieved their operational triumphs if they had not had a profound understanding of the whole range of military activities that Clausewitz excluded from consideration. In the second place, no campaign can be understood, and no valid conclusions drawn from it, unless its logistical problems are studied as thoroughly as the course of operations; and as Dr Martin van Creveld has recently pointed out in his book, *Supplying War*,[3] logistical factors have been ignored by 99 military historians out of 100 – an omission which has warped their judgements and made their conclusions in many cases wildly misleading.

Clausewitz's dogmatic assertion of priorities – his subordination of the logistical element in war to the operational – may have owed something to a prejudice common to all fighting soldiers in all eras. It certainly owed much to his reaction against the super-cautious 'scientific' generals whose operational ineptitude had led Prussia to defeat in 1806. But it cannot be denied that in the Napoleonic era it *was* operational skill rather than sound logistical planning that proved decisive in campaign after campaign. And since Napoleon's campaigns provided the basis for all strategic writings and thinking throughout the nineteenth century, 'strategy' became generally equated in the public mind with *operational* strategy.

But the inadequacy of this concept was made very clear, to those who studied it, by the course of the American Civil War. There the masters of operational strategy were to be found, not in the victorious armies of the North, but among the leaders of the South. Lee and Jackson handled their forces with a flexibility and an imaginativeness worthy of a Napoleon or a Frederick; nevertheless they lost. Their defeat was attributed by Liddell Hart, whose analyses seldom extended beyond the operational plane, primarily to operational factors, in particular, to the 'indirect approach' adopted by Sherman. But, fundamentally, the victory of the North was due not to the operational capabilities of its generals, but to its capacity to mobilise its superior industrial strength and manpower into armies which such leaders as Grant were able, thanks largely to road and river transport, to deploy in such strength that the operational skills of their adversaries were rendered almost irrelevant. Ultimately the latter were ground down in a war of attrition in which the *logistical* dimension of strategy proved more significant than the operational. What proved to be of the greatest importance was the capacity to bring the largest and best-equipped forces into the operational theatre and to maintain them there. It was an experience that has shaped the strategic doctrine of the US armed forces from that day to this.

But this capacity depended upon a third dimension of strategy, and one to which Clausewitz was the first major thinker to draw attention: the *social*, the attitude of the people upon whose commitment and readiness for self-denial this logistical power ultimately depended. Clausewitz had described war as 'a remarkable trinity', composed of its political objective, of its operational instruments, and of the popular passions, the social forces it expressed. It was the latter, he pointed out, that made the wars of the French Revolution so different in kind from those of Frederick the Great, and which would probably so distinguish any wars in the future. In this he was right.

With the end of the age of absolutism, limited wars of pure policy fought by dispassionate professionals became increasingly rare. Growing popular participation in government meant popular involvement in war, and so did the increasing size of the armed forces which nineteenth-century technology was making possible and therefore necessary. Management of, or compliance with, public opinion became an essential element in the conduct of war. Had the population of the North been as indifferent to the outcome of the Civil War as the leaders of the Confederacy had initially hoped, the operational victories of the South in the early years might have tipped the scales. The logistical potential of the North would have been of negligible value without the determination to use it. But given equal resolution on both sides, the capacity of the North to mobilise superior forces ultimately became the decisive factor in the struggle. Again Clausewitz was proved right: *all other factors being equal*, numbers ultimately proved decisive.

Technical Advances

In one respect, in particular, other factors were equal. The Civil War was fought with comparable if not identical weapons on both sides, as had been the revolutionary wars in Europe. The possibility of decisive *technological* superiority on one side or the other was so inconceivable that Clausewitz and his contemporaries had discounted it. But within a year of the conclusion of the American Civil War, just such a superiority made itself apparent in the realm of small arms, when the Prussian armies equipped with breech-loading rifles defeated Austrian armies which were not so equipped. Four years later, in 1870, the Prussians revealed an even more crushing superiority over their French adversaries thanks to their steel breech-loading artillery. This superiority was far from decisive: the Franco-Prussian War in particular was won, like the American Civil War, by superior logistical capability based upon a firm popular commitment. But technology, as an independent and significant dimension, could no longer be left out of account.

In naval warfare, the crucial importance of technological parity had been apparent since the dawn of the age of steam, and in colonial warfare the technological element was to prove quite decisive. During the latter part of the nineteenth century, the superiority of European weapons turned what had previously been a marginal technological advantage over indigenous forces, often counterbalanced by numerical inferiority, into a crushing military ascendancy, which made it possible for European forces to establish a new imperial dominance throughout the world over cultures incapable of responding in kind. As Hillaire Belloc's Captain Blood succinctly put it: 'Whatever happens, we have got/The Maxium gun, and they have not.' Military planners have been terrified of being caught without the contemporary equivalent of the Maxim gun from that day to this.

So by the beginning of this century, war was conducted in these four dimensions: the *operational;* the *logistical;* the *social* and the *technological.* No successful strategy could be formulated that did not take account of them all, but under different circumstances, one or other of these dimensions might dominate. When, in 1914-15, the operational strategy of the Schlieffen Plan, for the one side, and of the Gallipoli campaign, for the other, failed to achieve the decisive results expected of them, then the logistical aspects of the war, and with them the social basis on which they depended, assumed even greater importance as the opposing armies tried to bleed each other to death. As in the American Civil War, victory was to go, not to the side with the most skilful generals, and the most courageous troops, but to that which could mobilise the greatest mass of manpower and firepower and sustain it with the strongest popular support.

The inadequacy of mere numbers without social cohesion behind them was demonstrated by the collapse of the Russian Empire in 1917. But the vulnerability even of logistical and social power if the adversary could secure a decisive technological advantage was equally demonstrated by the success of the German submarine campaign in the spring of 1917, when the Allies came within measurable distance of defeat. The German Empire decided to gamble on a technological advantage to counter the logistical superiority which American participation gave to their enemies. But they lost.

The Inter-war Thinkers

From the experience of the First World War, different strategic thinkers derived different strategic lessons. In Western Europe, the most adventurous theorists considered that the technological dimension of war would predominate in the future. The protagonists of armoured warfare in particular believed that it might restore an operational decisiveness unknown since the days of Napoleon himself — the first two years of the Second World War were to prove them right. Skilfully led and well-trained armed forces operating against opponents who were both militarily and morally incapable of resisting them achieved spectacular results.

But another school of thinkers who placed their faith in technology fared less well; this school included those who believed that the development of air power would enable them to eliminate the operational dimension altogether and to strike directly at the roots of the enemy's *social* strength, at the will and capacity of the opposing society to carry on the war. Instead of wearing down the morale of the enemy civilians through the attrition of surface operations, air power, its protagonists believed, would be able to attack and pulverise it directly.

The events of the war were to disprove this theory. Technology was not yet sufficiently advanced to be able to eliminate the traditional requirements of operational and logistical strategy in this manner. Neither the morale of the British nor that of the German people was to be destroyed by air attack; indeed, such attack was found to demand an operational strategy of a new and complex kind in order to defeat the opposing air forces and to destroy their logistical support. But operational success in air warfare, aided by new technological developments, did eventually enable the Allied air forces to destroy the entire logistical framework that supported the German and Japanese war effort, and rendered the operational skills, in which the Germans excelled to the very end, as ineffective as those of Jackson and Lee.

Technology had not in fact transformed the nature of strategy. It, of course, remained of vital importance to keep abreast of one's adversary in all major aspects of military technology, but given that this was possible, the lessons of the Second World War seemed little different from those of the First. The social base had to be strong enough to resist the psychological impact of operational setbacks and to support the largest possible logistical build-up by land, sea and air. The forces thus raised had then to be used progressively to eliminate the operational options open to the enemy and ultimately to destroy his capacity to carry on the war.

The Social Dimension

The same conclusions, set out in somewhat more turgid prose, were reached by the strategic analysts of the Soviet Union — not least those who in the late 1940s and early 1950s were writing under the pen name of J.V. Stalin. But Marxist military thinkers, without differing in essentials from their contemporaries in the West, naturally devoted greater attention to the social dimension of strategy — the structure and cohesiveness of the belligerent societies. For Soviet writers this involved, and still involves, little more than the imposition of a rigid stereotype on the societies they study. Their picture of a world in which oppressed peoples are kept in a state of backward subjection by a small group of exploitative imperialist powers, themselves domestically vulnerable to the revolutionary aspirations of a desperate proletariat, bears little resemblance to the complex reality, whatever its incontestable value as a propagandistic myth. As a result their analysis is often hilariously inaccurate, and their strategic prescriptions either erroneous or banal.

But the West is in no position to criticise. The stereotypes which we have imposed, consciously or unconsciously, on the political structures that surround us, have in the past been no less misleading. The Cold War image of a world which would evolve peacefully, if gradually, towards an Anglo-Saxon style of democracy under Western tutelage if only the global Soviet-directed Marxist conspiracy could be eradicated was at least as naïve and ill-informed as that of the Russian dogmatists. It was the inadequacy of the socio-political analysis of the societies with which we are dealing that lay at the root of the failure of the Western powers to cope more effectively with the revolutionary and insurgency movements that characterised the post-war era, from China in the 1940s to Vietnam in the 1960s. For in these, more perhaps than in any previous conflicts, war really was the continuation of political activity with an admixture of other means; and that political activity was itself the result of a huge social upheaval throughout the former colonial world which had been given an irresistible impetus by the events of the Second World War. Of the four dimensions of strategy, the social was here incomparably the most significant; and it was the perception of this that gave the work of Mao Zedong and his followers its abiding historical importance.

Military thinkers in the West, extrapolating from their experience of warfare between industrial states, naturally tended to seek a solution to what was essentially a conflict on the social plane either by developing operational techniques of 'counter-insurgency', or in the technological advantages provided by such developments as helicopters, sensors or 'smart' bombs. When these techniques failed to produce victory, military leaders, both French and American, complained, as had the German leaders in 1918, that the war had been 'won' militarily but 'lost' politically — as if these dimensions were not totally interdependent.

In fact, these operational techniques and technological tools were now an ancillary to the main socio-political conflict as the tools of psychological warfare had been to the central operational and logistical struggle in the two world wars. In those conflicts, fought between remarkably cohesive societies, the issue was decided by logistic attrition. Propaganda and subversion had played a marginal role, and such successes as they had achieved were strictly geared to those of the armed forces themselves. Conversely, in the conflicts of decolonisation which culminatated in Vietnam, operational and technological factors were subordinate to the socio-political struggle. If that was not conducted with skill and based on a realistic analysis of the societal situation, no amount of operational expertise, logistical back-up or technical know-how could possiby help.

Nuclear Strategy

If the social dimension of strategy has become dominant in one form of conflict since 1945, in another it has, if one is to believe the strategic analysts, vanished completely. Works about nuclear war and deterrence normally treat their topic as an activity taking place almost entirely in a technological dimension. From their writings not only the socio-political but the operational elements have quite disappeared. The technological capabilities of nuclear arsenals are treated as being decisive in themselves, involving a calculation of risk and outcome so complete and discrete that neither the political motivation for the conflict nor the social factors involved in its conduct — nor indeed the military activity of fighting — are taken into account at all. In their models, governments are treated as being as absolute in their capability to take and implement decisions, and the reactions of their societies are taken as little into account as were those of the subjects of the princes who conducted warfare in Europe in the eighteenth century. Professor Anatol Rapoport, in a rather idiosyncratic introduction to a truncated edition of Clausewitz's *On War,* called these thinkers 'Neo-Clausewitzians'.[4] It is not easy to see why. Every one of the three elements that Clausewitz defined as being intrinsic to war — political motivation, operational activity and social participation — are completely absent from their calculations. Drained of political, social and operational content, such works resemble rather the studies of the eighteenth-century theorists whom Clausewitz was writing to confute, and whose influence he considered, with good reason, to have been so disastrous for his own times.

But the question instantly obtrudes itself: in the terrible eventuality of deterrence failing and hostilities breaking out between states armed with nuclear weapons, how will the peoples concerned react, and how will their reactions affect the will and the capacity of governments to make decisions? And what form will military operations take? What, in short, will be the social and the operational dimensions of a nuclear war?

It is not, I think, simply an obsession with traditional problems that makes a European thinker seek an answer to these questions. If nuclear war breaks out at all, it is quite likely to break out here. And in Europe such a conflict would involve not simply an exchange of nuclear missiles at intercontinental range, but a struggle between armed forces for the control of territory — and rather thickly populated territory. The interest displayed by Soviet writers in the conduct of such a war, which some writers in the West find so sinister, seems to me no more than common sense. If such a war does occur, the operational and logistical problems it will pose will need to have been thoroughly thought through. It is not good enough to say that the strategy of the West is one of deterrence, or even of crisis management. It is the business of the strategist to think what to do if deterrence fails, and if Soviet strategists are doing their job and those in the West are not, it is not for us to complain about them.

But it is not only the operational and logistical dimensions that have to be taken into account; so also must the societal. Here the attention devoted by Soviet writers to the importance of the stability of the social structure of any state engaged in a nuclear war also appears to me to be entirely justifiable, even if their conclusions about contemporary societies, both their own and ours, are ignorant caricatures.

About the operational dimension in nuclear war, Western analysts have until recently been confused and defeatist. In spite of the activities of Defense Secretary Robert McNamara and his colleagues nearly 20 years ago, and in spite of the lip service paid to the concept of 'flexible response', the military forces in Western Europe are still not regarded as a body of professionals, backed up where necessary by citizen-soldiers, whose task it will be to repel any attack upon their own territories and those of their allies. Rather they are considered as an expendable element in a complex mechanism for enhancing the credibility of nuclear response. Indeed, attempts to increase their operational effectiveness are still sometimes opposed on the grounds that to do so would be to reduce the credibility of nuclear retaliation.

But such credibility depends not simply on a perceived balance, or imbalance, of weapons systems, but on perceptions of the nature of the society whose leaders are threatening such retaliation. Peoples who are not prepared to make the effort necessary for operational defence are even less likely to support a decision to initiate a nuclear exchange from which they will themselves suffer almost inconceivable destruction, even if that decision is taken at the lowest possible level of nuclear escalation. And if such a decision were taken over their heads, they would be unlikely to remain sufficiently resolute and united to continue to function as a cohesive political and military entity in the aftermath. The maintenance of adequate armed forces in peacetime, and the will to deploy and support them operationally in war, is in fact a symbol of that social unity and political resolve which is as essential an element in nuclear deterrence as any invulnerable second-strike capability.

So although the technical dimension of strategy has certainly become of predominant importance in armed conflict between advanced societies in the second half of the twentieth century – as predominant as the logistical dimension was during the first half – the growing political self-awareness of those societies and, in the West at least, their insistence on political participation have made the social dimension too significant to be ignored. There can be little doubt that societies, such as those of the Soviet Union and the People's Republic of China, which have developed powerful mechanisms of social control, enjoy an apparent initial advantage over those of the West, which operate by a consensus reached by tolerating internal disagreements and conflicts; though how great that advantage would actually prove under pressure remains to be seen.

Whatever one's assessment of their strength, these are factors that cannot be left out of account in any strategic calculations. If we do take account of the social dimension of strategy in the nuclear age, we are likely to conclude that Western leaders might find it much more difficult to initiate nuclear war than would their Soviet counterparts — and, more important, would be perceived by their adversaries as finding it more difficult. If this is the case, and if on their side the conventional strength of the Soviet armed forces makes it unnecessary for their leaders to take such an initiative, the operational effectiveness of the armed forces of the West once more becomes a matter of major strategic importance, both in deterrence and in defence.

Most strategic scenarios today are based on the least probable of political circumstances — a totally unprovoked military assault by the Soviet Union, with no shadow of political justification, on Western Europe. But Providence is unlikely to provide us with anything so straightforward. Such an attack, if it occurred at all, would be likely to arise out of a political crisis in central Europe over the rights and wrongs of which Western public opinion would be deeply and perhaps justifiably divided. Soviet military objectives would probably extend no further than the Rhine, if indeed that far. Under such conditions, the political will of the West to initiate nuclear war might have to be discounted entirely, and the defence of West Germany would depend not on our nuclear arsenals but on the operational capabilities of our armed forces, fighting as best they could and for as long as they could without recourse to nuclear weapons of any kind. And it need hardly be said that hostilities breaking out elsewhere in the world are likely, as they did in Vietnam, to arise out of political situations involving an even greater degree of political ambiguity, in which our readiness to initiate nuclear war would appear even less credible.

The belief that technology has somehow eliminated the need for operational effectiveness is, in short, no more likely to be valid in the nuclear age than it was in the Second World War. Rather, as in that war, technology is likely to make its greatest contribution to strategy by improving operational weapons systems and the logistical framework that makes their deployment possible. The transformation in weapons technology which is occurring under our eyes with the development of precision-guided munitions suggests that this is exactly what is now happening. The new weapons systems hold out the possibility that operational skills will once more be enabled, as they were in 1940-1, to achieve decisive results, either positive in the attack or negative in the defence. But whether these initial operational decisions are then accepted as definitive by the societies concerned, will depend, as they did in 1940-1, and in all previous wars, on the other two elements in Clausewitz's trinity: the importance of the political objective, and the

The Forgotton Dimensions of Strategy

readiness of the belligerent communities to endure the sacrifices involved in prolonging the war.

These sacrifices might or might not include the experience, on whatever scale, of nuclear war, but they would certainly involve living with the day-to-day, even hour-to-hour, possibility that the war might 'go nuclear' at any moment. It is not easy to visualise a greater test of social cohesion than having to endure such a strain for a period of months, if not years, especially if no serious measures had been taken for the protection of the civil population.

Such measures were projected in the United States two decades ago, and they were abandoned for a mixture of motives. There was, on the one hand, the appreciation that not even the most far-reaching of preparations could prevent damage being inflicted on a scale unacceptable to the peoples of the West. On the other was the reluctance of those peoples to accept, in peacetime, the kind of social disruption and the diversion of resources which such measures would involve. The abandonment of these programmes was then rationalised by the doctrine of Mutually Assured Destruction. And any attempt by strategic thinkers to consider what protective measures might have to be taken if the war which everyone hoped to avoid actually came about was frowned upon as a weakening of deterrence. But here again, there seem to have been no such inhibitions in the Soviet Union; and their civil defence programme, which some Western thinkers find so threatening, like that of the Chinese, seems to me no more than common sense. It is hard not to envy governments which have the capacity to carry through such measures, however marginally they might enhance the survivability of their societies in the event of nuclear war.

The Western position, on the other hand, appears both paradoxical and, quite literally, indefensible, so long as our operational strategy quite explicitly envisages the initiation of a nuclear exchange. The use of theatre nuclear weapons within Western Europe, on any scale, will involve agonising self-inflicted wounds for which our societies are ill prepared; while their extension to Eastern European territory will invite retaliation against such legitimate military targets as the ports of Hamburg, Antwerp or Portsmouth for which we have made no preparations at all. The planned emplacement of nuclear weapons in Western Europe capable of matching in range, throw-weight and accuracy those which the Russians have targeted on to that area may be necessary to deter the Soviet Union from initiating such an exchange. But it will not solve the problem so long as the Russians are in a position to secure an operational victory without recourse to nuclear weapons at all. Deterrence works both ways.

Implications for the West

It cannot be denied that the strategic calculus I have outlined in the above pages has disquieting implications for the defence of the West. We appear to be depending on the technological dimension of strategy to the detriment of its operational requirements, while we ignore its societal implications altogether — something which our potential adversaries, very wisely, show no indication of doing. But the prospect of nuclear war is so appalling that we no less than our adversaries are likely, if war comes, to rely on 'conventional' operational skills and the logistical capacity to support them for as long as possible, no less than we have in the past.

Hostilities in Europe would almost certainly begin with the engagement of armed forces seeking to obtain or to frustrate an operational decision. But as in the past — as in 1862, or in 1914, or in 1940-1 — social factors will determine whether the outcome of these initial operations is accepted as decisive, or whether the resolution of the belligerent societies must be further tested by logistical attrition, or whether governments will feel sufficiently confident in the stability and cohesion of their own peoples, and the instability of their adversaries, to initiate a nuclear exchange. All of this gives us overwhelming reasons for praying that the great nuclear powers can continue successfully to avoid war. It gives us none for deluding ourselves as to the strategic problems such a war would present to those who have to conduct it.

Notes

*   Reprinted from *Foreign Affairs*.
1.   Carl von Clausewitz, *Vom Kriege* (Dummlers Verlag, Bonn, 1972), Book 3, Chapter 1, p. 345.
2.   B.H. Liddell-Hart, *Strategy: The Indirect Approach* (Faber and Faber, London, 1954). Part of the book was originally published as *The Decisive Wars of History*.
3.   Martin L. van Creveld, *Supplying War: Logistics from Wallenstein to Patton* (Cambridge University Press, 1977).
4.   Anatol Rapoport (ed.), *Clausewitz On War* (Penguin Books, Harmondsworth, 1968), p. 60 passim.

NOTES ON CONTRIBUTORS

Chris Bellamy has served in the British army and has an MA in War Studies from Kings' College, London. He has written widely on Russian military history and affairs.

David Horner is a major in the Royal Australian infantry. He has a PhD from the Australian National University and served as a platoon commander during the Vietnam War. His first book, *Crisis of Command, Australian Generalship and the Japanese Threat, 1941-1943*, was published in 1978. He is the joint editor of *New Directives in Strategic Thinking*, which was published in 1981 and his next book is due out shortly.

N.E. Howard is Regius Professor of History at Oxford University. He was Professor of War Studies at Kings' College, London, from 1963 to 1968. His best known works are the *Franco-Prussian War* (1961), *Theory and Practice of War* (1965), *Studies in War and Peace* (1970) and the *Continental Commitment* (1972).

Ron Huisken has a PhD in international relations from the Australian National University. He has worked for the Stockholm International Peace Research Institute and for the disarmament division of the United Nations secretariat where he carried out research on the economic aspects of defence. He is the author of *Arms Limitation in South-east Asia* (1978).

Geoffrey Jukes has been a member of the Department of International Relations at the Australian National University since 1967. He is a specialist on Soviet military history and naval policy and on Soviet relations with the Third World. His publications include *Development in Soviet Strategic Thinking since 1945* (1972), *The Indian Ocean in Soviet Naval Policy* (1972), and *The Soviet Union in Asia* (1973).

Ravi Rikhye works in commerce and for the Indian Institute for Defence Studies and Analyses. He has contributed numerous articles on the problems of South Asian defence to the Institute's journal and is currently working on crisis management within the area.

K.R. Singh is an associate professor in the School of International Studies at the Jawaharlal Nehru University. His main publications include *The Indian Ocean: Big Power Presence and Local Response* (1977), *Iran: Quest for Security* (1980) and the *Persian Gulf: Arms and Arms Control* (1981).

Geoffrey Till is a lecturer at the Royal Naval College, Greenwich and at City University, London. His history of *Air Power and the Royal Navy* was published in 1979. He has a PhD in War Studies from Kings' College, London.

Philip Towle is a defence lecturer at Cambridge University. He has worked for the British Foreign Office and for Reuters news agency. He has a PhD in War Studies from Kings' College, London and was a senior research fellow in the Strategic and Defence Studies Centre of the Australian National University from 1978 to 1980. He is the author of *Naval Power in the Indian Ocean: Threats, Bluffs and Fantasies* (1980).

INDEX

Alexander 1, Tsar of Russia 40
Arms Control and Disarmament Agency 82
Australia: fear of Japan 17, 134, 139 passim; White Australia policy 140

Balfour, A.J. and Japan 112, 121-3
Bhutto, Z.A. 203
Bloch, I.S. and theory of war 15, 25
Britain: army in the nineteenth century 26-7; Convention with Russia in 1907 41; 50, 66; estimates of German power before 1914 127; power in the sixteenth and seventeenth centuries 13
Brooke-Popham, Air Chief Marshal underestimates Japanese aircraft 156-8

Cable, Sir James and Soviet power 19
censorship of war reporting 26
Chamberlain, Austen 144
Chamberlain, Joseph 114
Chamberlain, Neville 149
Chatfield, Admiral Lord 175-7
Chauvel, Lt General Sir Henry 142-4
China: Boxer uprising 115; importance of morale 21; Japanese war 114; Sino-Soviet dispute 48, 97; strength in Tibet 225-31; war with India 195 passim
Churchill, Sir Winston 16, 164
CIA: Chinese threat to India 199; Israeli power 241; Soviet military expenditure 73-8, 93
CID on Japanese military power 144-8
civil defence in the Soviet Union 271
Clarke, Sir George: Japanese power 116, 123; Russian power 41
Clausewitz, Karl von 49, 53, 267-8
coal and national power 12
Crimean War 47
Cuba crisis and nuclear weapons 24
Curtin, John 163-4
Curzon, Lord and Japan 113-17

Defoe, Daniel and Russia 38-9
Dillon, Dr E.J. and Soviet power 19

disarmament: campaign for nuclear disarmament 24; CSCE 28; negotiations in the 1920s 23; SALT 28

Egypt: nuclear weapons 256; peace treaty with Israel 239, 250-1; Soviet personnel in 245
Elizabeth I of England 13, 37

France: aeroplane production in the First World War 13; battleships before 1914 14; defeat in 1940 22, 105

Germany and Prussia: Anglo-German Naval Treaty 1935 186; evades Treaty of Versailles 181-3; Frederick the Great 11, 262; manoeuvres before 1914 127-8; military attachés 26; Russian fear of 48; Schlieffen plan 265; Second World War 94, 265

Heikal, Mohamed 255
Hitler, Adolf 16, 95
Hughes, W.M. 149-1

IISS: Arab-Israeli military balance 249; Pakistani tank strength 220-2; Soviet forces 81, 100, 194
Indian Intelligence Bureau 195-9
intentions and capabilities 49 passim, 88
Iran-Iraq war 246, 251-2
Israel: army training and skills 13, 20; power 237 passim

Japan: Australian fear of before 1941 17, 139 passim; British attachés in 27; Royal Navy underestimates 187-8; secrecy 155, 179, 187-190

Kashmir 200 passim
KGB 91-2
Khan, Ayub 204, 209
Khrushchev, Nikita: exaggerates

275

Soviet power 17, 89; ICBMs 99; Soviet forces 96
Korea 114, 121-2

Lansdowne, Lord 121-2
Latham, Sir John: China 150; Japan 155
Lavarack, Colonel J.D. 146-7, 151-2
Liddell Hart, Sir Basil 18, 261 *passim*

MacDonald, Sir Claude 116, 130
Menzies, R.G. 149, 156
military attachés: Japan 88, 91, 116-18, 122, 143-8; Moscow 52
Milton, John 38, 53
Morgenthau, Hans 12, 15, 18, 29
Muirhead-Gould, Captain G.L. 182-5
Mussolini, Benito 17
Murdoch, James 141

Napoleon I 40, 262
Nasser, Gamel Abdel 17, 255
naval attachés 148, 190
Nehru, Jawaharlal 199, 204
Niazi, General A.A.K. 210-12
nuclear weapons 24-5, 29, 254-6, 267-71

October 1973 War 246, 253-4, 256

Pakistan: air force co-operates with Arab states 222-5; loss of East Pakistan 210-13; rearms after 1971 216-20; war with India 200-10
Pearce, Sir George 140, 149
Peres, Shimon 241, 247

Piesse, Major E.J. 140
PLO 237, 243
Poland 21
population 12
Pound, Admiral Sir Dudley 189

Roberts, Field Marshal Lord 115, 119-20
Rommel, Field Marshal E. 18
Roskill, Captain S.W. 131, 174
Royal Navy: Japan before 1914 129-32; miscalculations between the wars 172-85
Russia and Soviet Union: Afghanistan 25, 41, 60-6, 90, 102, 117; Bloch, I.S. 26; civil defence 98; NATO 47-8; submarines 101

Sandys, Duncan 14
Singapore base 134, 144, 147, 153-5
Stalin, Joseph 20, 51-2, 266

Tse La Pass 195-8

United States: Civil War 262-3; debates on defence 16; Ford, Gerald 240; intervention in Indo-Pakistan war 213-16; race riots 23; Schlesinger, James 240

Vietnam War 13, 18, 266-7

Waters, Colonel W.H.H. and Soviet power 19, 59, 120, 124

Zero fighter 156, 177 *passim*

For Product Safety Concerns and Information please contact our EU representative GPSR@taylorandfrancis.com
Taylor & Francis Verlag GmbH, Kaufingerstraße 24, 80331 München, Germany

www.ingramcontent.com/pod-product-compliance
Lightning Source LLC
Chambersburg PA
CBHW070556300426
44113CB00010B/1277